Field Guide to Nonprofit Strategic Planning and Facilitation

Third Edition

By Carter McNamara, MBA, PhD

AUTHENTICITY CONSULTING, LLC
MINNEAPOLIS, MN USA

For reprint permission, more information on Authenticity Consulting, LLC, or to order additional copies of this or any of our other publications, please contact:

> Authenticity Consulting, LLC
> 4008 Lake Drive Avenue North
> Minneapolis, MN 55422-1508 USA
>
> 800.971.2250 toll-free
> 763.971.8890 direct
>
> http://www.authenticityconsulting.com

Trademarks
Authenticity Circles, Free Management Library, Free Nonprofit Micro-eMBA and Free Micro-eMBA are service marks of Authenticity Consulting, LLC, Minneapolis, Minnesota. "Leveraging the Power of Peers" is a registered mark of Authenticity Consulting, LLC, Minneapolis, Minnesota.

Credits
Cover design and illustrations by Erin Scott/Wylde Hare Creative, Woodbury, Minnesota.
Photographs © 2005 JupiterImages Corporation/Comstock.com, primary cover photo;
    © Teri McNamara/Impressions & Expressions and © Erin Scott/Wylde Hare Creative,
    secondary cover photos.
Clip art by Nova Development Corporation Art Explosion 750,000 Images.
Printed by Graphic & Printing Services, Big Lake, Minnesota.

Manufactured in the United States of America
First Edition February 2003
Second Edition June 2003
Third Edition December 2007

Waiver of Responsibility
Various Web addresses are referenced in this book. The author and publisher have no legal responsibility or liability for the currency or accuracy of these Web addresses or the content at these addresses.

Publisher's Cataloging in Publication Data
McNamara, Carter, 1953 -
    Field Guide to Nonprofit Strategic Planning and Facilitation / by Carter McNamara
    ISBN 1-933719-06-0
    ISBN 978-1-933719-06-3
    1. Strategic planning. 2. Nonprofits. 3. Facilitation. I. Title

Table of Contents

Introduction

Focus of Guidebook

When members of nonprofit organizations struggle with their strategic planning process or their plans ends up not being useful at all, it is rarely because their planning process did not include state-of-the-art techniques in facilitation or the latest models in strategic planning. Rather, it is because their process did not effectively address the most critical, "core" aspects of the strategic planning process. Guidelines in this guidebook are focused on those critical aspects.

This guidebook is focused on helping you accomplish organization-wide and/or program-specific, strategic planning processes for your nonprofit organization. Guidelines will show you how to conduct a simplified (not simplistic!) strategic planning process that is very realistic, flexible and suited to the nature of your typical nonprofit organization – thus, producing a strategic plan that is also very relevant to the future of your nonprofit organization.

One of the most effective approaches to ensuring a highly relevant strategic planning process and plan is to ensure a highly effective approach to facilitating the planning process itself. Therefore, this guidebook also provides complete guidelines to facilitating nonprofit strategic planning – one of the few strategic planning books to include that information for facilitators.

(Note that it is beyond the scope of this guidebook to provide comprehensive, step-by-step guidelines to organize and develop a strategic plan for a collaboration of nonprofit organizations. Although the process used to develop such a plan is generally similar to the process to develop a strategic plan for a nonprofit organization or program, there still are enough differences such that guidelines about strategic planning for collaboration should not be gleaned only from this guidebook.)

Audiences

This guidebook is designed to apply to a variety of situations, whether:

- Yours is a new or established nonprofit.

- You are conducting strategic planning for the first time or have done planning before.

- Your organization is facing several major, current issues or you are using planning just to "fine tune" things in your organization.

- You are facilitating the strategic planning process yourself or having someone facilitate the process for your nonprofit.

This guidebook will be extremely useful to you, especially if you are a:

- Founder or Chief Executive (Executive Director) of a nonprofit

- Member of a nonprofit Board of Directors

- Nonprofit leader, manager or supervisor

- Nonprofit management consultant

- Human resource and development professional working with nonprofits

Content of Guidebook

PART I includes guidelines to help you gain a clear understanding of how the strategic planning process guides the direction, structure and operations of all facets of nonprofit organizations. You will gain perspective on the overall strategic planning framework and the traits that are common to any strategic planning process. You will read about when to regularly schedule strategic planning, but that strategic planning is never really "done".

PART II includes step-by-step guidelines to customize and implement a strategic plan that is relevant, realistic and flexible. The planning process is divided into six overall phases, including:

1.   Preparing a "plan for a plan."

2.   Conducting situational analyses, external and internal to the organization.

3.   Establishing strategic direction for the organization, including mission (and vision and/or values, if preferred), goals and strategies. (Many small nonprofits do not identify strategies.)

4.   Action planning, including identifying who will be doing what (objectives) by when and what resources will be needed.

5.   Developing and communicating the strategic plan document.

6.   Implementing, monitoring and adjusting the plan.

PART III is written for the facilitator of the nonprofit strategic planning process, whether the facilitator is internal or external to the organization. The first set of guidelines in PART III is designed to ensure a highly collaborative, working relationship between the facilitator and planners from the nonprofit organization. The next set of guidelines is about the most common set of techniques used in facilitating the nonprofit strategic planning process. PART III ends with guidelines to address the most common challenges that arise during facilitation.

How To Use Guidebook

Do Not Be Intimidated By Size of Guidebook –
Do One Step at a Time

Imagine that you wrote down every step that it took to do your grocery shopping. The list of steps would seem so long to you that you would promptly feel overwhelmed and would never go shopping again! Yet, it is obvious that you can usually manage a shopping trip on your own. The first time that you went, you might have been rather careful, for example, you asked someone for directions, you checked a map, and you carefully watched where you were going. The next time that you went, you gave little attention to where you were going. You just did it.

The same is true for strategic planning. The first time, you might have no clear idea of what it means to successfully develop a strategic plan, yet you carry out the process one step at a time in order to develop and implement your plan. The next time that you do planning, it is not half as challenging as the first time. The second or third time around, you just do it.

This guidebook is carefully designed so that you can develop and implement your strategic plan – one step at a time, whether this is the first time that you have done strategic planning or you are experienced in the process. Do not be intimidated by the size of the guidebook.

Common Terms in Guidebook

Nonprofit

This guidebook makes frequent reference to the phrase "nonprofit organization" and the term "nonprofit". Those references are in regard to the organization for which strategic planning is being conducted.

Facilitator

The guidebook also refers to a strategic planning "facilitator". The facilitator is the person responsible to help planners design a strategic planning process and/or conduct that process for the nonprofit organization. The facilitator can be internal (a member of the nonprofit) or external to the nonprofit organization. Guidelines for getting a facilitator are referenced in the section, "Phase 1: Design Plan for Plan," in PART II.

Planners

This guidebook also makes frequent reference to the term "planners". A planner is anyone who is involved in the development of the strategic plan for the nonprofit organization, especially those people who regularly take part in planning meetings. The facilitator is usually not considered a planner.

Clients

Clients are the people who benefit from the services of a nonprofit. Some experts distinguish between primary clients and secondary, or supporting, clients.

Primary clients are the people who we intend to directly benefit from the services of the nonprofit. They might include, for example:

- Attendees to an art show

- Members of an association

- Citizens attending a civic event

- Grantees of a foundation

- Patients in a hospital

- Members of a congregation

- Students in a school

- Participants in social service programs

- Patrons to a library

Secondary clients are the people who indirectly benefit from the services of the nonprofit. They might include, for example:

- Organizations that collaborate with the nonprofit

- Special interest groups that support the purpose of the nonprofit

- Suppliers of materials to the nonprofit

Both types of clients could be considered as "stakeholders" to the nonprofit.

Other Key Terms

This guidebook also includes a Glossary on page 159 in Appendix A that provides definitions of these and other key terms in nonprofit strategic planning.

Conventions Used in Guidebook

Various formats are used to indicate the organization and relationship of the information included in this guidebook. It is important to be clear about the formats that are used because the guidebook sometimes refers readers to specific areas (sections, subsections, topics, etc.) in the guidebook, depending on the approach that the planners have customized to implement their strategic planning process.

- **PARTS**: The guidebook is divided into three major parts, including PART I, PART II and PART III, followed by Appendices with supplemental material.

- **Sections**: Each PART is divided into sections, such as the section, "Strategic Planning" in PART I. Titles of sections are centered at the top of the page.

- **Subsections**: The sections are divided into subsections. For example, the subsection "Strategic Planning Framework" is in the section, "Conducting Strategic Planning," in PART I.

- **Topics:** Sometimes topics are included in some sections and/or subsections. For example, the topics "Factors That Influence Approach to Strategic Planning" and "Variations from Strategic Planning Framework" are in the subsection, "Strategic Planning Framework," within the section, "Conducting Strategic Planning."

- **Subtopics:** Subtopics provide information about very specific items within an overall topic. For example, "Identifying Timelines in Action Plans" is included in the topic "Guidelines To Develop Action Plans" in the subsection "Develop Action Plans" in the overall section "Phase 4: Develop Action and Financial Plans."

Formats Used to Reference and Organize Information

References to other content within the Field Guide, other related

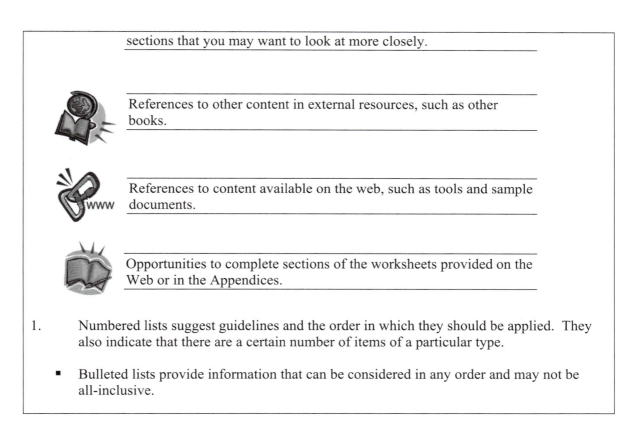

sections that you may want to look at more closely.

References to other content in external resources, such as other books.

References to content available on the web, such as tools and sample documents.

Opportunities to complete sections of the worksheets provided on the Web or in the Appendices.

1. Numbered lists suggest guidelines and the order in which they should be applied. They also indicate that there are a certain number of items of a particular type.

- Bulleted lists provide information that can be considered in any order and may not be all-inclusive.

"Crossroads" Topics to Help Planners Customize Their Planning

This guidebook is carefully designed to help planners customize their own strategic planning process, especially to ensure that their plans are relevant, realistic and flexible. Consequently, the guidebook directs planners to specific areas of the guidebook at various times, depending on the nature of the plan that planners customized for themselves. Some of the sections in this guidebook begin with a topic entitled, "Crossroads …" Points in that topic are meant to help you decide if the guidelines in that section should be followed now or later, depending on the planners' preferences for their planning process.

Reading Guidebook to Learn Strategic Planning?

If you are just interested in learning about strategic planning and do not intend to actually facilitate or develop a strategic plan now, then:

1. Start by reading PART I in order to understand the strategic planning process.

2. Read PART II to learn how to develop and implement a strategic plan.

3. Read PART III to learn about the role of strategic planning facilitator.

Ideally, you will arrange to take part in, or even facilitate, a strategic planning process. You might volunteer to work with an experienced facilitator so that you can get a feel for the strategic planning process. Learning about strategic planning is very much like learning how to ride a bike. You can read all you want to, but until you actually ride the bike, you really will not fully learn how.

Reading Guidebook to Develop Strategic Plan Now?

If you are planning to start strategic planning for your nonprofit organization soon (you are the "initiator" of the process), then:

1.   Read PART I to understand the overall strategic planning process. Even if you have worked in nonprofits for years, you still should read about the typical nonprofit organization, if only to gain a concise overview of the typical challenges when doing strategic planning with nonprofits. You might read PART I in half an hour or so.

2.   Carefully consider whether your organization is really ready for strategic planning. Guidelines for addressing that consideration are included in the subsection, "Ready for Strategic Planning?", in the section, "Phase 1: Design Plan for Plan," in PART II. Follow those guidelines now to discern if your nonprofit really is ready for strategic planning. You might choose to discuss the guidelines with others in your organization in order to make a careful decision about whether to go forward with strategic planning. The decision might take anywhere from a few minutes to a week to make.

3.   If you conclude that your organization is ready for planning, then follow the rest of the guidelines in "Phase 1: Design Plan for Plan." The guidelines will help you to consider:

- Whether to form a Planning Committee to oversee development of the strategic plan

- What will be the focus of the strategic plan

- How long of a time period that the plan will address

- How to customize the best strategic planning process for your organization

- Who will be involved in the planning process

- How to obtain a strategic planning facilitator, whether the facilitator is internal or external to your nonprofit organization

- What resources you will need

- The best schedule for your planning activities

- How to announce the strategic planning activities to the entire organization

Note that a Planning Committee, if used, is responsible to oversee development of the plan, not necessarily to do all the activities required to actually develop and/or implement the plan. Depending on the size of the organization, people other than the Committee members will likely be involved in the planning. Those people, along with Committee members, will comprise the planners for the nonprofit organization. The amount of time needed to follow all of the guidelines in the section, "Phase 1: Design Plan for Plan," might be anywhere from an hour to a week, depending on how long it takes to organize a Planning Committee, if used, and to discuss the guidelines.

4.   Identify someone to be the strategic planning facilitator, as considered in the previous step when designing a plan for a plan. Suggestions for finding and hiring a facilitator are included in Appendix E on page 193. It could take anywhere from a day to a couple of

weeks to find an external facilitator; otherwise, use of an internal facilitator might take less time.

5.   The planners and the Planning Committee, if used, should work with the strategic planning facilitator to follow the guidelines in Phases 2-5 in PART II in order to develop a strategic plan document. The Committee should decide whether to 1) work as a partner with the facilitator in an overall team effort to lead development activities or 2) have the facilitator lead the activities, including by conferring with the Committee. The length of time to develop a strategic plan can take anywhere from a few weeks to a few months. This guidebook recommends that planners proceed with planning at a fairly rapid pace; otherwise, momentum decreases and the process bogs down. A small- to medium-sized nonprofit might finish a strategic plan in as few as 15-20 hours of meetings over a month-long period.

Reading Guidebook To Facilitate Strategic Planning?

1.   Even if you are experienced at nonprofit strategic planning, you still might read PART I, especially if any of your planners will be reading that information to learn the strategic planning process. That way, you will know what they know about planning.

2.   To be successful at facilitating nonprofit strategic planning, you must understand nonprofits. If you are not familiar with nonprofit organizations, then you should read Appendix F: "Nature of Typical Nonprofit Organizations" on page 199.

3.   You might read PART III to ensure you know, or to remind yourself, how to accomplish a highly collaborative, working relationship with the planners from the nonprofit organization. You will also read about using some common techniques in facilitation.

4.   Carefully read the guidelines in PART II to prepare for guiding your planners to develop their strategic plan. Phase 1 is about preparing a "plan for a plan" and includes a significant amount of considerations about the internal workings of the nonprofit. The nonprofit organization might choose not to involve you in that phase.

5.   Meet with members of the Planning Committee to begin designing and developing the strategic plan by following guidelines in Phases 2-5 of PART II. You might need occasional reference to guidelines and techniques in PART III.

Who Should Have Guidebook

Ideally, at least the facilitator and every member of the Planning Committee should have a copy of this guidebook. If that is not practical, then the guidebook might be shared among the facilitator and members of the Committee. Ideally, they can 1) read the information in PART I to understand the strategic planning process and 2) work with each other to complete the plan for a plan by following the guidelines in the section, "Phase 1: Design Plan for Plan," in PART II.

Planners can share copies of the worksheets from this guidebook. See the topic included immediately below.

Worksheets To Copy or Download

This guide includes numerous worksheets that planners can use to collect and organize the results from their strategic planning activities. If the formats of the worksheets seem useful, the owner of the guidebook can make copies of the worksheets for use within their organization.

Or, guidebook owners can download a copy of all of the worksheets and use their computer's word processor to modify the worksheets for use within their organization. You will be able to fully use them by the time you start your planning activities.

To download a copy of the worksheets, point your Web browser to the Web address:
http://www.authenticityconsulting.com/pubs/SP_gdes/worksheets.doc
Then save the document to your computer's disk, for example, use the "Save As" command in your browser and name the file "worksheets".

Adapt Guidelines To Suit Structure of Board of Directors

Members of a nonprofit, governing Board of Directors can choose to organize themselves into a variety of structures. Probably the most common structure is the "policy Board" in which Board members establish certain broad policies, along with roles in the Board and organization, including Board officers, Board committees and a Chief Executive Officer. Not all Boards utilize these roles. "Working Boards," collective Boards or Policy Governance® Boards are different from policy Boards in this regard.

This guide provides guidelines and techniques primarily for the perspective of a nonprofit that utilizes a policy Board, probably the most common type of Board structure. However, you should adapt the guidelines in this guide to the particular structure and nature of your organization and Board.

See "Nature of Typical Nonprofit Organizations" on page 199 in Appendix F for more information about various Board structures.

"Jump Start" Some Strategic Planning Preparation Now?

Before planners start customizing and implementing their strategic planning process, they might start collecting some of the types of information that will be useful during subsequent planning activities, especially during the external analysis. Sources for that type of information are listed in Appendix B on page 165.

For example, you might:

- Sign up for any of the free, on-line newsletters and on-line discussion groups.

- Find out if there are trade journals about the types of services offered by your nonprofit. If so, subscribe to some of them. Try gain access to any on-line archives of articles from the journals.

- Schedule appointments with representatives from at least two potential funders. Explain that your nonprofit will be starting strategic planning and that you would like to talk to the representative as part of the external analysis phase of planning. Mention that you want to gain better understanding of the various community needs that are of interest to the funder and how those needs might be met.

- Schedule appointments with any experts about the services that your nonprofit provides, for example, with any researchers, educators and members from nonprofits that work with similar clients.

- Contact the planning office for your city, county or state/province, and ask if they have any resources that might help you to better understand the groups of clients that your nonprofit aims to serve.

In the USA, contact the local chapter of the National Council of Nonprofit Associations (at http://www.ncna.org/ or 202-962-0322). Ask how the Council might benefit your nonprofit organization.

Contact the United Ways of America or Canada (http://national.unitedway.org/index.cfm for United Way America or http://www.unitedway.ca/english/ for United Way Canada). Ask how their organization might benefit your nonprofit organization.

See the section "Basic Methods To Assess Client Needs" on page 191 in Appendix D for some ideas about how to start collecting information about possible new clients and what their needs might be. That information will come in handy later on during the internal analysis portion of the overall situational analysis.

About the Author

Carter McNamara, MBA, PhD, is a partner in Authenticity Consulting, LLC. He is founder and developer of the Authenticity Circles[SM] and Leaders Circles[SM] peer coaching group models, and the on-line Free Management Library[SM], Free Micro-eMBA[SM] and Nonprofit Micro-eMBA[SM]. Dr. McNamara has over 20 years of strategic planning experience and trainings, including in small nonprofits and for-profits, large for-profits and large university systems. Dr. McNamara holds a BA in Social and Behavioral Sciences, a BS in Computer Science, an MBA from the University of St. Thomas, and a PhD in Human and Organization Development from The Union Institute in Cincinnati, Ohio.

About Authenticity Consulting, LLC

Authenticity Consulting, LLC, publisher of this guidebook, is a Minneapolis-based consulting firm specializing in development of nonprofit organizations, management and programs. Authenticity co-founders, Carter McNamara and Andrew Horsnell, bring over 35 years of consultation experience, including services in facilitation, training, publications and presentations.

While many firms specialize in one or a few specific services to nonprofits, Authenticity brings a comprehensive and integrated approach to development with focus on building the capacity of the entire organization, including its governance, management and staffing, programs, marketing, finances, fundraising and evaluation. The firm also provides services in social entrepreneurship, including nonprofit business planning and development.

To deepen and enrich its capacity building projects, Authenticity also provides powerful, practical peer coaching group programs for networking, training, problem solving and support – either free-standing or to enrich other programs – through Authenticity Circles peer coaching group models. This unique, Action Learning-based, group coaching process ensures ongoing support and accountability among participants during the organizational planning and change process – few change models recognize and build in processes to ensure these two critical elements of any change process.

Authenticity Consulting, LLC, can be reached at 800-971-2250 for the United States office. For more information, see http://www.authenticityconsulting.com/ on the Web.

Acknowledgments

This Guidebook is the result of my learnings gleaned from almost 25 years of conducting or participating in the strategic planning process in a variety of types of organizations, including hospitals, start-up ventures, large for-profit corporations, universities and nonprofits. Along the way, I attended numerous courses and workshops on strategic planning, which described several different approaches to strategic planning. I also read a great deal about strategic planning, especially from several key sources listed in the bibliography of this guidebook. I am indebted to the trainers and writers who helped to provide these development experiences for me.

In 1997, the Management Assistance Program for Nonprofits (MAP) led the development of Strategic Planning Facilitation Workshops that I helped to design and facilitate with Christie Hammes of MAP and Ginnie Belden, consultant. The workshops were offered as a joint effort with the Minnesota Facilitators Network and the Amherst H. Wilder Foundation. The experienced nonprofit strategic planning facilitators who participated in those Workshops provided key input specifically to the section, "Challenges in Facilitating Strategic Planning," in this guide. I am indebted to MAP and these facilitators for their wisdom and contributions.

Other organizations and professionals in this field contributed, as well, both directly and indirectly. My appreciation goes to Greater Twin Cities United Way, Sandra Larson, Barbara Davis, Neil Gustafson, Michael Patton and Christie Hammes of MAP, in particular, for the content they shared for this guide.

I am indebted to the many clients who taught me a great deal about what works – and what does not work – when facilitating strategic planning with nonprofit organizations. I am also indebted to my business partner, Theresa McNamara, from whom I continue to learn while engaging in our continuing dialogues about successful approaches to strategic planning. Theresa is also the editor of many of our guidebooks. Lastly, she is my partner in life and is the reason that I am able to contribute resources to the nonprofit world in the first place.

PART I:

UNDERSTANDING

STRATEGIC PLANNING

Strategic Planning

What Is Strategic Planning?

Simply put, strategic planning is clarifying the purpose of an organization, where the organization wants to be in the future and how it is going to get there. Thus, strategic planning in a nonprofit organization means clarifying:

- The purpose, or mission, of the nonprofit organization.

- The desired status, or vision, for the nonprofit and its clients at some point in the future, usually in the next one to five years.

- How the nonprofit is going to achieve that status, including by analyzing the external and internal environments of the organization, establishing goals, perhaps implementing strategies to achieve the goals, and by operating according to certain overall priorities, or values.

- Action plans, including specifying who is going to be doing what (objectives) and by when in order to achieve the goals and/or implement the strategies.

- What resources are needed in order to implement the action plans, including budgeting for those resources, such as people, materials, equipment and facilities.

- How to make sure that the nonprofit is on track to get there, including by implementing, monitoring and adjusting plans.

Strategic planning can focus on one organization, numerous organizations involved in collaboration, or even on one or more programs in one or more organizations. Also, strategic planning can be carried out in any of a variety of approaches. You will soon read about the approaches most useful to nonprofits.

Analogy to Understand Strategic Planning

Perhaps one of the easiest ways to explain strategic planning is by using a simple analogy. The following table depicts a comparison between strategic planning for an organization to vacation planning for a family.

Strategic Planning		Vacation Planning
Strategic planning	~	Arranging a trip we will take
Mission	~	Why we are traveling, for example, relax, gain renewal, strengthen the family, educational experiences, etc.
Values	~	Our priorities in how we carry out our trip, for example, have a good time, listen, talk, quiet places, opportunities to meet new people, etc.
Vision	~	Where we want to end up and what we will be doing at our ultimate destination
External analysis (what we cannot control)	~	Checking the weather, road conditions, etc.
Internal analysis (what we can control)	~	Checking our available vacation time, condition of our car, who drives, etc.
Goals	~	Major stops along the way
Strategies (small organizations often do not identify strategies)	~	Major routes we will take to the major stops
Action planning	~	Who will drive each route, check the map, make reservations, etc.
Budgeting	~	Identifying how much money we will need to spend
Implementation and adjusting of plans	~	We get in the car and start our vacation, some roads are under construction and we change routes, etc.

What Is "Strategic"?

There are many types of planning, for example, project planning, business planning, staffing planning, financial planning, etc. The unique feature about strategic planning is that it is meant to be "strategic". Strategic planning experts suggest that a plan is strategic if it:

1.   Involves strong input and support from leaders in the organization.

2.   Was produced from careful consideration of the effects of potential changes in the external and internal environments of the organization.

3.   Is based on the future of the organization.

4.   Will have significant influence on the governance, leadership and operations of the organization.

5.   Will involve extensive use of the organization's resources during implementation of the plan.

An organization might not need its current plans to be long-range in order to be strategic. For example, if an organization is facing several, major issues that are internal to the workings of the organization, then it is prudent to develop short-term plans to address those internal issues before developing and implementing a plan that is more long-range in nature. While this point might seem obvious to you, it is amazing how many nonprofits set out to develop plans that are long-range (believing that that makes their plans more strategic), yet, at the same time, these nonprofits have so many internal issues that there is very low likelihood that their plans could ever being implemented successfully in the first place.

Experts often clarify the term "strategic" by comparing it to the term "operational". Operational activities are usually those that are focused on the day-to-day, or short-term, activities. In reality, the continuum between strategic and operational can become quite blurred.

All Else Flows from Strategic Planning in Nonprofit

Strategic planning has significant influence on many aspects of the nonprofit organization. That is why the process is so critical to the success of the nonprofit. For example, strategic planning influences:

- The identification of clients (primary and secondary) to be served by the nonprofit

- How the nonprofit serves the clients

- What resources are needed by the nonprofit, including people, time, materials, equipment, facilities and money

- How the resources are structured and aligned with each other, including Board, staff and programs

- Goals for the Board, Chief Executive officer and staff

- Organizational and program budgets

- Performance management, including of the organization, programs, Board and staff

Major Benefits of Strategic Planning

Strategic planning, when conducted and implemented effectively, can:

- Provide clear focus and alignment of resources in the organization, thereby producing more effective and efficient Board and staff operations

- Build strong teams within the Board and within the staff

- Acquaint staff and members of the Board

- Enhance satisfaction and meaning among members of the organization because they perceive clear contribution and value from their efforts

- Solve major, complex problems in the organization

- Improve conditions for clients, especially the primary clients of the nonprofit because programs are more focused and effective when delivering services

- Improve the image and credibility of the nonprofit because it appears well focused and organized

Experts remind us that the strategic plan document is not the most important benefit from the strategic planning process; rather the *strategic thinking* is. Strategic thinking includes carefully examining the external and internal environments of the organization and then deciding the best approaches (goals, optionally strategies, and action plans) needed to always ensure a good fit between the external and internal environments.

Conducting Strategic Planning

Strategic Planning Framework

There are a variety of approaches to strategic planning. Many of them are derived from the same common strategic planning framework.

The various approaches emphasize different types of activities and different orders. For example, some approaches attend to the mission only after having conducted the situational analysis (internal and external analyses). Some approaches emphasize strategic goals, while others emphasize strategic issues.

In general, the variations occur in the early stages of strategic planning: situational analysis; mission, vision and values statements; strategic issues and strategic goals. The latter stages tend to be performed in the same order, regardless of the particular approach being applied.

The diagram to the right gives an overview of the major phases and the possible order in which they might be performed. This guidebook will refer to the diagram to indicate where you are in the overall framework during the phases in PART II. Variations of this diagram show how different approaches to planning tend to be implemented. Keep in mind, you will be deciding how to customize your approach to best meet the needs of your organization.

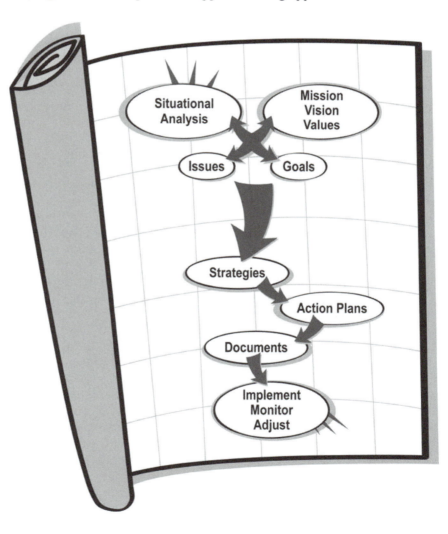

Factors That Influence Approach to Strategic Planning

Organizational factors that influence how planners customize their strategic planning process include:

- Culture of the organization

- Size of the organization and its programs

- Complexity of the organization, its programs and the needs of its clients

- Extent of strategic planning experience in the organization

- Extent of change sought by the organization

- Types of issues facing the organization

- Time available for strategic planning

- Personality of the most influential leader in the organization

Variations from Strategic Planning Framework

Organizations can customize strategic planning process in a variety of ways. This customization can be based on:

- Scope of the plan, for example, focused on organization, one or more programs, a collaboration of organizations or a combination of these

- Time span of the plan, for example, over one, two, three years or more

- Emphasis on particular parts of the framework, for example, on mission, vision, values, strategic issues, strategic goals and/or strategies

- The direction of the planning, for example, top-down, bottom-up and combined

- Originality of the planning, for example, build on an old plan or start a completely new plan

- Order of planning activities, for example, develop the mission statement first or later on after conducting the situational analysis, and identify strategies before establishing strategic goals or afterwards

- Different names for the strategic planning process, for example, goals-based planning, issues-based planning, organic (or holistic) planning and scenario planning

 See the section "Phase 1: Design Plan for Plan" on page 17 in PART II for an overview of the approaches to strategic planning and guidelines to help you select the best approach for your planning project.

Traits of Any Strategic Planning Process

Regardless of the strategic planning process that planners design for their nonprofit, they will likely discover the following traits as they carry out their particular planning process.

1. **The process is cyclical.**
   During planning, you will notice that it seems like planners keep cycling through similar sets of activities. This is very common in any approach to strategic planning, especially if planners are striving to conduct a planning process that is relevant, realistic and flexible.

2. **Different phases of the process might get different emphasis.**
   For example, olanners might spend much more time on identifying goals and strategizing to achieve those goals than on developing a mission statement.

3. **Planners can start anywhere in the strategic planning process.**
   Overall, the aims of the strategic planning process are quite simple: a) clarify the purpose of the organization, b) where it wants to be in the future and c) how it is going to get there. If planners start working on where to be in the future, they usually end up reflecting on the purpose of the organization, and later on about how to get there. They end up cycling through the various, major phases of the strategic planning process.

4. **Much of the strategic planning information is already in the minds of planners.**
   It is common among planners, especially when the strategic plan has been developed, to reflect that they already knew much of what they included in the plan. Some planners lament that, therefore, the planning process was not that successful. That is a major misconception. The goal of strategic planning is not to generate lots of new information. Rather, it is to verify and clarify information among members about the purpose and direction of their organization. One of the most powerful outcomes from the planning process is that it ensures complete understanding and agreement of information among all members of the organization, regardless of whether that information is entirely new or not.

5. **Mission is the "stake in the ground."**
   Regardless of their particular approach to planning, when planners become confused about what is best for their organization and what the organization should do in the future, they often find that they continue to go back to the mission statement for clarity and direction.

What Strategic Planning Will Not Do For You

Strategic planning experts assert that strategic planning is no substitute for effective leadership. Simply put, leadership is the ability to set direction for oneself or others and then influence oneself or others to follow that direction. There has been a recent explosion of books and publications about leadership. One of the reasons for this popularity about leadership is that, although organizations can have many well-designed plans, those plans will not get implemented unless there is effective leadership. So a strategic plan can end up being a useless stack of paper unless there is leadership to guide implementation of the plan.

Strategic planning also is no substitute for effective performance in the workplace. Effective performance is conducting activities that effectively and efficiently contribute toward achieving the goals of the organization. For example, an employee can have goals that are directly aligned with the goals of the organization, but if the employee does not work toward achieving his or her goals, then a strong plan will not help. On the other hand, an employee can be working quite successfully toward achieving his or her goals, but if those goals are not aligned with the overall goals of the organization, then arguably, the employee really is not performing effectively.

Strategic planning is no substitute for effective management. Effective management includes continued planning, organizing of resources, and monitoring usage of resources to ensure progress toward achieving the goals of the organization.

Myths About Strategic Planning

Strategic planning has received a great deal of attention over the past forty years, starting from when the process first was developed for use in the United States military. Since that time, a wide variety of approaches to strategic planning have emerged. Unfortunately, so have a few common myths. It is timely now to dispel those myths.

Myth of Complexity

Organizational leaders often believe that the issues in their organizations are very complex and, therefore, solutions to their issues must be complex, as well. So, for example, when developing a strategic planning process, they tend to value complexity in their process. However, the solutions to their issues are often based instead on mastering the basics about developing and implementing plans in a relevant, realistic and flexible fashion.

Myth of Novelty

One of the most effective ways to get attention to something is to give it a new name. For example, there has been an explosion of books about leadership and management over the past 10 years or so, including about approaches to planning. Many of the books suggest "new" approaches that, upon close examination, are not all that much different than those suggested by management books even 50 years ago.

Myth of the Guru

Unfortunately, many of us still believe that if a process was first proposed by a "big name" guru, then the process must be very effective. Ironically, one of the reasons that gurus become big in the first place is because they have learned the wisdom that is inherent in basic, best practices and espouse them on a regular basis. Too many of us doubt our own wisdom, including our ability to customize and implement our own planning process. You can develop your own plan, going step by step through the planning process.

Three Criteria for Effective Strategic Planning and Plans

A highly effective strategic planning process will produce a highly effective strategic plan. So what is a highly effective strategic planning process? How can we be sure that we have developed the best strategic plan for our organization? These are common questions among those who are new to strategic planning.

Unfortunately, there is no one, standard, specific strategic planning model that can be applied the same way in every situation. Experienced planners have learned that each time an organization does strategic planning, the process somehow seems different from the last time. Also, facilitators have learned that each time a particular approach to strategic planning is used, it seems different from the previous time that approach was used.

However, regardless of the particular approach to the planning or the environment of the nonprofit or the personality of the planners, the strategic planning process will always be highly effective if the process is relevant, realistic and flexible; thereby, producing plans that are relevant, realistic and flexible as well.

Realistic Planning and Plans

Strategic planning experts are well aware of what is probably one of the biggest problems in strategic planning among nonprofit organizations: far too often, the strategic planning process becomes so complex and demanding that members of the nonprofit simply cannot carry out the process because they have such limited resources in terms of people, time, money, materials, facilities, equipment, etc. Ultimately, the members conclude that a comprehensive, detailed strategic planning process does not really suit the nature of their nonprofit – and they are probably right. Consequently, many nonprofit leaders are even repulsed by the phrase "strategic planning" because it evokes such strong feelings of frustration and boredom.

A realistic planning process ensures that the members of the nonprofit have enough people, time and energy available to do the planning that is necessary to produce an effective strategic plan. Inexperienced facilitators soon learn that, when facilitating strategic planning with nonprofits, less is more. Bryson (1995) states, "In my experience, most organizations can demonstrate a substantial improvement in effectiveness if they simply identify and satisfactorily resolve a few strategic issues" (p. 36).

Flexible Planning and Plans

Inexperienced facilitators also learn that, even after a strategic plan document has been completed, it can be a major challenge for the nonprofit to work toward the goals and strategies identified in the plan. For example, sudden changes can occur in the nonprofit that cause goals and strategies to quickly become obsolete, such as when key staff members leave the organization, expected grants do not materialize, etc. Thus, to be highly effective in the long run, the strategic planning process must place a great deal of emphasis, not just on completing a strategic plan document, but on guidelines to actually implement, monitor and – especially – continually adjust the plan as necessary.

Relevant Planning and Plans

To be relevant, the strategic planning process must identify goals, strategies and action plans that position the nonprofit to use its strengths to take advantage of opportunities, while building on weaknesses to ward off threats. In addition, the process and resulting plan must include the strong buy-in, or ownership and commitment, of the key leadership in the organization, including of the Chief Executive Officer and members of the Board. Strong buy-in comes from a planning process that is developed and carried out in a highly collaborative fashion, always focused on the nature and needs of the nonprofit organization and the clients that the organization serves. Strong buy-in also comes from designing the planning process so that it is focused, not just on future-oriented goals and strategies, but also on current, major issues facing the organization.

When Should Regular Strategic Planning Occur?

There are a wide variety of reasons and scheduling for conducting strategic planning, for example, to start a new nonprofit or program. Nonprofits should conduct strategic planning on a regular basis, such as once a year or every two years.

See the section "Phase 1: Design Plan for Plan" on page 17 in PART II for guidelines about reasons for, and scheduling for, planning.

Annual strategic planning should occur relative to the timing of the beginning of the fiscal year. The table on the following page depicts a sample calendar of important annual activities, one of which is strategic planning.

Typical Calendar of Annual Activities in Nonprofit Organization

In the following sample calendar, the fiscal year begins on January 1.

	Yearly Board Activity	**Suggested Timing**
1.	Fiscal year begins	January (fiscal-year timing is often specified in the By-Laws and fiscal policies)
2.	Conduct Board Self-Evaluation (do once a year and in preparation for first Board retreat (might be 2/ year))	March-April (do shortly before evaluating Chief Executive)
3.	Evaluate Chief Executive (reference his or her progress towards last fiscal year's goals and job description)	April-May (do shortly after completion of last fiscal year)
4.	Review and update By-Laws, Board policies, insurances, personnel policies and Board staffing policies	April-June (do concurrent to Board and chief evaluations)
5.	Conduct first Board retreat (team building, address Board self-evaluation results, begin strategic planning, etc.)	April
6.	Begin recruiting new Board members	April-May (in time for June/July elections)
7.	Conduct strategic planning to produce organizational goals and resources need to reach goals	May-June-July (start planning in time for setting mission, vision, values, issues, goals, strategies, resource needs, funding needs, and getting funds before start of next fiscal year)
8.	Develop slate for potential new Board members	June-July (per By-Laws)
9.	Establish Chief Executive's goals for next year (as produced from strategic planning)	August (as organizational goals are realized from planning)
10.	Hold annual meeting and elect new Board members	July (per By-Laws)
11.	Draft next year's budget (based on resources needed to reach new strategic goals)	July-August-September
12.	Develop fundraising plan (with primary goals to get funds needed for budget)	July-August-September
13.	Conduct second Board retreat (address Board orientation/training, review Board/staff roles, re-organize or form new committees based on strategic goals, develop committee work plans, update Board operations calendar, review planning status, etc.)	August (in time to orient new Board members soon after they join the Board)
14.	Conduct fundraising plan (primarily to meet fundraising goals)	August-December

Strategic Management: Strategic Planning Never "Done"

It is deceptive to think that strategic planning is something that is done once a year and ends with a strategic plan document. Strategic planning is an ongoing process. Ever heard the phrase "strategic management"? To many people, that phrase might sound like a complex practice that is only affordable to large organizations with extensive resources. Not true. Basically, strategic management is the process of developing, implementing and adjusting strategic plans on a regular, cyclical basis in organizations.

The process is usually much more effective when carried out explicitly and in a highly focused, systematic fashion. So one of the best reasons to conduct an explicit, highly effective strategic planning process is because the process accomplishes ongoing, highly effective strategic management!

How Much Will Strategic Planning Cost?

This is a common question among those who are new to strategic planning. The success of the strategic planning process is based on the quality of the strategic thinking that goes into the overall strategic planning process. That thinking need not require extensive use of expensive consultants or materials. Therefore, the biggest cost in strategic planning is usually the salary and/or wages for the paid staff who participate in the planning sessions. The amount of time that they spend in planning meetings depends on the nature of the planning process, which, in turn, depends on the size and complexity of the nonprofit and its programs, organizational culture, extent of experience in planning among Board members and staff, and time available for planning,

Specific costs, other than salary and/or wages, usually include the cost of a strategic planning facilitator (unless a member of the Board or staff is the facilitator) and any planning materials, such as guidebooks, conference rooms, presentation equipment and stationery. Considering the potential strong, positive impact that can be achieved from strategic planning, these costs are minimal.

To Learn More About Strategic Planning

PART I of this guidebook includes a basic overview of the strategic planning process for nonprofits, certainly enough of an overview for planners to get started in the process. However, you might prefer to learn more about strategic planning; therefore, the following sources are listed. Note that planners will soon learn a great deal more about strategic planning as they develop and implement their own plan by following the guidelines in Phases 2-6 in PART II.

See the Glossary on page 159 in Appendix A to review various terms used in planning. This might be helpful as part of your effort to learn more about planning. See the Bibliography on page 273 for ideas about practical reference resources about strategic planning.

In addition, the topic "Strategic Planning" in the Free Management Library[SM] includes a number of free, miscellaneous articles at http://www.managementhelp.org/plan_dec/str_plan/str_plan.htm.

PART II:

RELEVANT, REALISTIC

AND FLEXIBLE

STRATEGIC PLANNING

Phase 1: Design Plan for Plan

You would not consider going on a family vacation without first planning your trip. The same is true for strategic planning. This phase in the process invites you to stand back and consider:

- Whether your organization is ready for planning

- How to form a Planning Committee to oversee development of the strategic plan

- Why you are planning now

- What you will focus your plan on

- How long of a time period that your plan will address

- How to customize the best strategic planning process for your organization

- Who will be involved in the planning process

- How to obtain a strategic planning facilitator

- What resources you will need

- The best schedule for your planning activities

At this point, your plan for a plan is comprised of your best estimates regarding the strategic planning process for your nonprofit. Planners should update their plan for a plan, even during the actual strategic planning process itself. The more experience you gain in strategic planning, the more accurate your plan for a plan will be.

 See "Worksheet #1: Plan for Plan" on page 212 for worksheets that you might complete as you progress through the guidelines in this section.

Ready for Strategic Planning?

A high-level leader of the organization should assess whether the nonprofit is ready for strategic planning. The considerations described in this subsection might be addressed by the Chief Executive Officer and/or Board Chair.

Minimum Requirements for Strategic Planning

As you consider the answers to the following questions, you might realize that you are not in a good position to do strategic planning right now. Following are some of the minimum requirements for starting strategic planning.

1. **Nonprofit has enough money to pay current expenses for next three months.**
   If your nonprofit does not have sufficient funds to pay current (already incurred) expenses over the next three months, then you might be better off attending to other, more focused types of activities, for example, targeted, short-term fundraising. More long-term

fundraising will likely require evidence of a well-developed strategic plan for the nonprofit organization to share with potential donors.

2. **Have confidence that plans will be implemented.**

    If your nonprofit has a history of completing various planning processes, but never really doing anything with the plans, then do not waste your time on strategic planning. Instead, attend to why the planning never seems to get anywhere. For example, your nonprofit might have a major leadership problem. Simply put, leadership is setting direction and influencing others to follow that direction. Without effective leadership, strategic planning can be a major waste of time.

3. **Absence of cynicism about planning.**

    If you sense that members of your Board and/or staff are highly cynical about strategic planning, then do not announce that your nonprofit will soon be undertaking strategic planning. Attend to the cynicism first – or, in your "plan for a plan," carefully attend to goals and strategies to first address the cynicism. Cynicism can be caused by continued disillusionment, especially where there once were high hopes. One of the best ways to address cynicism is to provide the cynics a chance to vent their doubts and frustrations. Then clearly explain why any past efforts at planning may have "failed" (maybe they did not fail at all), what you realistically expect from the this round of planning, and what you are going to do to ensure that this round is relevant, realistic and flexible.

4. **Doing a plan because members of the organization prefer to do a plan.**

    Be very careful about doing a plan only because someone outside the organization is demanding it. For example, funders often want to see a somewhat up-to-date strategic plan before they will consider granting funds. If a funder is not satisfied with your organization's planning, then you are faced with whether to develop a plan or not. If the leaders in your organization do not want to do planning at all, then do not start strategic planning right away. Your half-hearted attempts at strategic planning will likely produce a plan that seems uneven, unfocused and certainly not strategic. That could only make things worse between your organization and the funder.

    Rather than doing a poor attempt at strategic planning right away, instead have a "heart to heart" discussion among leaders in the organization. In your discussions, review the advantages of planning, various ways to do planning, and identify any means by which your organization can benefit from the planning process. If you still conclude that planning is a waste of time, then do not undertake strategic planning. However, you will still need to attend to finding ways to generate funds without an up-to-date strategic plan.

5. **Members of the Board can work together, as can members of the staff.**

    If there is a high degree of conflict among members of your Board and/or staff, then do not start strategic planning right away. Strategic planning, particularly the part about strategizing to address issues or achieving goals can get a little contentious. In an environment with lots of conflict, strategic planning could be toxic. Ironically, one of the reasons for the conflict could be that there is no clear focus and direction for the organization. Thus, strategic planning may even minimize conflict. So it might be useful to pursue planning, but be sure to get a facilitator with good skills in conflict management.

6. **Chief Executive will be in the organization, at least over next three months.**

    If your Chief Executive is on the way out, then you might not want to conduct a complete strategic planning process before the new Chief Executive is hired. Instead, you might benefit from having the new Chief Executive involved in the planning, so that he or she has input and ownership in the new plan.

7. **Various Board and staff members can afford at least 12-15 hours of meetings in next month or so.**
    Sometimes, the reality of a nonprofit organization is such that people are extremely busy and when forced to go to meetings, they end up coming late and leaving early. This is not a matter of someone being irresponsible as much as that they might be the only people who can deliver services to clients and the clients are lined up at the door. In that case, directing people to take part in strategic planning might be destructive to the staff and clients. Perhaps it would be best right now to attend to finding more short-term resources, cutting back on demands on staff, reducing the amount of services to clients, or conducting training on time and stress management.

Any Concerns About Doing Strategic Planning Now?

Even if none of the above-mentioned situations exist in your nonprofit, then you still should consider the following questions.

1. If you did strategic planning before, were there any problems with the approach to planning and/or with the approach to implementation of the plan? How will you avoid those problems this time around?

2. Are there any people who might be uncomfortable with the strategic planning process? How will you respond to those people?

3. Are there any major events coming up that might affect the strategic planning process? How will you manage those events?

4. How are you sure that your people have the time and energy to participate in the strategic planning process?

5. Can you be assured access to the people needed by the strategic planning process? How will you ensure access?

6. Is your organization really ready to do anything other than the routine? Sometimes leaders do strategic planning just because "it is the thing to do," but later on during planning, they keep resorting back to the same old way of doing things.

7. Other concerns you might think of?

Now Complete Part of "Worksheet #1: Plan for Plan"

See worksheet "1.1 – Is Nonprofit Ready for Strategic Planning?" on page 212 in "Worksheet #1: Plan for Plan" in Appendix G.

Organize Planning Committee?

At this point, key leaders in the organization have decided that the nonprofit is indeed ready for strategic planning. Now it is time to proceed through the rest of the guidelines for this phase, starting with considering whether a Planning Committee would be useful or not.

Responsibilities of Planning Committee

The overall responsibility of the Planning Committee is to oversee the development of the strategic plan. The Committee would not be conducting every activity in the planning process. Rather, the Committee would act as a body to:

1. **Complete a plan for a plan.**
    This includes careful design of a strategic planning process that suits the nature and needs of their nonprofit organization. Guidelines for completing the plan for a plan are included in this section.

2. **Recruit the strategic planning facilitator.**
    The facilitator might be internal (a member of the nonprofit organization) or external to the organization. If you decided on an external facilitator, the guidelines in Appendix E on page 193 about contracting with a consultant will be helpful at this point.

3. **Work with the facilitator.**
    This might include sharing suggestions and guidance, particularly when applying the guidelines in Phases 2-5 in PART II to develop the strategic plan.

4. **Monitor progress of development of plan by comparing progress to schedule.**
    The schedule is produced from following the guidelines in this section.

5. **Review tangible results from each step of the planning process.**
    This could include review of the completed worksheets that will be produced from each of Phases 2-5 in PART II.

Who Should Be on Planning Committee?

If the number of planners, including members of the Board and staff, for the nonprofit organization would total 10 people or less, then a Committee might not be needed. Rather, all of the planners would act as a body to carry out the above-listed responsibilities, in addition to participating in developing and implementing the strategic plan.

If a Committee would be useful, then, ideally, the Board Chair and Chief Executive Officer (CEO) take the lead in organizing the Committee. The Planning Committee should include 5-8 highly committed individuals. That range in size often seems to provide the most appropriate range of energy, participation and decision-making ability.

1. **The CEO should be on the Committee.**
    The CEO provides ongoing visible legitimacy to the planning process, along with ability to make decisions and provide historical information about the nonprofit. If there is a likelihood that the CEO will not be on the Planning Committee, then members of the Board and the CEO should have very clear and credible reasons for excluding the CEO from the Committee.

2.   **Include the person who is directly responsible to ensure the strategic plan is completed**. Usually that person is the CEO. The Board ultimately is responsible to ensure completion.

3.   **The Board Chair should be on the Committee**. The Board is responsible to establish the direction for the nonprofit, along with overall methods to work toward that direction. The direction and methods are decided during strategic planning. Thus, Board involvement in strategic planning is critical. Therefore, at least one member of the Board should be on the Planning Committee and usually it is best if that member is the Chair of the Board.

4.   **Attempt to include at least one experienced member of the Board**. This person should have been on the Board for at least a year and have strong knowledge of the nonprofit organization.

5.   **Include a "champion"**. The champion helps to maintain enthusiasm during the planning process.

6.   **Include someone to help administrate the process**. For example, this person would ensure that materials and facilities are provided for meetings and would document results of meetings.

7.   **Consider having the leader of each major program on the Planning Committee**. Programs play a critical when coordinating the implementation of goals and strategies from strategic planning, so program leaders often play a valuable role in strategic planning for the entire organization. Those leaders often have strong knowledge of the clients served by the nonprofit, as well.

Remaining membership of the Committee should be determined by following guidelines in the subsection, "Who Will Be Involved from Nonprofit?", included later on in this section, "Phase 1: Design Plan for Plan."

Now Complete Part of "Worksheet #1: Plan for Plan"

See "1.2 – Organize Planning Committee?" on page 214 in "Worksheet #1: Plan for Plan."

Why Do Strategic Planning Now?

It is important to identify why your nonprofit should be planning now. These are the reasons that you will use when explaining and justifying the planning process to yourself and others. The reasons also will be useful later on when evaluating whether the strategic planning indeed was successful for your nonprofit.

Here is a list of the typical types of comments that nonprofit leaders make when explaining why they are doing strategic planning. You might consider them when clarifying your reasons for conducting strategic planning now.

- "Our state budget must be cut by 30%. We're very likely to lose our state grant. What are we going to do?"

- "We keep getting all of these ideas for programs from members of our Board. What should we do?"

- "We really do not know how to allocate our resources, including our people, time, materials and money."

- "We want to be in charge of our destiny."

- "We're going through some life-cycle changes. We have been very entrepreneurial, making decisions by the 'seat of our pants.' We cannot be doing that anymore."

- "Our Board members keep arguing about the purpose of our organization!"

- "We seem stuck in the same old routines, never getting anywhere or doing anything new."

- "I wish that all of us were 'on the same page.' It seems that we all have different ideas about what we're about."

- "We need to defend why our nonprofit is doing what it is doing and how it is doing it."

- "Our Executive Director is leaving in May. We have a Board Search Committee, but the members are not sure what goals the new Executive Director should achieve."

- "I want to start a new nonprofit. Directions for starting a nonprofit keep asking for a strategic plan. What's that?"

- "It seems like we never have enough money. We're always raising funds to deal with one crisis after another."

- "Our funder wants a strategic plan. We have no clue how to do one!"

Now Complete Part of "Worksheet #1: Plan for Plan"

See "1.3 – Why Do Strategic Planning Now?" on page 215 in "Worksheet #1: Plan for Plan."

What Is Organizational Scope of Plan?

A strategic plan can be focused on the entire organization, one or more programs, or a collaboration of organizations or programs. (It is not within the scope of this guidebook to include guidelines to organize collaboration, conduct strategic planning for the collaboration and implement plans in the collaboration.)

Reasons To Focus Strategic Planning Organization-Wide

Frequently, strategic planning is focused on the entire organization and not just on one particular program. Depending on the approach to strategic planning, planning establishes: the mission, vision and/or values; goals and strategies; action plans and budgets for the entire organization. You should consider doing a strategic plan focused on the entire organization if any of the following is true:

1.   The organization has not done strategic planning in several years.

2.   Your nonprofit is quite new, for example, the nonprofit has not established: a mission, vision and/or values; goals and strategies; and clear assignments regarding who will be doing what and by when.

3.   The environments of your nonprofit (external and/or internal) are changing rapidly.

4.   Your nonprofit is experiencing frequent, internal problems.

5.   Decision-making seems difficult to achieve and ineffective to follow.

6.   There is prolonged conflict among staff and/or Board members.

7.   The organization has several programs that conflict for resources and clients.

See "Why Do Strategic Planning Now?" on page 21 for numerous reasons to conduct strategic planning.

Reasons To Focus Planning on Programs Only

Occasionally, planners focus strategic planning primarily on one or more programs, and not on the entire organization. Strategic planning focused primarily on a program can be used to ensure strong alignment between the program and the entire organization and between other programs, as well. You might consider doing a strategic plan focused primarily on one or more programs, especially if any of the following are true:

1.   The overall organization is stable and has successfully completed a strategic plan for the organization over the past year or two.

2.   The program is new.

3.   The program is expecting a major change in methods to deliver services to clients.

4.   Major changes are expected among the clients served by the program.

5.   The programs in the nonprofit are quite different from each other.

6.   The program is experiencing prolonged problems.

Special Considerations If Strategic Planning for Programs Only

The description of this guidebook specifies that guidelines are focused primarily on organization-wide strategic planning. However, if planners are using the guidelines herein to conduct strategic planning primarily for one or more of their programs instead, then they should address certain considerations, including that in a plan for *each* program:

1. There needs to be strong, focused planning around "inbound" marketing activities in order to identify, clarify and verify the groups of clients served by the program, their needs and how the program will meet those needs.

2. Perhaps there is even more reason to involve clients in development of the program plan than in the organization-wide strategic plan, although clients should be involved in the latter, as well.

3. Program staff should be very heavily involved in program planning, for example, administrators of the program and staff who deliver services to clients.

4. There may be more focus on developing certain, specific skills in order to serve clients in the program, such as trainers, counselors, artists and day-care providers.

5. There needs to be strong, focused planning around "outbound" marketing activities in order to advertise, promote and sell the services of the program. Certainly, outbound marketing activities are conducted for the organization, as well, and usually called public relations. However, outbound marketing plans should be done for each program, and probably in an even more robust fashion than done in public relations campaigns for an entire organization.

6. At least some of the goals in the program plan should include a strong outcomes focus, maybe even more than goals included in an organization-wide strategic plan. (Outcomes are changes in clients. An outcomes goal might be that clients obtain a high-school diploma, drive a car, pass a physical exam, etc.)

 Guidelines for the above special considerations are not emphasized in this guidebook. Thus, if planners are considering a plan focused mostly on one or more programs, and not on the entire organization, then they might consider the step-by-step guidelines in the guidebook, *Field Guide to Nonprofit Program Design, Marketing and Evaluation,* by this author.

Now Complete Part of "Worksheet #1: Plan for Plan"

 See "1.4 – What Is Organizational Scope of Plan?" on page 216 in "Worksheet #1: Plan for Plan."

What Strategic Planning Approach Might Be Used?

There are a variety of approaches to organizational planning, not all of them strategic, but still useful in any regard. This subsection describes the most common approaches to strategic planning for nonprofit organizations, including goals-based and issues-based strategic planning. In addition, descriptions are provided about organic (or holistic) strategic planning, and about the scenario planning technique, as well. Overall, the approaches include:

1.   Goals-based strategic planning

2.   Issues-based strategic planning

3.   Organic (holistic) strategic planning

4.   Scenario planning technique

A summary of these approaches is included near the end of this section. Also, near the end of this section, you will be asked to document your thoughts about which approach to use. Note that this subsection is entitled "What Strategic Planning Approach Might Be Used?," rather than "What Strategic Planning Approach Will Be Used?". At this point, you do not have to know for sure what approach will be used. You need only make your best guess.

Note that it is common for planners to choose one approach to planning, but eventually to find themselves conducting a mix of the various approaches.

See "1.5 – What Strategic Planning Approach Might Be Used?" on page 218 as you progress through the guidelines about selecting an approach to strategic planning.

Goals-Based Strategic Planning

How Is Goals-Based Strategic Planning Conducted?

Goals-based strategic planning is probably the most common form of strategic planning. The types of planning activities and their typical order are shown in the diagram.

Although planners conduct most or all of the activities laid out in the strategic planning framework, they place heavy emphasis on establishing clear goals to be achieved at some point in the future, for example, one, two or three years out. Subsequent activities in planning are focused very much on achieving the goals, especially when identifying strategies or developing action plans. Goals might be derived from reference to the situational analysis and the mission, vision and values.

Goals-based strategic planning is in contrast to the issues-based approach to strategic planning where planners place heavy emphasis on identifying strategic issues. Subsequent activities in issues-based planning focus on addressing the issues, especially when identifying strategies or action plans.

When Should Goals-Based Strategic Planning Be Considered?

Consider goals-based strategic planning if any of the following is true for your nonprofit.

1. Planners can identify goals in the future – not all planners can do that, especially if they are facing current, major issues. (Note that goals-based strategic planning tends to work from goals in order to identify strategies and action plans. Whereas, issues-based strategic planning tends to work from issues in order to identify goals (sometimes), strategies and action plans.)

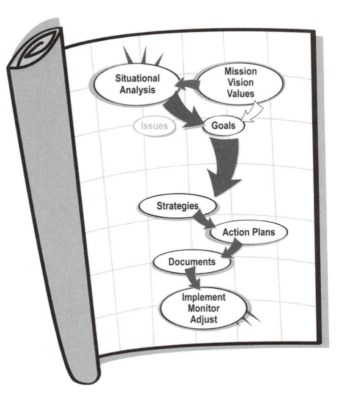

2. Planners have established a clear mission, vision and/or values statements, or scenarios before attempting to establish goals.

3. There are few, if any, very critical (especially internal) issues facing your organization.

4. The environments of your nonprofit (external and/or internal) are stable or, at least, predictable.

5. Decisions are often made in a top-down, hierarchical fashion.

6. Your nonprofit has successfully developed and implemented a complete strategic planning process before, especially a goals-based strategic planning process within the past two years.

7. Your nonprofit includes several, major programs, each of which might conduct its own focused planning and, thus, the program plans will need to be integrated into an overall organizational strategic plan. Having clear goals for the organization and programs often makes it easier to integrate the various plans.

8. Planners would like to accomplish a major change in direction for the organization or program(s) over the next year or so. Clear goals can establish clear direction, in addition to providing clear "signposts" along the way when following that direction.

Issues-Based Strategic Planning

How is Issues-Based Strategic Planning Conducted?

The issues-based approach is another common strategic planning process, which is also sometimes referred to critical-issues planning.

The types of activities and their typical order are shown in the diagram to the right. Issues-based planning might start with a situational analysis, and then move on to issues and action plans to address those issues. Mission, vision and values might be developed or updated afterwards. Goals might be established, but usually after addressing the issues and actions to address the issues.

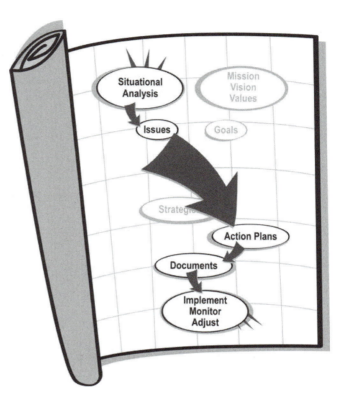

Issues-Based Strategic Planning Well Suited to Many Nonprofits

Many nonprofit organizations have very limited resources in terms of people, time and money. As a result, these nonprofits face a variety of major issues, for example, frequent shortage of funds, high turnover among members of the Board or staff, and extended conflict among members of the Board or staff. Here are several reasons why issues-based strategic planning is often the best approach to use with these organizations.

1. **Goals can quickly become obsolete.**
    Things can change quickly for struggling nonprofit organizations. Consequently, by the time the organizations have identified goals to achieve at some point in their future, their external or internal environments have changed to the extent that the goals are obsolete. Thus, their strategic plans can become obsolete as well.

2. **Intuitively, goals often come during or after strategizing.**
    Conventional approaches to strategic planning usually suggest identifying strategic goals before identifying the strategies or action plans to achieve the goals. Frequently, this order of activities is not as relevant as first identifying strategies and then identifying goals.

    To explain, strategies are a set of approaches used, ultimately, to carry out the purpose of the organization – strategies are an extension of the mission of the organization. The most targeted and suitable strategies often come, not from aiming at some particular end-point (goal) in the future, but from thinking about methods (strategies) to address a major challenge. Therefore, especially for struggling nonprofits, strategies derived from goals can seem awkward, even arbitrary.

3. **Quick attention to issues can increase planners' participation in planning.**
    If members of a nonprofit organization know that the organization is facing several major issues, then often those planners really struggle to participate in a planning process that is directing them to identify goals to achieve in the distant future. Instead, inviting planners to first identify major issues before identifying goals – if planners choose to establish goals at all – can immediately energize planners and, thereby, vest their participation and ownership in the strategic planning process.

Note that the issues-based approach to strategic planning is not intended to minimize the importance of establishing clear goals in the strategic planning process. Rather, the approach is intended to ensure that any goals are realistic and relevant to addressing major issues.

When Should Issues-Based Strategic Planning Be Considered?

You might consider using issues-based strategic planning for your nonprofit, especially if any of the following is true for your nonprofit.

1. Your nonprofit faces several, critical issues.

2. The nonprofit has very limited resources in terms of people, time and money.

3. There are expected to be major changes in the environments of your nonprofit (external and/or internal) over the next year or so.

4. The time span for your strategic plan can be one or two years, or at most three years out, rather than having to be for a longer term.

5. Planners struggle to identify clear goals for the future.

6. Planners are concerned about the continual "buy in" among members of the Board and staff.

Organic (Holistic) Strategic Planning

What Is Organic Strategic Planning?

Organization and management sciences today are placing a great deal of attention to naturalistic approaches to development. Probably the most prominent approach is called "self-organizing" systems. These are systems that develop primarily according to certain values, rather than according to specific procedures. Biological systems (people, plants, animals, etc.) are fine examples of self-organizing systems. They might grow in any variety of ways – ways which are rarely sequential in nature. However, these biological systems always develop according to certain key principles or values, such as propagation of their species and self-preservation.

The traditional approach to strategic planning can be highly linear, or sequential, in nature. In the traditional approach, planners might: first identify broad mission, vision and/or values statements; conduct a situational analysis; establish broad goals in accordance with the mission; identify strategies to achieve those goals (small nonprofits often skip this strategies); and develop specific action plans (objectives, schedules, responsibilities and resources) to implement those strategies. This linear approach is not well suited to all types of nonprofit organizations. Some organizations might prefer a more naturalistic planning process that allows all perspectives and activities in an organization to unfold over time. This planning process might be deemed "organic", that is, it emerges like that in natural systems, such as plants, animals and people. Some might prefer to call it "holistic."

See "Tool #2: Organic Philosophy of Problem Solving" on page 263 in Appendix H for the perspective of an organic or holistic planner.

How Is Organic Strategic Planning Conducted?

This is a rather unconventional approach to planning – certainly, an approach that some might argue is not strategic at all. However, the value of this approach is that it can match the nature of certain types of organizations much more closely than the traditional, linear approaches. It might even be argued that the linear approaches can even hurt these types of organizations as their members struggle to conform to a planning process that is quite contrary to their nature.

Meetings to identify mission, and especially vision, values and action plans, might be based on telling stories about "the best time that we ..." or "my wish is that ..." This approach is well developed in the emerging field of appreciative inquiry. Facilitation techniques, including stories, Round-Robin, brainstorming and voting might be used. .

Guidelines for these techniques are included in PART III of this guide. For information about appreciative inquiry, go to http://appreciativeinquiry.case.edu/.

When Should Organic Strategic Planning Be Considered?

Organic strategic planning might be suited to your nonprofit if one or more of the following is true for your nonprofit:

1.   The vision for your organization and its clients applies to a large group of people, and might take a very long time to achieve.

2.   The effort to achieve the vision might involve lots of very diverse people.

3.   The culture of the organization is quite averse to conducting orderly, sequential activities.

4.   The role of vision and values in your organization is extremely important.

5.   The culture of the organization highly values the working from the positive and telling of stories.

6.   If your organization expects funding from donors, it has confidence that it can obtain that funding without presenting a conventional strategic plan document with goals and strategies.

The focus of the process needs to be on the interaction among stakeholders as much, or more, than on achieving certain, specific results. Stakeholders are people or groups of people who have a strong interest in the organization. Note that if the organic strategic planning process is preferred by planners, then the process probably should be applied to the entire organization, rather than specifically to one or more programs.

Scenario Planning Technique

How is Scenario Planning Conducted?

Some planners recognize scenario planning as a complete strategic planning process. Other planners consider scenarios to be a technique that can be used in any strategic planning process, especially to ensure rigorous visioning and strategizing during the process.

Scenario planning includes considerations of a comprehensive set of driving forces, or major influences, that can affect the nonprofit, programs and stakeholders well into the future. Driving forces are usually in regard to political, economic, societal and technological influences.

1.   Planners consider various, major driving forces and then develop various scenarios, or pictures of the nonprofit, clients and even society, at various points in the future, for example, 5 years, 10 years and 20 years.

2.   Typically, planners develop a worst-case scenario based on the assumption that things will turn out for the worse in some or all of the various driving forces that are most relevant to the nonprofit.

3.   Planners usually also develop a best-case scenario based on the assumption that things will turn out for the better in the relevant driving forces.

4.   Finally, planners might work from the worst-case and best-case scenarios to develop a nominal (or most realistic) scenario from which they might do visioning and establishing strategic goals. (Note that a scenario can often be larger than a vision statement because the scenario might depict the organization, its clients and especially relevant, major conditions in society at some point in the future.)

5.   It is up to planners whether they choose to scope their scenarios to the organization and its clients or to also depict broader elements of society, as well.

See "Worksheet #4: Environmental Scan" on page 241 in this guidebook for guidelines and a tool to develop scenarios. The reader should not conduct the scenario technique at this point in the guidebook, but rather wait until following the guidelines later in PART II, when customizing and developing the strategic plan.

When Should Scenario Planning Technique Be Considered?

Scenario planning can be useful, especially with other approaches to strategic planning, if any of the following are true:

1.   Planners have concerns that their planning might not effectively consider future trends and how those trends affect their nonprofit.

2.   Planners prefer to develop, and work from, a comprehensive, clear vision for their organization and its clients, but they struggle to create that vision.

Summary of Approaches to Strategic Planning

The following table depicts a summary of highlights from the above descriptions of useful approaches to strategic planning for nonprofit organizations. When reviewing the table, note that different approaches to strategic planning might use the same method when conducting a certain activity in planning. In the following table, "E" designates an essential activity, "R" recommended and "O" optional. "S" designates that the scenario planning technique might be particularly useful in that planning activity.

Summary of Major Approaches to Strategic Planning for Nonprofit Organizations			
Planning Activity	**Goals-Based Strategic Planning**	**Issues-Based Strategic Planning**	**Organic Strategic Planning**
Develop/clarify mission	E	E	E
Develop/clarify vision and/or values	O, S	O, S	E
Conduct external analysis	E, S	E, S	E
Conduct internal analysis	E	E	R
Identify strategic issues	O	E	O
Establish strategic goals	E	O	O
Identify strategies (small nonprofits might skip)	E	E	O
Develop action plans	E	E	E
Develop budget	E	E	R
Develop Strategic Plan document	R	R	R
Authorize Plan	E	E	E
Implement, monitor and adjust plans	E	E	E

For example, planners who are using the goals-based or issues-based approaches to strategic planning might conduct an external analysis by using the same, comprehensive, detailed assessment tools.

In contrast, organic strategic planning might conduct an external analysis through use of ongoing stories and discussions among stakeholders. Planners who are conducting the organic strategic planning process might also choose to identify the mission, and especially vision, values and action plans, by sharing stories among stakeholders. These planners might not attend to strategic issues, goals and strategies.

Now Complete Part of "Worksheet #1: Plan for Plan"

See "1.5 – What Strategic Planning Approach Might Be Used?" on page 218 in "Worksheet #1: Plan for Plan."

How Might Strategic Planning Approach Be Followed?

At this point, you do not have to know for sure how the approach will be followed. You need only make your best guess.

Do You Want a Written Strategic Plan?

A common lament among strategic planning experts is that nonprofit organizations do not do strategic planning. Actually, many nonprofits organizations very frequently do strategic planning – it is just that they do it implicitly, that is, their plans are not directly expressed in written form. Among the highly diverse types of nonprofit organizations, some might choose not to document a strategic plan, although many strategic planning experts assert that it is wise to document your plan.

You might choose not to document a strategic plan if:

1.   Your organization is very small and does not need any funding from donors, or

2.   Your nonprofit conducted a very comprehensive strategic planning process within the past two years and the environments (external and internal) of your nonprofit are very stable.

Note that if a written strategic plan will exist for the entire organization, then program plans should be written, as well.

Organizational Direction of Planning Activities

Strategic planning can be done from the bottom-up (starting from the bottom of the organization and "rolling up" plans to an organization-wide plan) or from the top down.

Top-Down Planning

Top-down planning is often preferred if any of the following is true about the nonprofit.

1.   It has a very effective Board of Directors, including members who are representative of the stakeholders of the nonprofit.

2.   It has frequent turnover of staff.

3.   It is spread across a wide geographic area, so it is difficult for staff to interact.

4.   It has very experienced members of the Board and senior management.

5.   It has a culture that highly values the power of its upper management.

Top-down planning is usually focused on the entire organization, rather than specifically on programs. Planners could do top-down planning when plans are focused primarily on programs and not the entire organization; however, in that case, the programs would likely have to be fairly large for that planning approach to be useful at all.

Bottom-Up Planning

Bottom-up planning might be preferred if any of the following is true:

1.   Members of the Board of Directors are difficult to organize and/or engage.

2.   Planning will be focused mostly on one or more programs.

3.   Staff have strong expertise in the nonprofit's programs, including the clients' needs and how those needs are met.

4.   Members of the Board and management are quite new to the nonprofit.

As with top-down planning, bottom-up planning is usually focused on the entire organization, rather than specifically on programs. Planners could do bottom-up planning when plans are focused primarily on programs and not the entire organization; however, in that case, the programs would likely have to be fairly large for that planning approach to be useful at all.

The bottom-up approach carries some risk that the overall strategic plan will not be aligned with the mission of the organization, the plan will be focused too much on day-to-day detail, and the Board will not have ownership in the plan.

> Separate plans formed during bottom-up planning must be "rolled up" or integrated together. Guidelines for this activity are included later on when needed in Phase 4 of PART II.

Concurrent (Combined) Planning

Usually, organizations end up with an overall, concurrent process that includes an integration of top-down and bottom-up planning. In this approach, planners need to be very careful to communicate about who is developing which plans and how they will be combined.

Experts assert that the best forms of planning usually include strong participation from both members of the Board and staff, if possible. This participation often leads to more relevant, realistic and flexible strategic plans. Board and other nonprofit leaders might attend closely to the mission, vision and/or values statements; external analysis; internal analysis; and goals and strategies. Concurrently, program staff might attend closely to internal analysis, goals and strategies, and action planning (including budgeting). Then the planning information produced by the Board members, leaders and program staff is combined.

Originality of Plan – Incremental Change or Fresh Start?

The plan can be developed by making incremental (often minor) adjustments to a previous version of a strategic plan or by following a "zero-based" approach in which all aspects of the plan are developed from a fresh start. Many organizations end up using a combination of these approaches.

Your organization might resort to incremental planning if:

1.   The environments of your nonprofit (external and internal) are quite stable, and

2.   The organization did strategic planning in the last year or two, and

3.   The strategies and action plans of the previous version of the strategic plan proved to be quite useful to the nonprofit.

Now Complete Part of "Worksheet #1: Plan for Plan"

See "1.6 – How Might Strategic Planning Approach Be Followed?" on page 223 in "Worksheet #1: Plan for Plan."

What Is Time Span for Plan?

The time span of the strategic plan is usually the period of time in which the strategic goals in the plan are intended to be implemented. It is very common that the time span of a nonprofit strategic plan is three years to five years. Note that the time span for goals might be three years, but the span for action plans is one year.

1. The higher the rate of change expected in the external environment of the nonprofit, the shorter might be the time span for the strategic plan.

2. The more that an organization is expected to expand in the future, for example, over a wide geographic area with many regional offices, the longer the time span might be.

3. Many times, the time span of a plan also depends on the particular type of strategic planning approach preferred by planners, but the approach should not be the only determinant of the time span of the plan.

For example, during a three-year strategic planning process, planners might focus their planning on situational analyses, goals and strategies, with a three-year time span in mind. However, they might be wise to focus their detailed action planning (specifically who will be doing what by when) to be especially over the next 12 months or fiscal year. That approach is appropriate because planners usually conduct strategic planning on a yearly basis; thus, action plans will be updated successively for each year of the three-year plan. Organic planning might focus on very short-term activities, for example, over the next three to six months with intention of updating the plan 2-4 times per year.

When developing their plan, planners might refer to "short-term" and "long-term" matters regarding their strategic plan. Planners should think about what those two terms mean regarding the time span of their plan. For example, for a three-year strategic plan, short-term might mean over the next six to 12 months, while long-term might mean over the entire three-year span of the plan.

Scenarios can be used as a technique to generate vision, goals and strategies that can be used in various approaches to strategic planning. Thus, planners might choose to develop scenarios well out into the future, for example, five or 10 years. However, those scenarios would probably be used to help develop vision, goals and strategies that apply to a closer period of time, for example, one, two, three or five years.

NOTE: Guideline in this guidebook often suggest that planners focus their detailed planning on, "especially, the next 12 months or fiscal year." Development of the mission, vision, values, any scenarios, situational analysis, goals, strategies and action plans can be focused farther out in time. Whether the plan extends one, two or three years out or more, planners still should focus their analysis very closely on the next 12 months or fiscal year.

Now Complete Part of "Worksheet #1: Plan for Plan"

See "1.7 – What Time Span Will Be Used?" on page 226 in "Worksheet #1: Plan for Plan."

What Is Schedule for Developing Plan?

Length of Overall Planning Process

The length of the planning process is the amount of time required to produce a strategic plan document. The length of the process depends on:

- Whether the nonprofit or program(s) has done planning before (the more experience, the less time that might be required)

- The complexity of the nonprofit's environment, issues and programs (the more complex, the more time that might be required)

- Whether the culture prefers short or long meetings

- How much time the nonprofit is willing to commit to the process

- If any crises occur during the process, for example, key people leave the organization or funding is cut.

For nonprofits with very limited resources, attempt to complete a strategic plan document in as little as 15-20 hours of meetings and during a one-month period; otherwise, momentum might be lost and the planning effort may stop altogether. This approach might still include doing work on the process between meetings, for example, researching external trends, and drafting statements and documents.

Scheduling and Duration of Meetings

There is no standard rule about the number of meetings required in the process, when to have them and how long each will be.

Often, the first meeting in the strategic planning process is held away from the regular work facilities, often called a retreat meeting. The retreat is usually longer than a typical business meeting, for example, a half-day or full-day long.

It is often best to have planning meetings at most two to three weeks apart. Otherwise, it is too easy to lose momentum between meetings as people get back to being highly involved in the day-to-day workings of their jobs and lives.

Think about when meetings seem to work best in your organization. For example, some organizations seem to have the most productive meetings early in the day, while others have them in the afternoon.

In the first meeting, attempt to establish dates for all future meetings. This helps to ensure that meetings accommodate the schedules of all of the planners.

Always consider how planners can get planning done between meetings, too (their "homework"). For example, research can be done, documents can be drafted, and documentation of meeting results can be distributed. Guidelines throughout PART II include suggestions for various homework activities.

Note that the most important factor in accomplishing complete attendance to meetings is leadership support. Therefore, always ensure the Board Chair and/or the Chief Executive sends meeting notices to each planner who should attend.

Sample Planning Sequence and Schedule

The table on the following page depicts an example of a brief, goals-based, strategic planning format and schedule. The format and schedule used by planners depends on their results from following the guidelines provided in this section, "Phase 1: Design Pan for Plan."

Now Complete Part of "Worksheet #1: Plan for Plan"

See "1.8 – What Schedule Might Be Used?" on page 227 in "Worksheet #1: Plan for Plan."

Example of Brief Goals-Based Strategic Planning Format and Schedule

Hold half-day retreat to start planning process with planners.

1. Board Chair and Chief Executive Officer explain benefits of strategic planning, provide planning guide and schedule. Time is allocated for discussion, questions and answers.
2. Organizational profile is reviewed.
3. Tools of external analysis are explained and assigned to key Board and staff.
4. Tools for internal analysis are explained and assigned to key Board and staff.
5. All of the next planning meetings are scheduled.
6. Certain planners are asked to start the external and internal analyses, and provide resulting information to all planners. All planners start to think about strategic goals.
7. Meet two weeks later in another half-day retreat.

In next half-day Board retreat, identify strategic goals.

1. Brief review and update of mission, vision and/or values statements.
2. Discuss external and internal analysis results.
3. Identify and rank top 5-8 strategic goals. (No strategies are identified yet.)
4. Each member is asked to think about strategies before next meeting.
5. Meet two weeks later in another half-day retreat.

In next half-day retreat, finalize strategies and begin drafting plan.

1. Strategies are identified, clarified and ranked for each strategic goal.
2. Brief update of mission, vision and/or values statements.
3. Group of staff asked to propose action plans (including budgets) before next meeting.

In half-day staff meeting, review action plans.

1. Each action plan is reviewed and fine-tuned.
2. Subcommittee asked to draft strategic plan document.
3. Plan later reviewed by Chief Executive and passed on to Board for approval.

In the next Board meeting, Board members authorize the strategic plan document.

1. Board members discuss and approve the drafted plan document.

Who Will Be Involved from Nonprofit? How? When?

Consider the following guidelines regarding who should be involved, how and when.

1.   **Involve those who are responsible for composing and implementing the plan.**
     It is critical that people who are responsible for plan (composing, implementing, monitoring, it, etc.) have "buy in" – commitment and ownership – in the planning process. Otherwise, the resulting plan will very likely not be relevant and realistic – it is highly unlikely that the plan will be fully implemented, if at all. The rule of thumb is to involve at least those people who will be responsible to oversee and/or implement any portion of the plan. The best way to get this buy-in is to involve those people in the planning process. If it is not practical to have all key people involved in all stages, then try to involve key people in certain phases of the planning activities.

2.   **Different types of members may be needed more at different phases of planning.**
     Board members should be highly involved in the external analysis and determining the overall direction for the organization (its mission, vision, values, goals and strategies). Staff might take a lead role in conducting the internal analysis and developing action plans to implement each strategy.

3.   **Members of the Board should be involved.**
     One of the major responsibilities of the Board is to establish the overall direction of the nonprofit and ensure that the nonprofit follows that direction. The Board carries out this responsibility primarily by overseeing the development and implementation of policies and plans, especially the strategic plan. Therefore, the Board should take part in development of the strategic plan, official approval of plan document and tracking the implementation of the plan, as well.

4.   **You will need a "champion" for the planning process.**
     The champion is someone who continues to help planners realize the importance of the planning process and their participation in it. Sometimes the champion can be the facilitator; but if the facilitator is someone from outside the organization, then you will be better off still to have an internal champion – or the importance of the planning process and motivation might be lost when the facilitator leaves.

5.   **You will also need a "sponsor" for the planning process.**
     The sponsor is the official role in the organization that is responsible for providing the authority and resources for people to carry out the planning process. Often, the sponsor is the Board Chair or the Chief Executive Officer.

6.   **As much as possible, involve external stakeholders in the planning.**
     Nonprofits exist to meet a major need in the community. Therefore, members of the community (external stakeholders) should be involved as much as possible in strategic planning, particularly when collecting information about the needs in the community and how the nonprofit might meet those needs. For example, potential funders are very important to involve in your planning. Plan to interview funders about their knowledge of trends in the areas of your programs, their impressions of your organization and what they would like from your organization in the future. Attempt to include the organization's clientele, community leaders, members of nonprofits that serve similar groups of clients, collaborators, etc. Especially if members of the Board are not representative of the various

groups of stakeholders, then the organization should ensure more representation of external stakeholders in planning.

See "Worksheet #3: Stakeholder Analysis" on page 239 for a list of possible external stakeholders.

7. **Always include in the group at least one person who can make decisions.**
   This person comes in handy, for example, if the planners get stuck, particularly when establishing strategies and/or action plans. People who can make decisions are usually the Board Chair, Chief Executive Officer and/or program managers.

8. **Involve someone to administrate the process**.
   This person would, for example, arrange meetings, help with facilities, and monitor status of planning between planning meetings. One of the most important results from the various planning discussions is the documentation of the results; otherwise, planning meetings can seem like an ongoing series of chit-chats. The administrator can produce that documentation. Thus, the administrative role is very important in the planning process.

9. **There should be one person who is ultimately responsible for the planning.**
   That person is the clear authority and focus to ensure that strategic planning continues in an orderly and continuous fashion. Ultimately, that person ensures that the planning does not stop altogether because people did not realize who was going to do what and when in the process.

10. **Often an "initiator" first proposes the process.**
    That might be the person who first obtained this guidebook and talked others into starting the strategic planning process. The initiator does not necessarily have to be part of the group of planners.

11. **In general, if there is any doubt about including someone, include him or her**.
    It is worse to exclude someone who is useful to the planning process than to have one or two extra people in the process who prove to not be useful at all.

12. **Organize a Planning Committee?**
    If the preceding criteria produce a group of more than 8-10 members, then consider forming a Planning Committee.

See "Organize Planning Committee?" on page 20 in "Phase 1: Design Plan for Plan."

The next topic is about the strategic planning facilitator. Note that the Chief Executive Officer typically should *not* be the strategic planning facilitator. The role of the facilitator is to help the group of planners to design their strategic planning process and then conduct that process in a highly effective and efficient fashion. That responsibility requires complete and continual attention to the goals, status and overall quality of the planning process, including making prompt recommendations and adjustments to the process as necessary.

The CEO needs to be able to participate completely in the strategic planning process, especially in analyzing information about the external and internal environments of the nonprofit, and then making recommendations and decisions about strategic goals, strategies and action plans. That level of participation in not practical if the CEO is also focused on managing the strategic planning process. In addition, if the CEO is also the facilitator, then the facilitator role might have far too much influence when guiding the planning process, even to the extent that planners are inhibited from participating completely.

Now Complete Part of "Worksheet #1: Plan for Plan"

See "1.9 – Who Will Be Involved from Nonprofit? How? When?" on page 228 in "Worksheet #1: Plan for Plan."

Need Outside Help? How? When? How To Get It?

Need Outside Facilitator?

The job of facilitator is to help the group members to customize their strategic planning process and then follow that process in an effective and efficient fashion. A nonprofit should seriously consider getting an outside facilitator (that is, someone to facilitate who is not a member of the nonprofit) if any of the following is true:

1.   The nonprofit has not conducted strategic planning before.

2.   For a variety of reasons, previous strategic planning was not deemed successful.

3.   There appears to be a wide range of ideas and/or concerns among organization members about strategic planning and about current organizational issues to be addressed in the plan.

4.   There is no one in the nonprofit who members feel has sufficient facilitation skills.

5.   No one in the nonprofit feels committed to facilitating strategic planning for the nonprofit.

6.   Leaders believe that an inside facilitator will either inhibit participation from others or will not have the opportunity to fully participate in planning themselves.

7.   Leaders want an objective voice, that is, someone who is not likely to have strong predispositions about the nonprofit's critical issues and ideas.

Typically, the facilitator is also useful to train planners about the strategic planning process, including the variety of approaches available and how they might be modified.

You might get a better impression of how a facilitator can help your nonprofit by reviewing the information in PART III of this guide. See the guidelines on page 193 in Appendix E if you do choose to hire a facilitator. Those guidelines will ensure that the process goes smoothly for you and results in a very successful consultancy for your nonprofit.

Need Other Expertise?

There are other types of experts who can come in handy during strategic planning. Consider the following.

1. **Expert on trends in your nonprofit's programs**
   This kind of expertise comes in handy, particularly during the external analysis portion of strategic planning when planners are considering the effects of external influences on the nonprofit, its programs and clients. For example, if your nonprofit provides day-care services, you will benefit from the advice of someone who follows trends in legislation about day-care and knows patterns of work among single-family households.

2. **Researchers**
   Researchers are often at the leading edge of generating and applying new knowledge. Strategic planning is all about situating the organization for the future. Therefore, your nonprofit might benefit from contact with researchers in various fields. For example, if your nonprofit attempts to meet any of the needs of the homeless, then it might be useful to consider the results of research among the homeless, such as where they stay at night, where they migrate during different seasons and what their most important needs are.

3. **A pair of hands**
   It might be useful just to have someone help with stuffing envelopes to send invitations to meetings, taking notes, moving equipment, etc.

For sources of assistance, see the subsection, "Organizations Assisting Nonprofits" in Appendix B on page 165.

Now Complete Part of "Worksheet #1: Plan for Plan"

See "1.10 – Outside Help Needed? How? When? How To Get It?" on page 229 in "Worksheet #1: Plan for Plan."

What Materials Are Needed? When? How To Get Them?

Now that you have identified the expertise (people) that you need, think about what other resources you might need during the process and when you will need them. Think about:

- Materials (books about strategic planning, flipcharts, markers, etc.)

- Equipment (overhead projectors, flipchart stands, white boards, etc.)

- Facilities (conference rooms, retreat centers, etc.)

Now Complete Part of "Worksheet #1: Plan for Plan"

See "1.11 – What Materials Are Needed? When? How To Get Them?" on page 230 in "Worksheet #1: Plan for Plan."

Conventions for Terms

It is common for new planners to be confused and concerned about usage of certain terms in planning, especially "goals" versus "objectives" and "strategies" versus "tactics". This confusion can significantly slow down and detract from the quality of the strategic planning process, so it pays to give some thought to these terms before you begin your planning.

Ironically, it often does not make a huge difference as to whether a priority is really a goal, strategy, objective or tactic at first because the difference becomes apparent as planners continue to develop and refine their plans. For example, what they first call a goal might later become a strategy. The most important activities during planning are to 1) identify "What is important to accomplish?," 2) identify "How to accomplish it?," and 3) then to be consistent about usage of terms.

Goals and Objectives

Goals and objectives are usually in regard to the question, "What is important to accomplish?" Experts in planning suggest that goals and objectives be described in specific terms, including use of specific numbers or percentages, for example, "Train 300 people." That way, a person knows if they have achieved the goal or not.

Whether a priority is a goal or an objective depends on the preferences of the planners. Planners should establish whether goals are superior or inferior to objectives. For example, if goals are superior to objectives, then it takes a series of objectives to accomplish an overall goal. Planners should select one type of relationship between goals and objectives and then be consistent throughout the planning process.

NOTE: This guidebook follows a convention to refer to "goals" as high-level, major accomplishments to be achieved in order to work toward the overall mission and to "objectives" as subordinate tasks that must be achieved, in total, in order to achieve the overall goals.

Strategy and Tactics

Strategies and tactics are usually in regard to "How do we accomplish it?" One might recognize a strategy or tactic if it is in regard to an activity needed to accomplish a goal or objective. For example, "Build a training curriculum," "Recruit students" and "Conduct trainings" might be strategies or tactics to achieve the goal "Train 300 people". Small nonprofits often skip strategies.

Whether a priority is a strategy or a tactic depends on the preferences of the planners. Planners should establish whether strategies are superior or inferior to tactics. Nonprofit organizations often do not include use of the term tactic unless the organization is large enough to have several "layers" of plans, for example, an overall strategic plan, department plans, program plans, group plans, and individual performance or career development plans.

NOTE: This guidebook follows a convention to refer to "strategies" as overall methods that must be implemented in order to achieve a goal and "actions" as subordinate activities that must be conducted in order to implement the strategies. (Objectives and actions are referred to primarily in the section, "Phase 4: Develop Action and Financial Plans.")

Terms in Different Types of Plans in Organization

If an organization has several layers of plans, then what might be an objective in the organization plan might also be a goal in a program plan. Similarly, what might be an objective in a program plan might also be a goal in the employee's plan.

In the following example, goals are considered superior to objectives, and strategies are superior to tactics.

Organization Plan	Program Plan	Employee Plan
Goal		
Strategy		
Objective	Goal	
Tactic	Strategy	
	Objective	Goal
	Tactic	Strategy
		Objective

Now Complete Part of "Worksheet #1: Plan for Plan"

See "1.12 – Any Conventions for Use of Terms?" on page 231 in "Worksheet #1: Plan for Plan."

Provide Planning Guide to Planners?

At this point, it can be very useful to assemble a basic planning guide for the planners. The guide can be very helpful when describing the customized strategic planning process and how the planners are to participate in the process. The guide might include:

1.   Cover sheet with title and date

2.   Brief explanation of the major reason for conducting strategic planning now

3.   Brief description of the approach to strategic planning as designed by the Planning Committee

4.   Listing of who will be involved in the planning and when, including a planning schedule

5.   Brief description of the organizational scope of the plan

6.   Brief description of the time span of the plan

7.   Brief description of the role of the Planning Committee, if used

8.   Listing of who can be contacted with any questions about the strategic planning process for the nonprofit

9.   Any other sources of information about strategic planning

At this point, not all of the planners might have been identified. The planning guide can be provided to planners as they become known and participate in the strategic planning process. Who will be responsible to assemble the guide? To whom will the guide be provided? Who will provide it?

Note that the contents of a planning guide could be very useful during training about strategic planning. The consideration of whether to conduct focused training is included a little later on in this section.

Now Complete Part of "Worksheet #1: Plan for Plan"

 See "1.13 – Provide Planning Guide to Planners?" on page 232 in "Worksheet #1: Plan for Plan."

Develop Profile of Organization

The profile is used to portray highlights about the organization to planners so they see the entire "picture", past and current, before they get started with their planning. The profile describes, for example:

1.   Highlights from the history of the organization:

    a) When was it started?

    b) Who started it and why?

    c) What was/were the first program(s), if any, and whom did they serve?

2.   Any significant events during its history, for example:

    a) Major awards?

    b) Mergers? Collaborations?

    c) Grants or cuts in funding?

3.   Any trends that planners should know about, for example:

    a) In funding?

    b) In staffing?

    c) Among clients?

4.   The decision-making style of the organization:

    a) Top-down or highly participative?

    b) Rational/sequential or organic/unfolding?

    c) Other?

5.   Description of current or expected program(s). This is an important activity during the profile, whether the nonprofit is new or already established. If the nonprofit is new, then planners should start thinking about what specific program(s) their nonprofit might provide. Programs play a major role in implementing goals and strategies from strategic plans. The section, "Nonprofits Programs, Configurations and Types" on page 199 in Appendix F will be helpful.

6.   Other information that planners should know about now? (Note that upcoming activities in the strategic planning process soon will involve more detail about the internal and external activities in regard to the nonprofit, including the opportunities and threats and the strengths and weaknesses facing the organization.)

Now Complete Part of "Worksheet #1: Plan for Plan"

See "1.14 – Develop Organizational Profile" on page 233 in "Worksheet #1: Plan for Plan."

How Will You Get "Buy In" When Announcing Process?

To ensure a highly relevant, realistic and flexible strategic plan, it is critical that the planning process is able to gain and maintain the complete commitment and ownership of all planners. Probably the most critical point in which to start cultivating the buy-in is when first announcing the strategic planning process. The announcement must be done carefully to help planners quickly realize and accept the need for the process, yet not react that the process is just another fad, or "silver bullet," intended to "save the day."

Here are some suggestions to consider.

1.   Usually, strategic planning is first considered and approved during a Board meeting with the CEO present. They discuss:

    a) Why strategic planning should be done now

    b) Organizational focus of the plan

    c) Benefits of the process

    d) When the process should start and stop

    e) How to convey the Board's and management's complete support of the process

2.   The process is announced by the CEO and maybe a Board member to a group of leaders among nonprofit staff, especially those who will be involved in the development and implementation of the plan. They discuss the same information discussed in the Board meeting, as listed above. Special care is given to ensuring sufficient time for reactions, questions and suggestions.

3.   If the staff is sufficiently large, then the process is announced (ideally by the CEO) in an additional meeting with these staff members. Again, special care is given to ensuring sufficient time for reactions, questions and suggestions.

4.   The announcement is accompanied with an official memo. The memo should reiterate reasons, benefits, start and stop dates, and management's full support of the strategic planning process.

5.   Any previous strategic planning activities should be mentioned in meetings, including successes, failures and what is being done to avoid failures this time around.

6.   The list of participants in the Planning Committee, if used, should be mentioned.

7.   The name of one contact person is provided for any staff members who might have any concerns, questions or suggestions about the upcoming process.

8.   The starting date of the planning process is provided.

Guidelines throughout this guidebook are carefully designed to ensure continued buy-in among planners during the development and implementation of the strategic plan.

Now Complete Part of "Worksheet #1: Plan for Plan"

See "1.15 – How Will You Get Buy-In When Announcing Process?" on page 235 in "Worksheet #1: Plan for Plan."

How Will Planners Be Trained About Strategic Planning?

By now, some of the planners (especially those in a Planning Committee, if used) have a fairly good sense of how they might approach strategic planning for their nonprofit. It is important that all the planners in the process understand what the approach might be. Thus, it is useful to conduct some basic training about the strategic planning approach.

Usually, the strategic planning facilitator is involved in the design and delivery of this training. The training might occur after the strategic planning process is announced to the entire staff, as explained above.

Here are some guidelines to consider when designing the training. Note that the contents of a planning guide, if used, may prove to be particularly useful during this training.

1. Do some training even if participants do not feel they need it. Brief training will get planners on the "same page" about strategic planning.

2. The training need only be about half an hour long.

3. In the training, review:

    a) A brief explanation of the major reason for conducting strategic planning now

    b) Overview of the strategic planning process for the nonprofit, including the scope, time span and approach to planning

    c) Listing of who will be involved and how, during the process

    d) Discussion of the schedule for planning activities

    e) Listing of who can be contacted with any questions about the strategic planning process for the nonprofit

4. Design the training to be highly interactive, for example, allow planning members to ask questions right away as they have them.

5. Provide time near the end of the training for members to ask questions, voice concerns and make suggestions.

Now Complete Part of "Worksheet #1: Plan for Plan"

See "1.16 – How Will Planners Be Trained About Strategic Planning?" on page 236 in "Worksheet #1: Plan for Plan."

Congratulations! At this point, you have customized an approach to strategic planning that will closely match the nature and needs of your nonprofit organization! The rest of the guidelines in PART II will guide you, step by step, through the process to customize your approach even more as you develop and implement your strategic plan.

Phase 2: Conduct Situational Analysis

Strategic planning is the process of ensuring a good fit between the external and internal environments of the nonprofit organization so that the nonprofit is positioned to perform effectively, well into the future. The situational analysis includes close examination of these environments and is a critical stage in the overall strategic planning process. The situational analysis usually includes both an external analysis and internal analysis.

Mission Statement or Situational Analysis First?

Crossroads for Planners

The mission statement should describe the overall purpose of the nonprofit, including the community needs to be met by the nonprofit. Many strategic planning experts assert, therefore, that nonprofits should begin the strategic planning process by developing or clarifying a mission statement for the organization (and vision and/or values statements, if preferred).

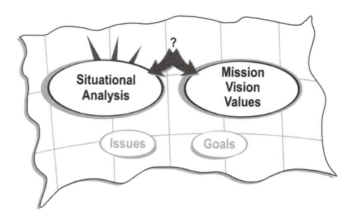

However, in some situations, planners can easily get bogged down when drafting a mission statement. For example, they can end up quibbling over certain words in the mission statement and sometimes end up producing a very generic set of sentences. Therefore, depending on the particular approach to strategic planning, planners might have a more clear sense of an up-to-date mission after they have completed the situational analysis.

Proceed With Situational Analysis If:

Planners might skip attention to the mission, vision and/or values statements for now, and instead attend to conducting the situational analysis now, especially if one or more of the following is true:

1. Planners are not completely sure of the community need to be met by the nonprofit and the methods to meet that need. If there is any doubt about the needs or methods, then planners should conduct a situational analysis.

2. Planners have reviewed the mission, vision and/or values statements during the past 12 months and can readily conclude that there is no change to be made the statements.

3. Planners expect rapid change in the external environment that might impact the mission of the organization, depending on the direction, goals and strategies chosen by planners as a result of the situational analysis.

4. Planners already foresee several major issues that the organization must face and that the mission of the organization might change as a result, depending on how the issues are

addressed. (Planners in this situation might prefer to use the issues-based strategic planning process, as well.)

5.   The nonprofit is focusing strategic planning primarily on one or more programs now, and not on the overall organization.

Planners who are conducting the organic strategic planning process might conduct the entire situational analysis by facilitating frequent discussions and sharing of stories among groups of stakeholders regarding the nonprofit's mission, and especially, its vision and values statements and any action plans for members.

To complete the situational analysis, follow the rest of the guidelines for this phase.

Otherwise, Attend to Mission Statement

Planners might benefit from attending to the mission, vision and/or values statements now if one or more of the following is true:

1.   Their nonprofit is very new and planners have no sense of what the mission statement should be, but assume that they do have a very strong sense of who the clients are and what their needs are. (Be very careful about making that assumption.)

2.   Planners believe that the external environment of the nonprofit is fairly stable, or at least well understood by planners. (Be careful about making that assumption.)

3.   Planners prefer to conduct the goals-based strategic planning process and believe that goals can be established much more easily if a clearly worded mission statement has been developed. (Develop the mission, but then conduct the situational analysis.)

4.   Planners prefer to conduct the organic strategic planning process and want to begin identifying the mission, vision and/or values right away.

5.   The culture of the organization places strong priority on values and/or vision. (The role of values is usually very important to members of nonprofit organizations.)

See "Mission, Vision and Values Statements" on page 72 to develop or clarify the statements now.

Analyze External Environment – What We Cannot Control

It is usually best to start the situational analysis by conducting an external analysis, rather than the internal analysis. Otherwise, planners tend to get bogged down in particulars that are internal to their organization (the area that planners know best), leaving little time or energy for a critical analysis of the external environment.

Take External Analysis Very Seriously

Many nonprofit leaders believe that the external analysis is not worth their time in the planning process because they assume that they already know what is going on around their nonprofit organization. Besides, they rationalize, they do not have sufficient resources to conduct the analysis – or they would not know how to conduct the analysis even if they wanted to do so. During strategic planning, these organizations might build a beautiful ladder – but entirely on the wrong roof. They might do a wonderful job of only the internal analyses, resulting in very effective and efficient approaches to internal operations, as the nonprofit follows an overall, wrong direction for the entire organization! These organizations tend to operate in a highly reactive fashion because they are continually surprised about events that occur outside of their organizations.

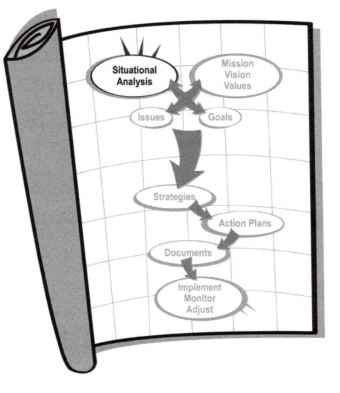

It is amazing how often, once planners do decide to engage in the external analysis, they find that they disagree about the influences around their nonprofit and about what should be done about them. The ensuing discussions among planners are the *essence* of the good strategic thinking – the type of thinking that is so critical, not only in strategic planning, but also in strategic management.

It is especially important for new nonprofits or nonprofits with new programs to conduct an effective external analysis. One of the biggest "turn offs" for funders is to read a grant application from a nonprofit in which it is clearly evident that the nonprofit shows little or no interest or understanding of its external environment, especially in regard to its competitors and collaborators. Planners should not charge ahead with plans for a new nonprofit without taking a very careful look at the external environment of the nonprofit.

Experts in strategic planning assert that a plan is not strategic, at all, if it does not include intentional and well-organized activities to conduct an external analysis.

What Is External Analysis?

An external analysis examines trends that are not within the control of the nonprofit, but that might impact it. Trends tend to be societal, technological, political, economic and/or environmental, in nature, for example, about:

- Availability of federal funds

- Demographic trends, especially trends among current or potential groups of clients

- The extent of access to labor and materials

- The nature of the competition (yes, even nonprofits compete with each other for markets, grants, employees, etc. – for-profits are beginning to compete with nonprofits, too)

- Recent changes in laws and regulations

- Recent or pending legislation

- Societal attitudes (liberalism, conservatism, individualism, etc.)

- Technological changes, including how services might be delivered

- Trends in donations among local donors

The external analysis should also include examination of:

- Stakeholders' impressions of the organization, including funders', clients', community leaders', volunteers', special interest groups', etc.

- Future actions of potential competitors and collaborators

Ultimately, from the external analysis, planners want to identify any major opportunities or threats that the organization might be facing. Board members can play a major role in this analysis because, ideally, members of the Board represent a cross section of members of the community and, thus, they often have a broader view of the external environment than members of the staff do.

Activities in an external analysis can include:

- Client analysis

- Competitor analysis

- Collaborator analysis

- Analysis of other stakeholders

- Environmental scan

- Identification of opportunities and threats facing the organization

Some planners might use the phrase "environmental scan" to refer to all of these activities in an external analysis. Some planners might consider collaborators and competitors to be stakeholders, and, thus, to be included in a stakeholder analysis.

Some planners refer to "spheres" of influence when referring to various kinds of stakeholders. The internal ring includes stakeholders that the organization has some control over, for example, Board members, staff and volunteers. The middle ring includes those that the organization has some influence over, for example, clients, funders, competitors, collaborators, suppliers and community leaders. The outer ring includes areas of concern to the organization, regarding political, economic, societal and technological trends.

Crossroads: Which External Analysis Activities, In Which Order?

If planners have very limited resources for planning, including very limited time, then they should start with an analysis of the primary clients of the nonprofit. One of the most important things for a nonprofit to know is "Who are our primary clients and what do they need from us?" That knowledge can come from conducting a client analysis. Afterwards, planners might attend to analyses of stakeholders and the broader environment (environmental scan), as time permits. If time permits, they could attend to analyses of potential collaborators and competitors, as well.

Some planners might prefer to start their external analysis by working from a very broad perspective and then continuing to sharpen their focus by reducing the scope of their analyses. These planners might benefit most by starting with an environmental scan and then conducting analyses of stakeholders and clients. If time permits, they could analyze potential collaborators and competitors, as well.

Conduct External Analysis of Primary Clients, Collaborators, Competitors and Other Stakeholders

Guidelines for the various analyses are included immediately below. Worksheets to conduct analysis in each of these areas are referenced at the end of this topic and are included in Appendix G on page 211.

Because of the similar nature of activities in these analyses, consider using the same group of planners to conduct all of the activities.

 See Appendix D on page 185 for guidelines on data collection. The guidelines provide practical means to obtain information from a variety of stakeholders.

Note that the planners should not attempt to identify or discuss what the nonprofit should do in response to any information in the descriptions resulting from the analyses. Rather, the goal of the planners now is to finalize the descriptions.

Conduct Analysis of Primary Clients

Members of the nonprofit must have a very good understanding of the groups of clients served by the nonprofit and the needs among those various groups. It is critical that they understand the needs of the primary clients – the people who directly benefit from the nonprofit's services. Usually that understanding is gained by conducting a thorough marketing analysis, with extensive focus and detail about specifically identifying and verifying groups of clients, their needs and how a nonprofit can reliably meet those needs. Market research uses a variety of techniques to learn about clients, for example, conducting surveys, interviews and focus groups.

The strategic planning process – especially if designed to be realistic – usually does not include thorough market analysis. Instead, the strategic planning process now tries generally to identify:

1. What groups of primary clients do we serve now? What do they want from us now? Are we providing what they want? How do we know? What do they need from us now? Are we providing what they need?

2. Are there new groups of clients that we might serve? If so, how?

3. Might we do more in the future for our current groups of clients? If so, what?

4. In the future, how can our nonprofit more specifically identify and verify whether our nonprofit is reliably meeting the needs of current and new clients?

Planners must be very careful when assuming that they really know the needs and wants of their nonprofit's clients. That assumption can easily get the nonprofit in trouble. Visible signs of that kind of trouble are low usage of programs and continued lack of funding for programs.

Another careful consideration is the difference between what clients want versus what they need. Often, clients will come to a service based on what they want. They stay with the service based on what they need. Thus, planners need to focus time and energy on really understanding who their clients are and what those clients want and need.

Some kinds of programs, such as arts programs, often do not see themselves as dealing with client "needs" as much as with client interests. Still, it is often more useful for program planners to translate the clients' interests to be in terms of clients' needs, if possible. For example, regarding an arts program, clients have need for stimulation, diversification and emotional intelligence, which, in turn, cultivates their interest in art.

 See "Basic Methods To Assess Client Needs" on page 191 in Appendix D for basic methods to identify new clients and their needs. See "Analyze Internal Environment – What We Can Control" on page 60 for guidelines to analyze how groups of clients are currently being served.

 It is not within the scope of this guidebook to provide detailed guidelines for conducting a complete market analysis. Those guidelines are included in the guidebook, *Field Guide to Nonprofit Program Design, Marketing and Evaluation,* by this author.

Conduct Analysis of Stakeholders

Stakeholders are any group of people who are interested and can be affected by the operations of your nonprofit. They have a "stake" in the future of the nonprofit. They might be considered as secondary clients.

It is absolutely critical for the nonprofit's planners to know what stakeholders think about, and want from, the planners' nonprofit. This is extremely important information that can be used to ensure the long-term success and funding of the nonprofit. Stakeholders include, for example:

- Past, present and future funders

- Past, present and future volunteers

- Regulators

- Special interest groups, etc.

- Unions

- Various leaders in the community

Clients, competitors and collaborators are also groups of stakeholders, but the analysis of these three groups is done a little differently than analysis of the above-listed stakeholders.

It is useful to rate the importance of each of the major groups of stakeholders listed above. The rating depends on the nature of the programs in the nonprofit and the clients served by those programs.

It is very useful to be able to interview members of the various groups and, ideally, conduct a focus group among them. This might sound like a major challenge, but very often people love to take part in experiences where they are asked about their opinions. Appendix D on page 185 includes guidelines to conduct interviews and focus groups.

Conduct Realistic Environmental Scan

When conducting a scan, it is important to be simple (not simplistic) and practical, and not to get bogged down in extensive analysis of various external driving forces that might affect the nonprofit. However, do not merely glance at a list of various types of forces and immediately shy away from doing any thinking about them, at all.

There are a variety of approaches to conducting an environmental scan, ranging from quite formal (such as methodically applying various assessments to a specific range of topics) to much less formal activities (such as having conversations with peers, occasionally reading various publications, etc.).

This guidebook recommends that an environmental scan be conducted by either conducting a driving-forces impacts analysis or using the scenario planning technique.

Conduct Analysis of Collaborators

It is common today that funders want to see evidence of collaboration among the nonprofits that they fund. Collaboration, when carried out carefully, can be a windfall, or major benefit, for all parties involved. Therefore, it is important to understand who your potential collaborators are and how you might work with them.

Conduct Analysis of Competitors

Some people might recoil at the thought of nonprofits having "competitors". Nonprofits do have competitors. They compete for clients and they compete for funding. Lately, various for-profit organizations have begun to focus their products and services on nonprofit markets. Therefore, it is critical, when setting the course for the future of a nonprofit, to understand who the competitors are and how their actions might affect the nonprofit.

Useful Worksheets for External Analyses

Appendix G on page 211 includes these worksheets for conducting your analyses:
"Worksheet #2: Primary Client Analysis"
"Worksheet #3: Stakeholder Analysis"
"Worksheet #4: Environmental Scan"
"Worksheet #5: Collaborator Analysis"
"Worksheet #6: Competitor Analysis"

To complete the above analyses, the group of planners should clarify, analyze, correct and agree on the description of information from each worksheet listed above. Often, the discussion-group technique is best for this activity. Guidelines for the discussion technique are included in PART III.

If planners chose to use the scenario planning technique, then they might update their scenarios after conducting the various other external analyses, for example, analyses of primary clients, stakeholders, collaborators and competitors.

Identify Top Opportunities and Threats Facing Organization

The key "output", or tangible result, from the external analysis is identification of the major opportunities and threats facing the organization over the time span of the strategic plan. Opportunities and threats are usually future-oriented in nature.

What Are Opportunities?

An opportunity is usually some seemingly positive situation in the current or future environment for the nonprofit. For example:

- Increasing number of people who might need the services of the nonprofit

- More access to those clients

- Useful technologies to deliver services more effectively to clients

- Likelihood of strong relationships with various stakeholders

- Changes in laws and regulations that make for more favorable conditions in which the nonprofit can operate

Note that opportunities and threats can seem very similar. What might seem like an opportunity to one person might seem like a threat to another because not enough of the opportunity seems present to that other person. Any differences in perspective among planners will be clarified soon in this external analysis.

What Are Threats?

A threat is usually some seemingly negative situation in the current or future environment for the nonprofit, for example:

- Decreasing number of people who might need the services of the nonprofit

- Less access to those clients

- Little innovation from which to deliver services more effectively to clients

- Less likelihood of strong relationships with various stakeholders

- Changes in laws and regulations that make for much less favorable conditions in which the nonprofit can operate

The following table might apply to a new homeless shelter.

Example of Opportunities and Threats Information	
Opportunities	**Threats**
- Strong, unmet need in community - Many people seeking help from us - Possibility of collaboration with other nonprofits	- Donations are decreasing in our area - Increasing apathy in society about homelessness - Laws making it very difficult for homeless to remain in our area and hear about us

Each Planner Identifies a List of Possible Opportunities and Threats

It is important that each planner have some time alone with the external analysis information for at least several days before attempting to identify opportunities and threats. Then:

1.   Review the external analysis information to generate a list of the most important, 5-8 opportunities for the organization during the time span of the strategic plan, especially over the next 12 months or fiscal year. Consider "important" to be in terms of potential positive impact on the organization.

2.   Record them on "Worksheet #7: Opportunities and Threats."

Repeat steps 1-2 to identify threats. Consider "important" to be in terms of potential negative impact on the organization.

Group Develops Ranked Lists of Opportunities and Threats

1.   **Compile a list of all of the opportunities mentioned by all of the planners.**
Use the Round-Robin technique with the entire group of planners to compile one preliminary, overall list of all of the potential opportunities recommended by each planner. Avoid duplication of the same opportunity on the overall list. Guidelines for the Round-Robin technique are included in PART III.

Note that the planners should not attempt now to identify or discuss what the nonprofit should do in response to the opportunities. However, planners can ask questions to ensure understanding of the descriptions of the opportunities.

2. **Ensure that the overall list is indeed complete.**
    Consider:

    a) Are there any obvious opportunities missing from the list? If someone suggests one, then put it on the list.

    b) Use a brainstorming technique to generate more ideas about opportunities? Guidelines for the brainstorming technique are included in PART III.

3. **Ensure that the list is well integrated.**
    Have a short, focused discussion about the opportunities *in relationship to each other.* Planners should not attempt to strategize how to address the opportunities. Rather, they should consider:

    a) Is there any duplication of opportunities?

    b) Can any of the opportunities be combined with others?

    c) Should any of the opportunities be divided into one or more other opportunities?

    d) Are some or all of the opportunities interconnected somehow?

4. **Develop a final, ranked list of the most important 5-8 opportunities.**
    If planners are used to a highly interactive approach to decision making, then they might use group discussion to rank an overall list of opportunities. Guidelines for the discussion technique are included in PART III.

    If planners are not convinced that group discussion will produce a ranked list in a timely fashion, then they might use a voting method to rank an overall list of opportunities. Guidelines for the voting technique are included in PART III.

 See "Worksheet 7: Opportunities and Threats" on page 248 to record the final, ranked list of opportunities.

Repeat steps 1-4 with the group, this time to compile and rank an overall list of threats. Consider "important" to be in terms of potential negative impact on the organization.

The group will do further analysis on their final lists of opportunities and threats later on in the strategic planning process.

Analyze Internal Environment – What We Can Control

What Is Internal Analysis?

A comprehensive internal analysis will examine the quality of performance of all major, internal aspects of the nonprofit organization, including:

- Board operations

- Strategic planning

- "Inbound" marketing (collecting information about groups of clients, their needs and how to reliably meet those needs)

- Program planning

- Staffing and supervision

- Financial management

- "Outbound" marketing (advertising, promotions and sales)

- Fundraising

- Facilities management

- Evaluations

From the internal analysis, planners try to identify the major strengths and weaknesses in the organization. Staff may play a major role during the internal analysis because they often have strong understanding of what is going on inside the organization.

Planners conducting the organic approach to strategic planning might choose to skip the internal analysis, and instead choose to proceed with creating action plans according to their mission, vision and/or values.

Use Assessments to Analyze Internal Systems

Too often, staff assumes that they know what is going on in their nonprofit because they work there almost every day. The biggest problem with that assumption is that staff may be so close to the problems that they only see the symptoms of the problems, not the real causes of the problems. Therefore, it is critical to conduct the internal assessment in a comprehensive fashion, ideally with the assistance of someone from outside the organization who is skilled at assessing organizations and generating recommendations to address any issues.

Nonprofit Management Indicators Tool

One of the more comprehensive and practical tools for conducting an internal assessment is the Checklist of Nonprofit Management Indicators developed by the Greater Twin Cities United Way. The tool helps members of the organization to do conduct a quick, comprehensive assessment of all major, internal aspects of their nonprofit organization. By using the assessment, each person indicates whether he or she thinks a particular aspect of the nonprofit needs attention or not. Each person's responses can be compared to "best practices" regarding that particular aspect of the nonprofit. The results of the assessment give a fairly good impression of how the nonprofit is doing overall when compared to best practices for nonprofits in general.

See the Management Indicators tool on page 171 in Appendix C.

Although the Indicators assessment is quite comprehensive, it can be completed by almost anyone in about thirty minutes. To use the assessment:

1.　Consider having each Board member complete the assessment and if that is not practical, then have each Board officer and/or the Chairs of Board committees complete the assessment.

2.　The Chief Executive Officer should complete the assessment.

3.　Consider having each staff member complete the assessment if the total size of staff is less than 5-8 members. If the total size of staff is more than that, then consider having staff management complete the assessment (for example, program managers and supervisors of staff).

4.　Ideally, the completed assessments are sent to someone outside of the organization who can analyze the results for the nonprofit organization. Analysis would include a) compiling the responses by totaling the number of responses for each question; and b) generating a report that highlights which areas of the nonprofit need the most attention, from comparing responses to best practices.

If it is not practical to have the staff and Board members complete the assessment, then each planner might complete the assessment and then analyze their own results. Afterwards, in the entire group, planners can share their results, including conclusions about how the nonprofit might be doing when compared to best practices in nonprofits.

Other Assessments

There are a variety of other assessments that can be used for nonprofits. One of the more popular is the Drucker Foundation Self-Assessment Tool. The tool can be used to help organizations to answer what management guru, Peter Drucker, calls the five most important questions for a nonprofit organization, including:

1.　What is our mission?

2.　Who is our customer?

3.　What does the customer value?

4.　What are our results?

5.　What is our plan?

The guidelines in this guidebook address these five questions, through the activities in Phases 2-5.

More information about this Tool is available at
http://www.pfdf.org/leaderbooks/sat/index.html on the Web.

Another assessment tool is the McKinsey Capacity Assessment Grid. The Grid provides a comprehensive set of questions about seven aspects of nonprofit organizational capacity. Questions allow respondents to indicate their views about each aspect along a continuum of performance.

The guidelines in this guidebook address these five questions, through the activities in Phases 2-5.

More information about the Grid is available at
http://venturephilanthropypartners.org/learning/reports/capacity/toc.pdf
on the Web.

Consider Results of Program Evaluations

Organizations usually conduct some form of program evaluation, whether informally or formally. For example, staff often asks clients if programs are useful to them. Or, they hear various comments from clients about program services. This information is extremely valuable to the nonprofit.

There are a variety of types of program evaluation. For example, members of the organization might evaluate a program to:

- Be sure that it is implemented as intended when the program originally was designed (an implementation evaluation).

- Make the delivery of services more effective and efficient (a process evaluation).

- Assess whether a program is achieving its goals or not (a goals evaluation).

- Assess the extent of outcomes achieved by participants in the program (an outcomes evaluation).

During the internal analysis, planners want to collect as much useful information as possible regarding the success of programs, including their processes, goals and outcomes. If the nonprofit has not established a systematic, formal evaluation process, then planners still might gain a great deal of information now by talking to program staff and as many clients as possible.

From this information, try to get an impression of the following for each program:

1. Is the program operating according to the ongoing design preferred by the program planners?

2. Is the delivery of services effective and efficient?

3. Is the program achieving the goals intended for the program when the program was established?

4. Are clients achieving the outcomes that the program desired for its clients?

Note that it is not within the scope of this guidebook to provide comprehensive guidelines to design and implement a systematic program evaluation process. Those guidelines can be found in the guidebook, *Field Guide to Nonprofit Program Design, Marketing and Evaluation,* by this author.

Two Most Forgotten Internal Priorities

The overall area of risk management tends to be forgotten during the internal analysis, especially in regard to facilities management and succession planning. Consider the following questions. Then take a hard look at the various threats that were identified during the external analysis activities. Are there any other risks to address?

Facilities Management

1.   What if the computer systems quit working, for example, a computer disk was ruined or a computer virus ruined files?

2.   What if someone broke into the facility and robbed the place?

3.   What if there was a fire in the facilities?

Often, these important considerations are forgotten and not included in organizational assessments. Are there other risks faced by your organization?

Planners need not come up with ideas now about how to address these risks. Rather, their goal now is to identify the risks or needs for risk management plans.

Succession Planning

Succession planning can occur in one of two ways: either in a proactive, planned fashion or in response to a crisis.

What if the Chief Executive Officer or other key staff member suddenly quit his or her job or was struck with a serious illness? Would other members of the nonprofit organization know what to do?

Identify Top Strengths and Weaknesses of Organization

The key "output", or tangible result, from the internal analysis is identification of the major strengths and weaknesses of the organization. Note that strengths and weaknesses are usually oriented to past and current activities within the organization.

What Are Strengths?

A strength is usually some seemingly positive situation in the current environment for the nonprofit, for example:

- Demand for the nonprofit's services

- Methods to deliver services

- Motivation among members of the Board and/or staff

- Expertise among staff

- Management systems

- Public image

- Relationships with stakeholders

Also, strengths and weaknesses can seem very similar. What might seem like a strength to one person might seem like a weakness to another because not enough of the strength seems present to that other person. Any differences in perspective among planners will be clarified soon in this internal analysis.

What Are Weaknesses?

A weakness is usually some seemingly negative situation in the current environment for the nonprofit, for example:

- Ineffective methods to deliver services

- Low motivation among members of the Board and/or staff

- Little expertise among staff

- Ineffective management systems

- Poor, or no, public image

- Poor, or no, relationships with stakeholders

The following table might apply to a new homeless shelter.

Example of Strengths and Weaknesses Information	
Strengths	**Weaknesses**
▪ Passionate, motivated people ▪ Respected organization ▪ Many volunteers ▪ Respected CEO	▪ Lack sufficient funding ▪ Lack overall, organizational direction ▪ Weak Board of Directors ▪ Lack expertise in staffing and supervision ▪ Lack expertise in financial management and fundraising ▪ Lack sufficient facilities

Each Planner Identifies a List of Possible Strengths and Weaknesses

Planners use the same procedure that they used to identify opportunities and threats. The procedure is repeated here, but customized to identifying strengths and weaknesses.

It is important that each planner have some time with the internal analysis information for at least several days before attempting to identify strengths and weaknesses. Consider "important" to be in terms of potential positive impact for the organization. Then:

1. Review the internal analysis information to generate a list of the most important, 5-8 strengths for the organization during the time span of the strategic plan, especially over the next 12 months or fiscal year. Consider "important" to be in terms of potential positive impact on the organization.

2. Record them on "Worksheet 8: Strengths and Weaknesses."

Repeat steps 1-2 to identify weaknesses. Consider "important" to be in terms of potential negative impact on the organization.

Group Develops Ranked Lists of Strengths and Weaknesses

1. **Compile a list of all of the strengths mentioned by all of the planners.**
    Use the Round-Robin technique with the entire group of planners to compile one preliminary, overall list of all of the strengths recommended by each planner. Avoid duplication of the same strength on the overall list. Guidelines for the Round-Robin technique are included in PART III.

    Note that the planners should not attempt now to identify or discuss what the nonprofit should do to use the strength. However, planners can ask questions to ensure understanding of the descriptions of the strengths.

2. **Ensure that the overall list is indeed complete.**
    Consider:

    a) Are there any obvious strengths missing from the list? If someone suggests one, then put it on the list.

    b) Use a brainstorming technique to generate more ideas about strengths? Guidelines for the brainstorming technique are included in PART III.

3. **Ensure that the list is well integrated.**
    Have a short, focused discussion about the strengths *in relationship to each other*. Planners should not attempt to strategize how to use strengths now. Rather, they should consider:

    a) Is there any duplication of strengths?

    b) Can any of the strengths be combined with others?

    c) Should any of the strengths be divided into one or more other strengths?

    d) Are some or all of the strengths interconnected somehow?

4. **Develop a final, ranked list of the most important 5-8 strengths.**
    If planners are used to a highly interactive approach to decision making, then they might use group discussion to rank an overall list of strengths. Guidelines for the discussion technique are included in PART III.

If planners are not convinced that group discussion will produce a ranked list in a timely fashion, then they might use a voting method to rank an overall list of strengths. Guidelines for the voting technique are included in PART III.

See "Worksheet 8: Strengths and Weaknesses" on page 249 to record the final, ranked list of strengths.

Repeat steps 1-4 with the group, this time to compile and rank an overall list of weaknesses. Consider "important" to be in terms of potential negative impact on the organization.

The group members will do further analysis on their final lists of strengths and weaknesses later on in the strategic planning process.

Identify Strategic Issues or Establish Goals?

Crossroads for Planners

Identification of strategic issues is critical to planners who have chosen to conduct the issues-based approach to strategic planning. Planners who have chosen to conduct the organic approach to strategic planning might skip the identification of issues altogether.

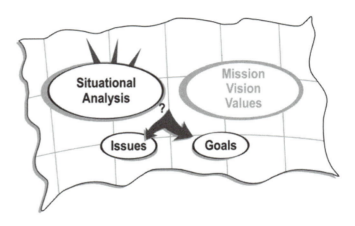

Planners who have chosen to conduct the goals-based approach to strategic planning may prefer not to identify strategic issues now, or at all, but rather to establish strategic goals right after having completed their situational analysis. That decision should be made carefully. Often, the identification of strategic issues, right after completing the situational analysis, can provide certain, key benefits to planners, including that identification of issues now can:

- Re-energize planners merely by recognizing and naming the issues that they sense from having completed the external and internal analysis.

- Refocus planners by carefully analyzing and organizing the various issues.

- Increase the credibility of the strategic planning process by clarifying that it recognizes the major issues that are facing the organization and then arranges for how those issues can be addressed.

See "Establish Goals Now?" on page 88 in the section "Phase 3: Establish Strategic Direction" if planners have still chosen to establish goals now.

What Are Strategic Issues?

Strategic issues are the most important challenges for the organization to address during the term of the strategic plan, especially during the next 12 months or fiscal period. Strategic issues are identified by reviewing the information from the situational analysis. The identification of strategic issues is particularly important for planners who are conducting an issues-based strategic planning process. These planners still should attend to external and internal analyses before identifying the strategic issues facing their organization.

The nature of the particular strategic issues that are identified during strategic planning depends, in particular, on the nature of the nonprofit's external and internal environments, programs and clients. In general, strategic issues are often in regard to:

- Extent of participation in programs by clients (too many, not enough)

- Availability of suitable workforce (not enough)

- Likelihood of donations (decreasing)

- Changes in costs of resources (people, materials, equipment, facilities, etc.)

- Changing laws and regulations

- Effectiveness of programs (ineffectiveness of process or progress toward goals and/or outcomes)

- Effectiveness of leadership in the nonprofit (ineffective planning and performance management)

- Effectiveness of management (ineffective obtaining, organizing and evaluating of resources)

These issues can be caused by any range of external and internal influences regarding the organization. The following table depicts strategic issues that might face a new homeless shelter. The numbers indicate the ranking of the issues in terms of the likely order in which to address the issues.

Example of Strategic Issues

1. How do we strengthen and develop our Board so it can be more effective in helping to set direction and raise funds? If we do not develop the Board, our strategic planning will not be effective. This should be addressed soon – maybe before all of the other issues. It affects the entire organization!

2. How do we establish overall direction for our nonprofit? Should we try to cut back or increase our services? Should we collaborate? These matters must be addressed in our strategic planning and soon. This issue affects all of the other strategic issues. It affects the entire organization!

3. How do we enhance our management skills? We're concerned that we will not be able to implement our strategic plan without more leadership and management skills. Our strategic plan is useless without these skills.

4. How can we get more money in the future, especially when donations seem to be decreasing? We cannot do any kind of expansion, even if we decide to do so, unless we get more money. This affects the entire organization, and especially any programs that we decide to start or expand. We need to decide this over the next year.

5. How can we serve more homeless clients in our area, especially when current, and likely new, laws are disenfranchising our clients from our services? We need to address this over the next year or two. This is an organizational issue, and specifically affects our programs for the homeless.

6. How do we respond to increased competition? We need to decide which programs have potential competition, probably over the next year or so. If we do not do anything about this, we'll continue to blame our programs, when our problem might really be competition that we just do not know about.

Criteria for Issue To Be Strategic

Organizations have a lot of issues – that is the nature of their existence. However, not all issues are strategic in nature. Strategic issues tend to be:

1. In regard to the information from the situational analysis

2. Important (long-term impact and solutions), rather than urgent (short-term crises)

3. Something that the organization can do something about

4. A major problem if the organization does nothing about

5. Focused on the organization, in total, or at least on a program

Select Most Important Strategic Issues To Address

Keep Spirits Up and Manage Any Conflicts During This Activity

This part of the planning process can be very engaging. It can also be a rather dispiriting experience for planners because they are faced with what seems a myriad of issues. To address this situation, it is important for the facilitator and planners to remind themselves that:

- They are going to pick only the most important strategic issues to address in the strategic plan (for example, top 5-8), especially during the next 12 months or fiscal year.

- The list of issues will provide a great deal of direction to the organization.

- The organization will only do what it can and when it can, regarding the issues.

- In the meantime, the organization is becoming a better organization for having faced the issues.

Each Planner Identifies a List of Possible Strategic Issues

Planners can use the same procedure that they used to identify the SWOT information (SWOT is an acronym for strengths, weaknesses, opportunities and threats). The procedure is included again below, this time customized to identifying strategic issues.

It is important that each planner be able spend some time alone with the SWOT information before attempting to identify strategic issues. Consider the guidelines in the above topic, "Criteria for Issue To Be Strategic." Then:

1.   Identify of an important strategic issue that the organization should address, especially over the next 12 months or fiscal year. Describe the issue, including how it relates to SWOT information, what will happen if the organization does nothing about it, and how it is important and not just urgent. Consider "important" to be in terms of potential negative impact on the organization.

2.   Try to categorize the issue according to:

   a)   An organization-wide issue or program-specific issue?

   b)   Short-term or long-term issue?

3.   Attempt to describe the issue in terms of a question, for example, "What can we do about …?", "How can we improve …?", "How do we …?", "How should we …?" and "What if …?".

4.   Record the issue on "Worksheet #9: Strategic Issues."

Repeat steps 1-4 until all of the most important 5-8 strategic issues have been identified.

Group Develops Ranked List of Strategic Issues

1.   **Compile a list of all of the strategic issues mentioned by all of the planners.**
   Use the Round-Robin technique with the entire group of planners to compile one preliminary, overall list of all of the strategic issues recommended by each planner. Avoid

duplication of the same issue on the overall list. Guidelines for the Round-Robin technique are included in PART III.

Note that the planners should not attempt now to discuss what the nonprofit should do to resolve an issue. However, planners can ask questions to ensure understanding of the descriptions of the strategic issues.

2.   **Ensure that the overall list is indeed complete**.
Consider:

   a) Are there any obvious issues missing from the list? If someone suggests one, then put it on the list.

   b) Do the issues tend to be mostly focused on internal matters? If so, then maybe more externally focused issues should be included? (Sometimes planners can use the strategic planning process primarily to vent by voicing all of their frustrations about the internal workings of their nonprofit. In that situation, the resulting list of issues may not be all that strategic at all.)

   c) Use a brainstorming technique to generate more ideas about opportunities? Guidelines for the brainstorming technique are included in PART III.

3.   **Analyze each issue to be sure that it is indeed strategic**.
For each issue, one at a time, consider the guidelines in the above topic, "Criteria for Issue To Be Strategic." Planners might use the discussion technique during those considerations. The discussions are very important to strategic thinking in the organization. If an issue is deemed not to be strategic, then planners might put it on the "parking lot." Guidelines for the parking lot technique are included in PART III.

4.   **Ensure that the list is well integrated.**
Have a short, focused discussion about the threats *in relationship to each other*. Consider:

   a)   Is there any duplication of strategic issues?

   b)   Can any of the issues be combined with others?

   c)   Should any of the issues be divided into one or more other issues?

   d)   Are some or all of the issues interconnected somehow?

   e)   If one or more of the issues is addressed, might it resolve any of the others?

   f)   Might it be useful to combine any issues that are in a similar category, for example, the short-term, long-term, organization-wide or program-wide issues?

5.   **Develop a final, ranked list of the most important 5-8 strategic issues.**
Planners can rank the list according to the issues that have the most potential negative impact and/or the order in which the issues might be addressed. The choice is up to the planners.

If planners are used to a highly interactive approach to decision making, then they might use group discussion to rank an overall list of issues. Guidelines for the discussion technique are included in PART III.

If planners are not convinced that group discussion will produce a ranked list in a timely fashion, then they might use a voting method to rank an overall list of issues. Guidelines for the voting technique are included in PART III.

See "Worksheet #9: Strategic Issues" on page 250 to record the final, ranked list of strategic issues.

Attend to Solutions (Goals, Action Plans) Soon After Identifying Strategic Issues

It is very important that planners not wait more than a week or two after finalizing the list of strategic issues in order to start strategizing to address each issue. Otherwise, planners might despair about the magnitude of the issues and become disillusioned about the planning process, in general. Guidelines to strategize are included in the next section, "Phase 3: Establish Strategic Direction."

If the planners have not yet visited their mission, vision and values statements, they might do so now by following the guidelines in the next section. The analysis of the issues often gives more focus and direction to planners, which can be useful in further developing, reviewing or updating those statements.

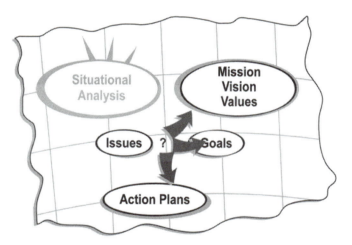

In addition, planners might prefer to create goals at this point. For issues-based planners, this might be done simply by rewording the identified issues to specific goals, if they choose to establish goals, at all. Guidelines to address goals are in the next section.

In any case, be sure that your process allows for quick movement to identifying strategies and/or action plans.

Phase 3: Establish Strategic Direction

Planners establish the strategic direction for an organization by:

- Developing or updating a mission statement (and sometimes a vision and/or values statements, as well)

- Establishing strategic goals (though not all organizations may want to establish goals)

- Identifying strategies to achieve the goals or address strategic issues

Mission, Vision and Values Statements

Various Perspectives on Statements

One of the first activities for planners, when establishing direction for their nonprofit, is to develop, or review, its mission statement. The mission statement succinctly describes the overall purpose of the organization. A vision statement describes what nonprofit leaders want the organization and its clients to look like at some point in the future. The values statement describes what nonprofit leaders want as overall priorities in the nature of how the nonprofit should operate. Board members, in particular, as responsible to ensure that at least a mission statement is articulated and referenced regularly by the organization.

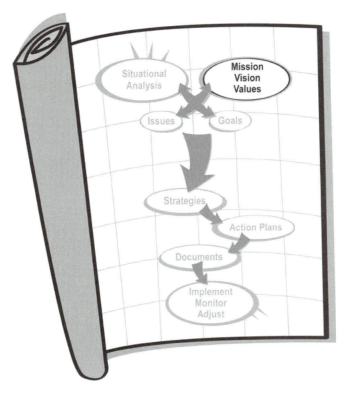

Some planners define the mission statement as including information about the organization's vision and values, as well. Likewise, some people refer to the vision statement as also including the mission and/or values information. The nature of the content and sizes of these statements can vary widely, ranging from a few phrases or sentences to several pages each.

Various Approaches to Developing Statements

An organization must have a mission statement to include on various legal and public documents, for example, when they file for incorporation with their state, provincial or federal agency. In addition to a mission statement, some planners also prefer to attend to a vision and/or values statement, as well. The order in which they develop them is up to the planners. Each subsection below includes guidelines to help planners assess if they want to develop a vision and/or values statement, along with attending to their mission statement. Planners who choose to attend to a vision and/or values statement should consider these activities soon after attending to their mission statement because the nature of the activities is very similar.

Planners who choose to conduct an organic strategic planning process will very likely want to attend to all three forms of statements at this time because the statements provide strong, ongoing focus for the frequent meetings among stakeholders.

Note that the most important part of attending to the statements is not to produce a particular, written statement. Rather, the most important parts of the process are the often spirited discussions among Board and staff members regarding what should be the content described in the statements.

There are a wide variety of approaches to developing statements, depending on:

- How well members of the organization understand their clients and their clients' needs

- Effectiveness of discussions and decision-making among members of the Board and staff

- Value of inclusiveness and consensus in decision making among members of the Board and staff

- Importance of each of the three kinds of statements to the organization

- Time available to develop the statements

The guidelines included in this subsection for developing a mission, vision and/or values statements are designed to promptly produce acceptable statements in a very practical fashion. Certainly, some experts and planners would disagree with the guidelines, not because they might not produce acceptable statements, but because they might not be according to the strong preferences and values they have about the extent of participation when developing the statements. As with any of the guidelines in this guidebook, planners have the prerogative to vary from the guidelines and design their own approaches.

If planners find themselves getting bogged down when trying to develop or update any of the statements, then they should strongly consider moving their attention to establishing strategic goals and/or identifying strategies, the next two subsections in this section about establishing strategic direction. After planners have attended to the goals and/or strategies, they can return to the statements, probably with more focus and clarity regarding what should be on the statements.

(Some parts of the guidelines for developing a mission, vision and/or values statements are quite similar and duplicated across the three sections. That extent of duplication was unavoidable in order to ensure clear usability as you develop each type of statement.)

Develop Mission Statement

What Is Mission Statement?

The mission statement describes the overall purpose of the organization, usually including a description of the types of clients that it serves and the needs that it attempts to help those clients to meet.

The mission statement is very important because it serves as the "compass" for all operations in the organization. A clear mission statement can provide strong, ongoing focus and direction among Board or staff members, thereby reducing conflict, as well. For example, if Board members are faced with deciding whether to implement a new program, they should first ask themselves if the nature of the new program is consistent with the nonprofit's mission.

Particularly for new nonprofits, the wording is extremely important. When the nonprofit registers with the appropriate state (or provincial or federal) agency to be incorporated, it must provide its mission statement, usually in an Articles of Incorporation, which is a public document. If the nonprofit applies for tax-exempt and or/ charitable status (in the United States, applications are to the Internal Revenue Service), it must provide its mission statement on the application. The decision as to whether an organization should be tax-exempt and/or charitable can rest on the wording of the mission statement.

Some planners differentiate between a mission statement, purpose statement and slogan.

- A mission statement might be the largest and most descriptive, and could be a paragraph or more than a page long. The reader might benefit from doing a quick search for "mission statement" on the Web to view the wide range of designs for mission statements.

- A purpose statement is often one sentence that starts with "To ...", for example:

   "To support individual and community development in Minneapolis by ensuring all adults between the ages of 18 and 65 achieve gainful employment in the community."

- A slogan is usually a very short phrase that is frequently repeated in the nonprofit's literature, for example:

   "We bring good things to life." [®] (This slogan is a registered trademark of the General Electric Company.)

Preparation for Writing or Reviewing Mission Statement

Whether the nonprofit already has a mission statement or is developing a mission statement for the first time, planners should carefully prepare for writing or reviewing their mission statement.

1.   Review the information generated from the situational analysis, in particular, what primary clients and stakeholders say that they want from the nonprofit. Think about any particular results, or outcomes, that seem most useful for current and potentially new groups of clients.

2.   Establish up-to-date criteria for evaluating a mission statement. The criteria might be established, by first having one or more planners recommend a set of criteria and, next, getting reactions from members of the Board and key staff in order to finalize the criteria. Consider the following as criteria for the new mission statement:

   a)   Clearly understandable by people internal and external to the organization (strong requirement)

   b)   Succinctly describes the purpose of the organization (strong requirement)

   c)   Succinctly describes the overall type(s) of client served by the nonprofit (strong requirement)

d) Provides sufficient focus and direction that members of the Board and staff can reference the mission when making major decisions (strong requirement)

e) Succinctly describes the particular need(s) met by the nonprofit (recommended)

f) Mentions the particular results (new knowledge, skills and/or conditions) that the nonprofit tries to help its clients to achieve (recommended)

g) Differentiates the nonprofit from other nonprofits in the area (recommended).

h) Conveys strong public image (recommended)

i) Mentions the communities in which the nonprofit operates (optional)

j) Mentions any particular strengths and opportunities identified during the situational analysis (optional)

3. Do not forget any requirements of the nonprofit as established in various legal documents, including: Articles of Incorporation, church laws, government regulations, requirements to maintain charitable status, national by-laws, requirements to maintain foundation status, etc. Those requirements might closely determine the mission of a nonprofit, including how much it can be changed, if at all.

See "Reviewing and Approving Mission Statement" on page 76 if the nonprofit already has a mission statement.

Writing New Mission Statement

While there is no one standard approach to writing a new mission statement, the following approach can be very practical and adaptable for a wide variety of types of organizations. This approach recognizes that, no matter how tightly focused the members of the Board and key staff are when discussing information about the mission, it almost always helps if they have a draft of a mission statement to look at during their discussions.

1. Identify a group of four to six people to develop the mission statement, including one person who will do the writing. Depending on the size of the strategic planning group, the writing group and planning group might be the same.

2. The writing group should draft at least one version of a mission statement and review the version against the evaluation criteria. They should mark their statement as "draft".

3. Members of the group might generate the draft by using the story and/or brainstorming technique to creatively generate descriptive words and phrases. The group should not attempt to develop the "perfect" mission statement. Rather, they should develop a draft that at least seems to meet the evaluation criteria. The brainstorming technique is described in PART III of this guidebook.

4.   The group of writers presents the draft, along with criteria to evaluate the draft, to the members of the Board of Directors and key members of the staff, for their review and decisions about the draft.

 See "Worksheet #10: Mission, Vision and Values" on page 251.

Reviewing and Approving Mission Statement

Members of the Board and key staff should engage in participative discussions about the wording of the current, or newly drafted, mission statement, before attempting to make a decision about the statement. This meeting should be scheduled for no more than an hour and a half. Do not attempt to completely rewrite the statement in this meeting. They might make a decision about the statement, including to:

1.   Start with an hour-long, open discussion about the statement, including comparison to each of the evaluation criteria.

2.   Mention what they like and do not like about the statement.

3.   Write their "like"s on one sheet of paper and the "dislike"s on another sheet of paper.

4.   Note that, at this point, members might decide to provide their favorite version of the mission statement to people outside of the nonprofit in order to get their "like"s and "dislike"s, as well.

5.   Provide the lists to the writing team with directions for them to revise a draft of the mission statement.

Repeat the guidelines in the subtopics, "Writing New Mission Statement" and "Reviewing and Approving Mission Statement," until a final version of the statement has been accepted by the members, including official approval by the Board of Directors.

Note that planners might adjust their mission statement during the rest of the activities in strategic planning.

Planners might put the mission statement on the wall. That way, they can continually reference the mission during their planning activities, for ongoing focus and direction.

"Chasing the Money"

It is important that leaders in the nonprofit continue to focus their mission on meeting a certain, specific need in the community. When it is very difficult for nonprofits to get donations or otherwise obtain revenue from fees, it can be very seductive consider changing the mission. Leaders might think about changing the nonprofit's mission to focus on any kind of activity that might bring in money to the nonprofit, regardless of whether that activity is directly in regard to the specific community need. Some nonprofit experts call this strategy "chasing the money" because the nonprofits are, in effect, doing whatever they can to get money and stay in existence, rather than focusing primarily on meeting a community need. Nonprofit leaders must be very reluctant to change their mission. Certainly, they can modify certain wording in the mission statement. But the primary purpose of the nonprofit, that was declared when the nonprofit was established, should remain the same.

An exception to this recommendation is when a nonprofit discovers certain unmet needs that may be stronger than the need which was the focus of the original mission. In that case, the nonprofit might change its mission to more accurately reflect the nonprofit's efforts to meet the newly identified unmet needs. The nonprofit still is responsible to verify that the unmet need exists and how it might be met, along with notifying relevant stakeholders of the change in mission. The change in mission might mean that certain laws and regulations are suddenly relevant to the nonprofit. These regulations might result in a change to the tax-exempt and/or charitable status of the nonprofit or they might impact the procedures that the nonprofit must follow in meeting the client needs.

Develop Vision Statement

What Is Vision Statement?

The vision statement provides vivid description of the organization and its clients at some point in the future. The purpose of the vision statement is to provide direction and motivation for members of the organization, in addition to that provided by the mission statement. Another benefit of the vision statement is that it can be used to help identify strategic goals, either by working backwards from what must be accomplished in order to achieve the vision. A vision often drives the direction for "organic" strategic planning planners, as well.

Note that a scenario is usually larger in size than a vision statement, and often includes a more complete depiction of the organization, along with its clients and even significant conditions in society at some point in the future.

Preparation for Writing or Reviewing Vision Statement

Similar to a mission statement, whether the nonprofit already has a vision statement or is developing a vision statement for the first time, planners should carefully prepare for writing or reviewing their vision statement.

1. Review the information generated from the situational analysis, in particular, what primary clients and stakeholders say that they want from the nonprofit. Think about any particular results, or outcomes, that seem most useful for current and potentially new groups of clients.

2. Establish up-to-date criteria for evaluating a vision statement. The criteria might be established, by first having one or more planners recommend a set of criteria and, next, getting reactions from members of the Board and key staff in order to finalize the criteria. Consider the following as criteria for the new vision:

    a) Clearly understandable by people internal and external to the organization (strong requirement)

    b) Depicts the desired future state of the organization and its clients at some point in the future (strong requirement)

    c) Inspirational to members of the organization and key stakeholders (strong requirement)

d) Depicts the environment in which the nonprofit operates and how clients benefit from the nonprofit's services (strong requirement)

e) Depicts the strengths and opportunities regarding the organization and as identified during the situational analysis (recommended)

See "Reviewing and Approving Vision Statement" on page 79 if the organization already has a vision statement.

Writing New Vision Statement

Similar to the writing of a mission statement, there is no one standard approach to writing a new vision statement. The following approach can be very practical and adaptable for a wide variety of types of organizations. The approach recognizes that, no matter how tightly focused are the members of the Board and key staff when discussing information about the vision, it almost always helps if they have a draft of a vision statement to look at during their discussions.

When writing the vision statement, consider the following guidelines.

1. Identify why you are doing a vision statement. What is the purpose of the statement? How will it be used?

2. Identify a group of four to six people to develop the vision statement, including one person who will do the writing. Depending on the size of the strategic planning group, the writing group and planning group might be the same.

3. Nonprofits exist primarily to serve clients, not to develop and operate organizations. Therefore, first develop a vision statement around future conditions for the client, rather than conditions in the organization.

4. Some planners might prefer to establish a vision by imagining from the present to the future, and others by imagining from the future to the present. In general, for nonprofits with limited resources, it might be better to work from the present to the future, particularly if developing a strategic vision. That approach can be easier for planners to conceptualize and often results in a much more realistic, and therefore meaningful, strategic vision.

5. Planners might choose to use the story and/or brainstorming techniques to generate their vision. Also, planners might choose to use scenario planning at this point in order to ensure robust visioning activity.

See "What Strategic Planning Approach Might Be Used?" on page 25. See "Worksheet #4: Environmental Scan" on page 241 for guidelines to develop scenarios.

6. Members of the writing group should draft at least one version of a vision statement and review the version against the evaluation criteria. They should mark their statement as "draft".

Members of the group might generate the draft by using a brainstorming technique to creatively generate descriptive words and phrases. The group should not attempt to develop the "perfect" vision statement. Rather, they should develop a draft that at least seems to meet the evaluation criteria. The brainstorming techniques is explained in PART III of this guidebook.

7.   The group of writers presents the draft, along with criteria to evaluate the draft, to the members of the Board of Directors and key members of the staff, for their review and decisions about the draft.

Developing the vision can be one of the most enjoyable parts of planning, but the part where time easily gets away from you. If you find that visioning is taking, for example, half a day, then consider proceeding with other phases of the planning process and coming back to visioning later. Otherwise, planners can become frustrated and bored when attending to more detailed matters, such as establishing action plans.

 See "Worksheet #10: Mission, Vision and Values" on page 251.

Reviewing and Approving Vision Statement

Planners can follow the same guidelines in the above-referenced subtopic, "Reviewing and Approving Mission Statement," until the vision statement in approved.

Note that planners might adjust their vision statement during the rest of the activities in strategic planning.

Planners might put the vision statement on the wall to provide focus and direction for the remainder of their planning activities.

Develop a Values Statement

What Is Values Statement?

Values represent the core priorities in how the organization chooses to operate and to be viewed by stakeholders, both inside and outside the organization. Values are increasingly important in strategic planning, especially as the planning processes attempt to accommodate diverse cultures with diverse values, perspectives and opinions.

Leaders in the nonprofit should be careful that their attention to values is well beyond developing a values statement. Members of the organization can become quite cynical if they perceive that the leaders in the organization are not making attempt to operate according to the stated values in the workplace. In this case, members might believe that the values statement was developed primarily for appearance. Therefore, be sure that the values are visited often and truly guide decisions in the organization. Similar to the mission and vision statements, the values statement should be widely communicated to all stakeholders, for example, on walls in offices and on stationery.

Values are put into operation by continually referring to the values in discussions among staff and members of the Board. Leaders in the nonprofit might take the advice of Bob Kniffin, previous Vice President of External Affairs, at Johnson and Johnson (J&J) company. The way that J&J handled an ethical issue (the "Tylenol scare" crisis) in the 1980s is probably one of the most inspiring and enlightening examples of how to successfully deal with a major ethical issue in business. Kniffin was one of the key players in helping J&J to handle the crisis so effectively. Kniffin said that it was not the J&J Credo (a form of a code of ethics) that helped J&J to handle the crisis so well. Rather, it was the ongoing "challenge sessions" that the company regularly held in order for each person to clarify their own perspective and commitment to the J&J Credo.

An example of a brief, concise values statement might be:

"We believe that:

- Employment provides opportunity for adults to develop community and themselves;

- Every person deserves opportunity for gainful employment;

- Gainful employment of all citizens is a responsibility of all citizens."

Preparation for Writing or Reviewing Values Statement

Similar to mission and vision statements, whether the nonprofit already has a values statement or is developing a values statement for the first time, planners should carefully prepare for writing or reviewing their values statement.

1. Identify why you are doing a values statement. What is the purpose of the statement? How will it be used?

2. Review the information generated from the situational analysis, in particular, what primary clients and stakeholders say they want from the nonprofit. Think about any particular results, or outcomes, that seem most useful for current and potentially new groups of clients.

3. Establish up-to-date criteria for evaluating a values statement. The criteria might be established, by first having one or more planners recommend a set of criteria and, next, getting reactions from members of the Board and key staff in order to finalize the criteria. Consider the following as criteria for the new values statement:

    a) Understandable by people internal and external to the organization (strong requirement)

    b) Depict the top priorities in how the nonprofit wants to operate in order to meet the needs of clients and other stakeholders (strong requirement)

    c) Depict the top priorities in how the nonprofit wants to operate in order to address current challenges in the workplace (strong requirement)

    d) Depict how the nonprofit wants to be viewed by staff and external stakeholders (strong requirement)

    e) Will be adhered to, as much as possible, by all members of the Board and staff (strong requirement)

Writing New Values Statement

See "Reviewing and Approving Values Statement" on page 82 if the organization already has a values statement.

Similar to the writing of mission and vision statements, there is no one standard approach to writing a new values statement. The following approach can be very practical and adaptable for a wide variety of types of organizations. The approach recognizes that, no matter how tightly focused are the members of the Board and key staff when discussing information about the values, it almost always helps if they have a draft of a statement to look at during their discussions.

When writing the values statement, consider the following guidelines.

1.   Identify a group of four to six people to develop the values statement, including one person who will do the writing. Depending on the size of the strategic planning group, the writing group and planning group might be the same.

2.   Establish four to six core values from which the organization would like to operate. Planners might choose to use the story and/or brainstorming techniques to identify their values for the organization. Consider what might be valued by staff, clients, the local community, funders and collaborators.

3.   Be careful to notice any differences between the values that the organization prefers and what might be its true values (the values actually reflected by members' behaviors in the organization).

        One approach to identify preferred values and actual values is as follows. Record each preferred value on a flash card, and then have each planner rate the values with 1, 2 or 3 in terms of the priority needed by the organization with 3 indicating the value is very important to the organization and 1 is least important. Then go through the cards again to rate how people think the values are actually being enacted in the organization, with 3 indicating the values are fully enacted and 1 indicating the value is hardly reflected at all. Then address discrepancies where a value is highly preferred (ranked with a 3), but hardly enacted (ranked with a 1). Incorporate actions to align actual behavior with preferred behaviors into the strategic plan.

4.   Next to each value, attempt to include short descriptions of behaviors that reflect those values.

5.   Members of the writing group should draft at least one version of the statement and review the version against the evaluation criteria. They should mark their statement as "draft".

        Members of the group might generate the draft by using a brainstorming technique to creatively generate descriptive words and phrases. The group should not attempt to develop the "perfect" statement. Rather, they should develop a draft that at least seems to meet the evaluation criteria for the values statement. The brainstorming technique is described in PART III of this guidebook

6.   The group of writers presents the draft, along with criteria to evaluate the draft, to the members of the Board of Directors and key members of the staff, for their review and decisions about the draft.

 See "Worksheet #10: Mission, Vision and Values" on page 251.

Reviewing and Approving Values Statement

Planners can follow the same guidelines in the above-referenced subtopic, "Reviewing and Approving Mission Statement," until the values statement is approved.

Note that planners might adjust their values statement during the rest of the activities in strategic planning.

The following table provides an example of a values statement that associates preferred behaviors with each value.

Example of Values Statement	
Leadership ▪ Model corporate vision, mission and values, as well as these team values **Responsibility and Integrity** ▪ Participate – say what you believe ▪ Work to know who will do what and by when ▪ Do what you say you are going to do when you say you are going to do it ▪ Take initiative! **Respect** ▪ Actively listen and acknowledge my viewpoint ▪ Recognize the value of my job – ask for my help and realize that I have other priorities ▪ Be sensitive to my values, my culture – reap the richness of diversity ▪ Be friendly and thoughtful to all	**Teamwork** ▪ Recognize others' contributions and successes ▪ Cooperate with fellow staff members and support their efforts ▪ Support decisions and strategic objectives ▪ Do not take ourselves too seriously – have fun! **Creativity** ▪ Encourage thinking "outside the box" ▪ Encourage discussion around points of disagreement or uncertainty ▪ Challenge the status quo ▪ Envision possibilities ▪ Allow yourself to experiment, fail and try again
- Actively work for the common good -	

Thanks to The Management Assistance Program for Nonprofits of St. Paul, Minnesota, for inclusion of this version of their values statements.

Ensure Strategic Thinking for Goals and Strategies

This subsection explains some useful guidelines to ensure that planners are indeed strategic when addressing their goals and/or strategies. (Not all organizations will want to establish strategic goals or strategies. Organic planners might skip goals and strategies altogether. Small nonprofits might go from goals to action plans.) As previously mentioned, probably the most important outcome from the strategic planning process is the capacity for strategic thinking. Another important outcome from the strategic planning process is agreement, especially on goals and strategies. To help planners clarify their thinking – and have a common language – about goals and strategies, information is provided about the specific aspects and criteria for effective goals and strategies.

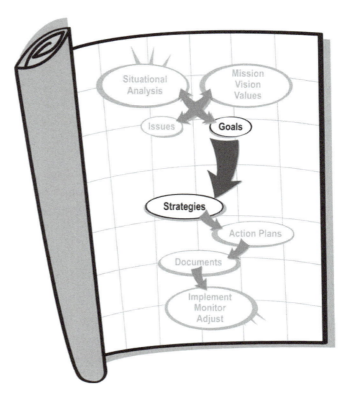

The subsection, "Conventions for Terms," in the section "Phase 1: Design Plan for Plan," explained that there can be some confusion among planners as to what to call a certain concept in planning. That subsection included recommendations that planners not overly worry about the differences. What is most important is to recognize the difference between "What is important to accomplish?" (these are usually goals or objectives) and "How to accomplish it?" (these are usually strategies or tactics). The differences emerge over time during planning. Keep that advice in mind when reading the following topic about types of goals and strategies.

Ensure Strategic Thinking

It is important that planners be as strategic as possible when identifying goals and strategies. Strategic matters consider potential changes to the external and internal environments of the organization, and can have significant effect on the governance, leadership and operations of the nonprofit. They usually involve extensive use of the nonprofit's resources, as well. Matters that are not strategic should not be included in the strategic planning process and plan. Planners should be thinking, especially about questions, such as:

- "How do we position ourselves if the future changes, and if it is not what we expected?"

- "How can we use our strengths to take advantage of opportunities, while strengthening our weaknesses and warding off threats?"

As review, strategic issues tend to be:

1. Directly in regard to the information from the situational analysis and/or mission, vision and/or values.

2. Important, rather than urgent.

3. Something that the organization can do something about.

4. A major problem if the organization does nothing about the matter.

5. Focused on the organization, in total, or at least on a program.

Dimensions of Goals and Strategies

Before identifying goals and strategies, it can help planners a great deal in their planning process if they are able to think clearly about all dimensions of the goals and strategies they are about to identify in their planning process. An understanding of these dimensions gives all of the planners a common language to use when describing and analyzing the goals and strategies.

Levels

1. **Organization-wide goals and strategies**
    These are in regard to matters that mostly involve the entire organization. They usually involve extensive use of resources from across the entire organization.

2. **Program goals and strategies**
    These are in regard to matters that mostly involve a specific program. They usually involve extensive use of resources from a particular program.

Timing

1. **Short-term**
    This is usually in regard to activities during the first quarter or third of the time span of the strategic plan, for example, over the next six to 12 months for a three-year plan.

2. **Long-term**
    This is usually in regard to activities over the entire span of the strategic plan, for example, over the next three years for a three-year plan.

Types

1. **Activities goals and strategies**
    These are accomplishments in regard to activities in the organization or programs – not in regard to changes in clients. Examples are: hire a Chief Executive Office, move into a new facility, or complete and approve a strategic plan. Activities goals and strategies can be organization-wide or program specific.

2. **Outcomes goals and strategies**
    These are accomplishments in regard to changes in clients from their participation in the nonprofit's programs, for example, clients obtain a high-school diploma, drive a car or pass a high-school equivalency test. Outcomes goals and strategies are usually associated with a program.

The distinction between activities and outcomes is very important, particularly to potential and current donors to the nonprofit organization. Funders are usually interested in funding efforts that contribute directly to producing the changes (outcomes) that the nonprofit is helping its clients to accomplish. Thus, during strategic planning, planners should attempt to identify which goals and associated strategies are in regard to outcomes, associate those outcomes with programs, and use those outcomes as credence when working with funders.

Resources

Resources to achieve goals and implement strategies are usually in terms of:

1.   People

2.   Materials

3.   Facilities

4.   Equipment

5.   Money

Criteria for Effective Goals and Strategies

When first establishing goals or identifying strategies, planners should consider the following criteria, including that the goals or strategies: (some planners might skip identifying strategies)

1.   **Convey methods that are understandable and explainable.**
     People should be able to read descriptions of the goals and strategies and understand what they mean. Occasionally, planners will be so close to the descriptions that they are the only people who can understand those descriptions in the strategic plan. Strategies also should be explainable to someone else. The planner who comes up with the idea of the strategy will need to explain his or her idea to other planners.

2.   **Be within the charter of the nonprofit organization.**
     Any goal or strategy should suggest activities that are within the focus of the nonprofit's legal description and any other official requirements on the nonprofit, for example, federal and state/provincial laws and church laws. For example, in the United States, it would be inappropriate for a charitable nonprofit to engage extensively in activities geared to influence a legislator to vote a certain way on pending legislation. Those activities would likely cause a government agency, the Internal Revenue Service (IRS), to conclude that the nonprofit was engaged primarily in lobbying, which is not a charitable activity in the United States. In that case, the IRS would take away the charitable status of the nonprofit organization.

3.   **Be within the nature and scope of the mission.**
     All activities in the nonprofit should be aligned with working toward the mission, especially top-level goals and strategies. The mission statement is the "compass" of the organization.

4.   **Consider strengths and opportunities, weaknesses and threats.**
     Ultimately, the definition of a good strategy is that it builds on strengths in order to take advantage of opportunities, while addressing weaknesses and facing threats to the organization.

5.   **Convey the level of application.**
        Planners should be able to discern if the goal or strategy might apply to the entire
        organization or a particular program.

6.   **Convey the type of activity.**
        Planners should be able to discern if the goal or strategy is oriented specifically to outcomes
        (changes in clients) or to general activities in the organization or program.

7.   **Convey some sense of timing.**
        Timing could be in regard to whether the goal or strategy is short-term or long-term, and
        even when it might start and stop.

8.   **Include estimates of resource requirements.**
        Resources would include people, materials, equipment, facilities and money. It is difficult to
        assess whether a goal or strategy is realistic or not without some sense of what is required to
        achieve the goal or implement the strategy.

9.   **Be realistic and achievable.**
        Achievement of the goal or implementation of the strategy should be possible within the
        constraints of current, or expected, timing and resources of the nonprofit organization.

10.   **Have predictable and acceptable effects on stakeholders, especially clients.**
        Once planners conclude that a goal or strategy qualifies as being understandable, legal and
        realistic, they must carefully consider any effects of the goal or strategy on those people who
        are served by, and interested in, the nonprofit. No goal or strategy should inadvertently
        harm a stakeholder. Even if it would not cause any harm, planners should carefully consider
        whether it might even be unacceptable to a certain stakeholder, or group of stakeholders.

11.   **Should have more of an upside than a downside.**
        The benefits of successfully achieving a goal or implementing a strategy should clearly
        outweigh the disadvantages if the goal or strategy is not addressed successfully.

The following table might apply to a new homeless shelter, where planners have chosen to conduct
an issues-based approach to strategic planning. The example goal and strategies are in regard to a
rather short-term strategic issue. Note that the planners in the homeless shelter chose to describe
their strategies in very specific terms, which, in any other strategic plan, could look like goals or
objectives.

Example of Goals and Strategies Information
Strategic Issue #1: "How do we strengthen and develop our Board so it can be more effective in helping to set direction and raise funds? If we do not develop the Board, our strategic planning will not be effective. This should be addressed soon – maybe before all of the other issues. It affects the entire organization!" (Some small nonprofits skip identifying strategies.) Goal #1: Complete Board Development by September 1, 2008. 1) Strategy 1.1: CEO proposes Board Development Plan to Board. Gain approval by April 1, 2008. 2) Strategy 1.2: Establish Board Development Committee by April 15, 2008, to oversee development and implementation of Plan. 3) Strategy 1.3: Hire consultant by May 1, 2008, to guide Board to develop and implement Plan. 4) Strategy 1.4: Conduct Board training by June 1, 2008. 5) Strategy 1.5: Consultant coaches Board Chair from May 1, 2008, until August 1, 2008. 6) Strategy 1.6: Board conducts Board self-evaluation and reviews results by September 1, 2008.

Tools To Identify Goals and Strategies

When identifying goals and strategies (selection of strategies is optional), planners are often faced with having to make decisions about how to work toward the mission of the organization or address major strategic issues. This guidebook provides several useful tools and guidelines that can help planners to think hard about what the goals and strategies should be for their nonprofit organization.

Appendix H on page 259 includes several useful tools to help planners identify strategies, including:

1.   **Guidelines to Problem Solving and Decision Making**
        This tool can come in handy, especially when analyzing strategic goals or issues and deciding what to do about them. This approach is in sharp contrast to the organic philosophy in the next tool.

2.   **Organic Philosophy of Problem Solving**
        The philosophy presents another viewpoint about "problems" and how they might be addressed. Planners who chose the organic approach to strategic planning might subscribe to this philosophy.

3.   **SWOT Grid Analysis**
        A strategy is indeed strategic if it uses the organization's strengths to take advantage of opportunities, while shoring up weaknesses to ward off threats. The Grid can be very useful to planners when ensuring that their strategies are indeed strategic.

4.   **Internal Nonprofit Organizational Problems and Strategies To Address Them**
        This tool helps planners to think about the specific kinds of issues in their organization and specifically what they might do about each.

5. **Guidelines to Successful Organizational Change**
The implementation of any major strategy involves change to the organization. This tool helps planners to think carefully about the change and how it can best be carried out.

Establish Goals Now?

Some planners might choose to identify strategies or even action plans after completing the situational analysis, especially if they are using the issues-based approach to strategic planning. In that case, they might go right to the sections about identifying strategies or action planning. Organic planners might skip goals altogether and go right to action planning. Goals-based planners will almost always proceed with goals after situational analyses.

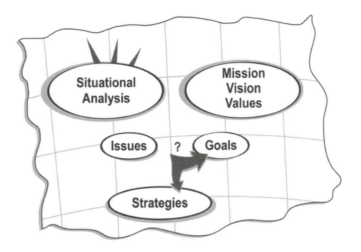

SMART Goals

In addition to the guidelines in the topic, "Criteria for Effective Goals and Strategies," ideally, goals are described as SMART, which is an acronym for:

- Specific – Someone should be able to conclude whether the goal was achieved or not.

- Measurable – Someone should be able to assess how much of the goal was achieved.

- Achievable – It should be realistic to achieve the goal in the allotted time.

- Relevant – The goal should contribute directly to the mission of the organization.

- Timely – There should be a relevant deadline for completion of the goal.

Note that different people associate different words with some of the letters in the acronym. For example, some associate the "A" with acceptable and/or the "R" with realistic and/or the "T" with traceable. It is up to the planners to choose what SMART means to them.

Not all goals are likely to be worded in a SMART fashion. One of the major advantages of wording goals to be SMART is that it can be much easier to recognize and explain why goals must be, or have, changed – that makes for a highly flexible plan. When a goal changes, it is usually not to the nature of the goal, but to the extent of the goal. For example, one might change the goal of "Training 300 students" to "Training 200 students." The nature of the goal (training students) is the same. The number of trained students is what changed.

Guidelines To Identify Strategic Goals

When identifying strategic goals, planners can use a process that is very similar to the process they used when identifying SWOT information (and strategic issues, if they attended to those activities in their planning process). Planners will be quite experienced at the process by now and can modify it according to the nature and needs of their organization.

Planners who have chosen to conduct the goals-based approach to strategic planning might choose to establish goals and then associated strategies primarily by referencing the situational analysis and the mission, vision and values statements.

Planners who have chosen to conduct the issues-based approach to strategic planning usually focus first on identifying strategies or actions (upcoming subsections), even before establishing goals (if they choose to establish goals at all). However, if these planners prefer, they might still establish goals after identifying strategies or actions by rewording each of strategic issues (from which strategies were derived in the first place) to specific goals to be achieved in the future. That way, each strategic issue becomes an overall goal, which the strategies or actions are to achieve.

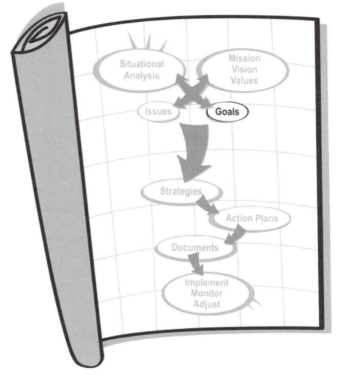

If planners get stuck when trying to establish goals, they might benefit from moving on and identifying strategies or action plans instead. The activity of strategizing often gives more clarity about the preferred future direction of the nonprofit; thus, giving more clarity about goals, as well.

Planners might benefit most from trying to start with the easiest goals to identify. That approach helps them to more quickly learn how to identify and articulate goals to themselves and others.

Each Planner Identifies a List of Possible Strategic Goals

Planners can use the same procedure that they used to identify the SWOT information. The procedure is included again below, this time customized to establishing strategic goals.

It is important that each planner be able to have some time alone with the mission, vision and/or values statements and any strategic issues before attempting to identify strategic goals. Consider the guidelines in the previous topics, "Ensure Strategic Thinking," "Criteria for Effective Goals and Strategies" and "Tools to Identify Goals and Strategies." Then:

1.   Identify an important strategic goal for the organization to achieve, especially during the next 12 months or fiscal year. Think about how the goal is related to the mission and SWOT information and about any effects on stakeholders. Consider "important" to be in terms of potential positive impact on the organization.

2.   Try to categorize the goal according to:

   a)   An organization-wide goal or program goal?

   b)   Short-term or long-term goal?

   c)   Activities goal or outcomes goal?

3.   Record the final, ranked list of goals.

 See "Worksheet 11: Strategic Goals" on page 255 to record the final, ranked list of goals.

Repeat steps 1-3 until the most important 5-8 goals have been identified.

Group Compiles Ranked List of Strategic Goals

Next, assemble all of the planners into a group and attempt to combine the goals across every planner's list into one overall, ranked list of potential strategic goals.

1.   **Compile a list of all of the goals mentioned by all of the planners.**
Use the Round-Robin technique with the entire group of planners to compile one preliminary, overall list of all of the potential goals recommended by each planner. Avoid duplication of the same goal on the overall list. Guidelines for the Round-Robin technique are included in PART III.

Note that the planners should not attempt now to identify or discuss what the nonprofit should do to achieve a goal. However, planners can ask questions to ensure understanding of the descriptions of the goals.

2.   **Ensure that the overall list is indeed complete**.
Consider:

   a)   Are there any obvious goals missing from the list? If someone suggests one, then put it on the list.

   b)   Do the goals tend to be mostly focused on internal matters? If so, then maybe more externally focused goals should be included? (Sometimes planners can use the strategic planning process primarily to vent by voicing all of their frustrations about the internal workings of their nonprofit. In that situation, the resulting list of goals may not be all that strategic at all.)

   c)   Are there sufficient outcomes goals (goals in regard to desired changes in clients)? If not, then add some. These goals will be useful when updating the design of each particular program for clients.

   d)   Use a brainstorming technique to generate more ideas about strategic goals? Guidelines for the brainstorming technique are included in PART III.

3.   **Analyze each goal to be sure that it is indeed strategic**.
        For each goal, one at a time, consider the guidelines in the previous topics, "Ensure Strategic Thinking" and "Criteria for Effective Goals and Strategies." Planners might use the discussion technique during those considerations. The discussions are very important to strategic thinking in the organization. If a goal is deemed not to be strategic, then planners might choose to put it on the "parking lot." Guidelines for the parking lot technique are included in PART III.

4.   **Ensure that the list is well integrated.**
        Have a short, focused discussion about the goals *in relationship to each other*. Consider:

        a) Is there any duplication of strategic goals?

        b) Can any of the goals be combined with others?

        c) Do any of the goals conflict with each other (the achievement of one goal would make it almost impossible to achieve another goal on the overall list)?

        d) Should any of the goals be divided into one or more other goal?

        e) Are some or all of the goals interconnected somehow?

        f) If one of the goals is achieved, might it achieve one or more of the others?

        g) Might it be useful to combine any goals that are in a similar category, for example, the short-term, long-term, organization-wide, program-specific, activities goals and outcomes goals?

5.   **Develop a final, ranked list of the most important 5-8 goals.**
        Planners can rank the list according to the goals that have the most potential positive impact and/or the order in which the goals might be addressed. The choice is up to the planners.

        If planners are used to a highly interactive approach to decision making, then they might use group discussion to rank an overall list of goals. The Guidelines for the discussion technique are included in PART III useful.

        If planners are not convinced that group discussion will produce a ranked list in a timely fashion, then they might use a voting method to rank an overall list of opportunities. The Guidelines for the voting technique are included in PART III useful.

   See "Worksheet 11: Strategic Goals" on page 255 to record the final, ranked list of goals.

Identify Strategies

Planners must decide now if they are identifying strategies to achieve strategic goals or address strategic issues. Small nonprofits might skip strategies and go right to developing action plans. Planners who chose to conduct the goals-based approach to strategic planning will be identifying strategies or action plans, probably by referencing the strategic goals. Planners who chose to conduct the issues-based approach to strategic planning will be identifying strategies or action plans, probably by referencing the strategic issues. Planners who have chosen to conduct the organic approach to planning might skip the identification of strategies altogether and do action plans.

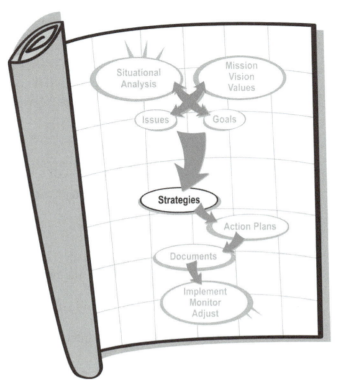

Guidelines To Identify Strategies

Agreement, particularly on goals and strategies, is often the most important outcome from the planning process for the members of the nonprofit organization. The top strategic goals or issues usually produce the most complex and contentious strategies. Therefore, meetings to reach agreement can sometimes be somewhat contentious. Therefore, guidelines recommend adequate time for individual reflection and even use of the consensus technique in the meetings.

When identifying strategies, realize that leaders in the nonprofit organization probably already have strategies that they are implementing – it is just that the strategies are implicit (not written down and discussed). Those implicit strategies can be vastly improved by ensuring that they are indeed strategic and discussed with other leaders in the organization. The following guidelines help in that regard.

Similar to identifying goals, planners might benefit most from trying to start with the easiest strategies to identify. Planners might do this by selecting the easiest goals or strategic issues to address. That approach helps them to more quickly learn how to identify and articulate strategies to themselves and others.

Each Planner Identifies a List of Possible Strategies

Planners can use the same procedure that they used to identify the SWOT information. The procedure is included again below, this time customized to identifying strategies.

It is important that each planner be able to have some time alone with the strategic goals or strategic issues information before attempting to identify strategies. Consider the guidelines in the previous topics, "Ensure Strategic Thinking," "Criteria for Effective Goals and Strategies" and "Tools to Identify Goals and Strategies." Then, for each strategic goal or issue:

1. Identify all of the strategies needed to address that goal or issue. For each strategy, think about how the strategy helps to address the goal or issue, any challenges in implementing that strategy and how that challenge might be met, any effects on stakeholders, and what resources might be needed to implement the strategy.

2. Try to categorize the strategies according to:

    a) Organization-wide or program-specific?

    b) Short-term or long-term strategy?

    c) Activities strategy or outcomes strategy?

 See "Worksheet #12: Strategies" on page 256 to record the choices of strategies.

Repeat steps 1-2 for each strategic goal or strategic issue until all goals or issues have been addressed.

Group Develops Strategies for Each Strategic Goal or Issue

The planners will finalize a list of the potential strategies for each strategic goal or issue, but following these steps for each goal or issue, one at a time:

1. **Compile a list of all of the strategies mentioned by all of the planners.**
    Use the Round-Robin technique with the entire group of planners to compile one preliminary, overall list of all of the potential strategies recommended by each planner. Avoid duplication of the same strategy on the overall list. Guidelines for the Round-Robin technique are included in PART III.

    Note that the planners should not attempt now to identify or discuss what the nonprofit should do to implement a strategy. However, planners can ask questions to ensure understanding of the descriptions of the strategies.

2. **Ensure that the overall list is indeed complete.**
    Consider:

    a) Are there any obvious strategies missing from the list? If someone suggests one, then put it on the list.

    b) Do the strategies tend to be mostly focused on internal matters? If so, then maybe more externally focused strategies should be included?

    c) Are there sufficient outcomes strategies (strategies in regard to desired changes in clients)? If not, then add some outcomes strategies. These strategies will be useful when updating the design of each particular program for clients.

    d) Use a brainstorming technique to generate more ideas about strategies? Guidelines for the brainstorming technique are included in PART III.

3.   **Analyze each strategy to be sure that it is indeed strategic.**
     For each strategy, one at a time, consider the guidelines in the previous topics, "Ensure Strategic Thinking" and "Criteria for Effective Goals and Strategies." Planners might use the discussion technique during those considerations. The discussions are very important to strategic thinking in the organization. If a strategy is deemed not to be strategic, then planners might choose to put it on the "parking lot." Guidelines for the parking lot technique are included in PART III.

4.   **Ensure the list is well-organized.**
     For all strategies across all goals or issues, consider:

     a)   Is there any duplication of strategies?

     b)   Can any of the strategies be combined with others?

     c)   Do any of the strategies conflict with each other (the implementation of one strategy would make it difficult to implement another strategy on the overall list)?

     d)   Should any of the strategies be divided into one or more other strategies?

     e)   Are some or all of the strategies interconnected somehow?

     f)   If one or more of the strategies is implemented, might it implement one or more of the others?

     g)   Might it be useful to combine any strategies that are in a similar category, for example, the short-term, long-term, organization-wide, program-specific, activities strategies and outcomes strategies?

5.   **Develop a final list of strategies for each goal or issue.**
     Unlike information about SWOT, goals or issues, it is not often useful to rank strategies because they tend to combine in a highly integrated fashion to address a goal or issue. Still, planners should finalize a list of strategies for each goal or issue.

     If planners are used to a highly interactive approach to decision making, then they might use group discussion to finalize the list of strategies. Guidelines for the discussion technique are included in PART III.

     If planners are not convinced that group discussion will produce a final list in a timely fashion, then they might use a voting method. Guidelines for the voting technique are included in PART III.

 See "Worksheet #12: Strategies" on page 256 to record the final list of strategies.

Update Statements, Strategic Goals or Strategic Issues?

Often, after planners have closely identified strategies, they realize some modifications that need to be made to the mission, vision and/or values statements; strategic goals or strategic issues from which the strategies were derived. Now is the time to go back and make those changes.

Phase 4: Develop Action and Financial Plans

Implementation plans are designed to ensure that the strategies that were identified during strategic planning are actually implemented in the workplace. Without well-designed implementation plans, strategic plans can end up as stacks of paper on peoples' shelves, unread and collecting dust.

Implementation plans usually include action plans and financial plans. Action planning ensures that strategies become individual responsibilities to be carried out on a regular basis. Action plans specify who will be doing what and by when in order to implement the strategies from the strategic plan. One of the ways to discern if an activity is in regard to action planning is if the activity actually refers to specific people, or positions, in the organization. Financial plans usually include the operating budget that corresponds to the expected revenue and expenses of the organization (or program) during the span of the strategic plan.

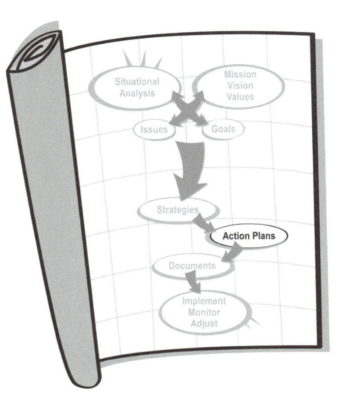

Planners who are conducting the goals-based and issues-based approaches to strategic planning will find that there is a natural progression from identifying strategies to developing action plans to implement the strategies. Planners who are conducting the organic approach to strategic planning might develop action plans primarily by sharing stories with stakeholders, probably during the same meetings in which they established their mission, vision and values.

"Planning Fatigue" at This Point?

At this point in planning, planners are sometimes fatigued from having completed the earlier phases of strategic planning. Consequently, action planning (which can demand a substantial amount of focus and detail from planners) can often seem tedious and overwhelming, especially as compared to earlier phases of strategic planning, which can often seem creative and stimulating in nature.

Sometimes planners simply stop the strategic planning at this point. Certainly, they will still have a strategic plan, of sorts. However, without focused action planning, their strategic plan might seem like useless philosophical statements to many, with no grounding in the day-to-day realities of the organization. Often, the extent of the planners' real commitment to the strategic planning process becomes apparent as planners undertake action planning.

If planners seem fatigued about the planning process at this point, then it might be beneficial for planners to go back and review the information they recorded in the "Worksheet 1.15 – How Will

You Get Buy-In When Announcing Process?" Leaders among the group of planners should remind other planners about the benefits of the planning process for the nonprofit organization and the many accomplishments that planners have achieved so far. It is useful to remind them, too, that much of what occurs in action planning is the same type of activities that members in the organization already do, including to figure out who is going to do what and then monitor that it occurs. Lastly, remind staff that action plans, like other kinds of plans, can be changed. Staff does not have to be correct the first time and every time about every facet of every detail in their action plans. The aim is to make best estimates, monitor the action plans, and then adjust them in the future, as needed.

Develop Action Plans

Typical Content of Action Plan

At it simplest, an action plan specifies:

1. What must be accomplished (objectives) to implement each strategy

2. Who is responsible to achieve each objective

3. The timing to start and complete each objective, or a deadline

4. What resources might be required

5. How the action plan will be monitored

6. Performance target

Action plans can be done in a wide variety of formats. The table on the following page depicts a rather specific, highly organized action plan. The planning information in the table might apply to a new homeless shelter, where planners have chosen to conduct an issues-based approach to strategic planning. The example action plan is in regard to a one strategy and goal to help address a rather short-term strategic issue.

Example of Action Plan Information				
Strategic Issue #1: "How do we strengthen and develop our Board so it can be more effective in helping to set direction and raise funds? If we do not develop the Board, our strategic planning will not be effective. This affects the entire organization!" Goal #1: Complete Board Development by September 1, 2008. 1) Strategy 1.1: CEO proposes Board Development Plan to Board. Gain approval by April 1, 2008.				
Action Plan for Strategy 1.1 **Objectives:**	**Dead-line**	**Responsi-bility**	**Budget**	**Monitor Status & Date**
1.1.1 Draft possible plan	2/15/08	CEO		
1.1.2 Develop case for plan	2/15/08	CEO		
1.1.3 Get on Board agenda	2/15/08	CEO		
1.1.4 Draft proposal	3/15/08	CEO		
1.1.5 Present proposal	4/1/08	CEO		
1.1.6 Gain authorization	4/1/08	CEO		
Performance target: approval of the Board Development Plan by Board.				

How Are Action Plans Developed?

Planners might have recognized by now that most of the information in an action plan can be obtained from descriptions of the various strategies identified in Phase 3. For example:

Type of Information in Action Plan	**Source of Information from Description of Strategies**
Description of objective	Analysis of description of methods in descriptions of strategies
Responsible position (in organization or program)	Reference to level of strategy (organization, program, etc.)
Timing	Description of timing of strategies
Budget	Description of resources in descriptions of strategies
Responsible to monitor (in organization or program)	Reference to level of strategy (organization, program, etc.)

Guidelines To Develop Action Plans

The design of an action plan depends on several factors, including: the extent and level of specificity, the range and complexity of the strategies, number of staff who participates in implementing the action plans, and the preferences of the members of the staff. Some nonprofit leaders prefer highly specific and organized action plans, while others prefer less formal plans. Thus, the time required to develop action plans depends on the same factors.

Planners might choose to organize the various strategies into related groups now, for example, according to organization-wide issues or specific programs. Strategies might also be organized according to certain functions in the organization, such as Board operations, staffing, marketing, financial management, fundraising and evaluations. The clarity of any grouping of strategies depends on how distinctly separate were the strategic issues or goals from which the strategies were derived. Personnel from specific programs might be used to develop the various action plans that are specific to their program.

Staff usually takes a strong role in developing action plans, depending on the particular Board structure of the nonprofit organization (see the subsection, "Diversity of Board Structures," in Appendix F: "Nature of Typical Nonprofit Organizations" on page 199). Organic planners might choose to identify action plans through use of the story technique with stakeholders. Other planners might develop their action plans in discussions with staff.

Similar to the identification of information about SWOT, strategic issues, goals and strategies, it is often best if developers of the action plans get a chance to consider strategies for at least a day or two on their own before they begin developing the action plans.

Planners might start with what seem to be the easiest strategies for which to develop an action plan. That way, they can more quickly learn how to develop action plans according to the nature and needs of their organization.

 See "Worksheet #13: Action Planning" on page 257 to develop action plans from the following guidelines.

Identifying Objectives in Action Plans

The activities of identifying objectives are actually a continuation of the strategic thinking activities. Although strategic thinking tends to focus on matters of a broad scope in and around the organization, the identification of objectives helps to ensure that the approaches to addressing those broad matters are indeed grounded in reality – thus, making strategies even more strategic.

Objectives should be derived, as much as possible, from analysis of the various strategies that were identified during earlier phases of the strategic planning process. The number of objectives in an action plan usually ranges anywhere from three to 10 or so. The number of objectives depends on the range, depth and complexity of the strategies in the strategic plan and on the degree of specificity preferred by planners. If the activities required to accomplish an objective in an action plan might involve a group of at least eight people or more, then members of the group might choose to identify the objectives in their action plan by using the same process that planners used to identify SWOT, strategic issues, goals and strategies information during the strategic planning.

If the action plan might involve a group of fewer than eight people and the group can use the discussion group method effectively, then they might identify their objectives by using discussion. Usually, an objective can be identified during discussions with staff around two questions in regard to a specific strategy:

- "What needs to be done (to implement the strategy)?"

- "How will that be done?"

Often, several repetitions of these two questions generate a number of objectives in regard to a specific strategy.

Some staff might find it easier to identify objectives by working backwards from an image of achievement of the goal or addressing the strategic issue. Other staff might find it easier to work forward from the present.

Note that, similar to specification of strategic goals, if objectives are described in a specific manner, than they are often easier to change in the future, as needed.

Assigning Responsibility for Objectives

It is usually best to think in terms of roles, or positions, in the organization at this point, rather than names of specific people. Sometimes those people leave the organization. Sometimes the action plan refers to a position that is not yet created in the organization. Sometimes, the objective might be assigned to a group of staff members. In that case, the objective still should be assigned to the one position that has specific responsibility to ensure that the group achieves the objective.

A common mistake made by planners when developing their action plans is to forget about the current workload already assigned to positions in the organization. This mistake usually results in action plans that do not get implemented because people are already very busy doing their current jobs in the workplace and, therefore, cannot find the time to do any new tasks, or objectives.

The manner in which a supervisor assigns an objective to a person is extremely important to the success of the objective. Skills in delegation are critical.

See "Delegation" on page 119 for more information.

Identifying Timelines in Action Plans

Usually, timing in a plan describes:

- When an activity to accomplish an objective is to start and/or stop.

- The deadline by which the objective is to be accomplished.

Timing is often the feature of action planning that planners seem to resent the most. The association of a particular time period puts pressure on the person who is responsible to accomplish the objective (otherwise, the person could wait forever!). Ironically, one of the advantages of associating timing with an objective is that it helps planners to ensure that accomplishment of the objective is realistic in the first place.

Associating timing with accomplishment of objectives is a very important management skill. Often, one of the biggest challenges for new supervisors is attempting to get any sense of accuracy about the time required for subordinates to accomplish tasks. Action planning can be a wonderful experience for management development.

1.   When identifying timing information, consider the scope of the objectives, the activities that must be conducted in order to accomplish the objectives, and the likely sequence of the activities. Those considerations often give planners a good sense of how long it might take to achieve a certain objective and even when the activity should start and stop.

2.   The extent of specification of the timing information depends on the scope of the objective to be accomplished. For example, if it might take someone six months to accomplish a particular task, then timing information might be described in terms of months. Smaller objectives might be associated with terms of weeks. Usually, the larger the organization and extent of strategies, the more likely that action plans should specify start and stop dates for accomplishments of objectives.

3.   Some planners simplify the action plan by including only a deadline by which the objective is to be achieved. While this certainly makes action planning easier, it also runs the risk of not being useful for planners and leaders when attempting to closely analyze the relevance and reality of the action plans.

4.   When identifying the timing information, planners often work backwards from a particular deadline, or they can work forwards from reasonable start date. Their approach often depends on the approach that they used earlier in their planning when identifying strategic issues and/or goals (they preferred to work forwards or backwards from a point in time).

5.   When identifying timing information, attempt to include the person who will be responsible for accomplishing the objective (this is in accordance with good planning practices as suggested throughout this guidebook).

6.   When identifying timing information, consider the responsible person's capabilities and consider current workload, especially if a particular person is being considered to accomplish an objective.

Identifying Resources in Action Plans

Resources are usually specified in terms of people, time, materials, equipment, facilities and money. Sometimes, planners simplify their action plans by including estimates of:

1.   Extent of personnel (number of people) needed to accomplish the objective and/or

2.   Amount of money that might be needed to support the resources required to achieve the objective. Usually, though, planners make mention of the money needed primarily to obtain and support any materials, equipment or facilities. They might leave out mention of budgeting information in regard to compensation for the people working to accomplish the objective, unless the scope of the objective is quite large and/or an independent contractor (consultant) is being included in the activity.

Careful planning and specification of resources can provide strong verification and justification, for example, when raising funds to implement parts of the entire strategic plan.

Identifying Who Will Monitor Action Plan and How

This includes specifying the position that will regularly monitor the status of the implementation of the action plan, along with the date of the last monitoring activity. Usually the responsibility for monitoring goes to the supervisor of the person responsible to accomplish the objective. Note that the Board of Directors is responsible to supervise the Chief Executive Officer (CEO) and, thus, would be responsible to monitor accomplishment of any objectives assigned to the CEO.

 Phase 6 includes extensive guidelines and tools regarding monitoring of the implementation of plans.

Performance Targets in Action Plans

The performance target is the specific result that is to be accomplished by implementing the action plan. Usually the target is the implementation of a strategy, but sometimes, it is difficult to ascertain the extent of implementation of a strategy without associating something more specific – that is the purpose of a performance target.

When setting targets, be careful to specify the units of measurement and the amount or percentage of that unit to be accomplished. For example, do not specify a target of "people," specify a target of "300 people."

Sometimes the description of an objective is not very specific. In that case, the specification of the target should be.

Finalize Action Plans – Integration and Reality Check

"Roll Up" Various Plans?

If planners have been using the guidelines to develop a variety of strategic plans for various subunits in their organization (for example, one for each program or region) and they prefer to "roll up" the plans into an organization-wide strategic plan, then now will be the time to start doing it. The "rolling up" starts, primarily by integrating the various action plans associated with each strategic plan. Guidelines in this section will help planners with that integration.

Ensure Action Plans Complete and Well Integrated

Once all of the various action plans have been drafted, then planners should carefully examine them to ensure that they are complete for each strategy and organized efficiently for the entire organization. At this point, action plans might exist for the entire organization or for programs (with or without the intention of "rolling up" the various programs plans into an overall organization plan).

For each action plan, one at a time, consider:

1.   Are there any obvious objectives missing from the plan? If someone suggests one, then put it in the plan. Consider using a brainstorming technique to generate more ideas for objectives. Guidelines for the brainstorming technique are included in PART III.

Next, consider all of the action plans for the overall strategic plan.

2.   Is there any duplication of objectives across different action plans?

3.   Can any of the objectives be combined for any one particular action plan?

4.   Do any of the objectives conflict with each other (that accomplishment of one objective would make it almost impossible to accomplish another objective on the overall list)?

5.   Should any of the objectives be divided into one or more other objectives?

6.   Are some or all of the objectives interconnected somehow?

7.   If one or more of the objectives is accomplished, might it contribute to more than one action plan?

8.   Might it be useful to combine any objectives that are in a similar category, for example, the organization plan or program plan?

Conduct Reality Check of All Action Plans

Once the action plans have been well integrated, then planners should carefully examine them to ensure that they are realistic. At this point, action plans might exist for the organization as a whole, or for each program (with or without the intention of "rolling up" the various programs plans into an overall organization plan). Consider the following for all of the action plans together:

1.   Are there enough people in the organization to attend to all of the objectives when specified across all of the action plans? For example, the action plans might specify that eight people are needed to work toward accomplishing objectives in March through June, but the nonprofit only has five people in the organization at that time.

2.   Is there enough money to support the budgets specified across all of the action plans? For example, if the action plans specify budgets that total $25,000, to support activities to work toward objectives from March through June, can the nonprofit provide that much money for that period?

3.   Are there enough materials, equipment and facilities to support the implementation of the various action plans? For example, across all of the action plans, if there needs to be two conference rooms available at the same time in March, can the nonprofit provide those facilities then?

4.   Are there any other "red flags" that become apparent from review of all of the action plans together?

Adjust Action Plans

First versions of action plans are usually modified later on somehow. It is rare that a nonprofit has all of the resources available to implement the action plans as first developed. Usually, the money needed to support the actions suggested in all of action plans is far more than the nonprofit can provide and/or much earlier than the nonprofit can provide it – even with rigorous fundraising. Usually the nonprofit has to arrange "fall back" or contingency plans that might include:

- Cutting back expectations and plans

- Providing more resources

- Moving deadlines farther out

It is much easier to adjust plans if the goals and objectives have been specifically described, for example, it is easier to adjust (probably reduce) an objective of "Draft fundraising plan to raise $50,000 by March 1" than to adjust an objective of "Do a fundraising plan."

Develop Performance Plans

Performance plans specify the planned "production" goals from the organization, its programs and/or major functions during the time span of the strategic plan. Usually, performance numbers are specified for each year in the time span. Be sure to include some outcomes goals that various programs will attempt to help clients to achieve. The following table depicts examples of performance numbers and the typical format of a performance plan. Note that the first goal is an outcomes goal and the rest are activities goals.

Examples of Programs' Performance Plans	2008	2009	2010
Literacy training (number of learners who pass a test each month)	500	600	700
Food shelf (clients served/ month)	300	400	500
Association members (total membership count per year)	400	500	600
Arts program (exhibits per month)	50	60	70
Organization (revenue from fees, in $1,000s)	100	125	130

Develop Staffing Plan

A staffing plan describes the types and amounts of expertise needed in the organization, including for current and new activities. Types of expertise are usually specified as kinds of positions, or jobs, in the organizations. The amount is sometime described in terms of "full-time equivalent" (FTE). For example, a full-time person would be represented by 1.0 FTE and a half-time person would be represented by 0.5 FTE.

A staffing plan can also include detailed financial information about compensation and benefits to staffing, along with any associated costs to obtain and support the staff, for example, training, equipment and supplies.

The following table depicts a simple staffing plan.

Staffing Plan (FTE)	2008	2009	2010
Chief Executive Officer	1.0	1.0	1.0
Housing Program Director	1.0	1.0	1.0
Transportation Program Director	1.0	1.0	1.0
Housing Program Staff	2.0	3.0	4.0
Transportation Program Staff	2.0	3.0	4.0
Secretary	1.0	1.0	1.0
Office Assistant	0.5	1.0	1.0
Total	**8.5**	**11.0**	**13.0**

Develop Other Associated Plans?

Often, it is useful to organize a variety of plans from the various types of information generated during the strategic planning activities. The choice is up to the planners.

 It is not within the scope of this guidebook to provide comprehensive guidelines to develop each of the following types of plans. That information is included in the *Field Guide to Nonprofit Program Design, Marketing and Evaluation,* by this author.

Program Plans

Program plans can be done in a wide variety of ways. Usually, they include description of activities required to develop and/or operate a specific program. The program plan can include sections about:

1. Program framework, including a logic model that depicts the inputs, processes, outputs and outcomes from the program

2. Marketing analysis, including description of

    a) "Inbound" marketing activities, including to identify and verify the certain groups of clients, their needs, methods to meet those needs, how those methods should be packaged, how those methods should be priced, etc.

b) "Outbound marketing activities, including advertising, promotions, sales and customer services

3. Community needs to be met by the program

4. Methods to meet the need (methods the program uses to deliver services)

5. Activities to develop the program "from the ground up"

6. Activities required during ongoing program operations

7. Goals of the program, usually for each of the next several years

8. Staffing plan for the program

9. Financial plans, including expected revenue and expenses of the program

Fundraising Plans and Proposals

An overall fundraising plan usually specifies:

1. The total of funds that will be required from donors

2. Potential sources of the funds

3. What sources will be approached

4. How they will be approached

5. Who will approach them and

6. When

In a fundraising proposal, there is usually clear description of a particular program, including description of:

1. The program

2. The community need to be met by the program

3. Method the program uses to meet the need

4. Why that program needs the money

5. How the money will be spent

6. Amount of money that is needed

7. How the program will verify (or evaluate) that the money is actually making a difference

Program Evaluation Plans

A program evaluation plan is usually in regard to a specific program and describes:

1. What management wants to be able to decide about a certain program

2. What information will be collected about the program in order to make that decision

3. How the information will be collected (what methods will be used)

4. Who will collect it

5. When it will be collected

6. How the information will be analyzed

There are numerous types of program evaluations. Probably the most significant are:

1. Outcomes evaluation, which clarify and determine the extent of achievement of certain, desired changes (or outcomes) by clients who participate in a program

2. Goals evaluation, which determines the extent to which a program has achieved certain, pre-established goals for the program

3. Process evaluation, which is geared to make the process more effective and efficient

4. Implementation evaluation, which is geared to identify the exact processes being used by a program and assess if those processes are the same as those intended when the program originally was designed

Advertising and Promotions Plans

These plans usually describe approaches to enhance the image of, or increase the demand for, a certain program in specific group of clients. The plans usually describe:

1. A specific group of clients (target market)

2. Key features and benefits of program to that market

3. A "unique value proposition," or description of why the group should use that program and not a program from a competitor

4. Key message(s) to convey to the group about the program

5. Methods/tools to convey the message(s)

6. Who will use the methods and when

Develop Operating Budget

Financial plans within strategic plans are usually in regard to the operating budget, or the expected revenue and expenses to operate the organization (or program) during the time span of the strategic plan. The Board of Directors must approve the operating budgets of the nonprofit organization. That approval can occur when approving the strategic plan, if the plan includes the operating budget.

How To Develop Basic Operating Budget

If yours is a new nonprofit, then you will not have much information that is verified from experience. As a result, you will need to make some estimates to the best of your ability – this is entirely reasonable.

When developing your budget, reference the sample operating budget format on the following page.

Step One – Select Time Period for Budget

It is common to develop operating budgets that depict activities over the nonprofit's fiscal period. The fiscal period is selected by the nonprofit to represent the official 12-month interval in which the nonprofit operations, including financial information, are reported and measured.

Step Two – Identify Expenses

It is typical for a nonprofit to start budgeting by identifying expenses. It is not at all uncommon among nonprofits that expenses exceed earned revenue (this is a called a deficit) and that the deficit is made up by revenue from fundraising when balancing a budget. However, some organizations might have established a policy not to have their expenses exceed their service revenue (revenue earned from services to clients, rather than from fundraising). This policy is certainly standard in the for-profit world when balancing a budget. If your nonprofit adopts this budget-balancing policy, then start your budgeting first by identifying your revenue (in Step Three), and afterwards, identifying your expenses. When identifying expenses,

1.   Estimate personnel costs, including:

   a) Costs for salaried personnel, for example, managerial or supervisory positions, including salaries and fringe benefits (plan 40% of salaries as fringe)

   b) Costs for hourly personnel, for example, secretarial support (plan 30% for fringe)

   c) Costs for any temporary employees

   d) Costs for contracted help (independent consultants), for example, accountants, lawyers and fundraisers.

   e) Costs associated with making those personnel productive, for example, training, membership dues, and travel

   f) Other(s)?

   Include these costs under "Personnel" in your budget.

2.   Estimate costs regarding facilities. Consider:

    a) Furniture (desks, chairs, file drawers, tables, wastebaskets, etc.)

    b) Other(s)?

Include these costs under "Facilities" in your budget.

3.   Estimate other costs. Consider:

    a) Tools

    b) Inventory (materials stored and/or sold to clients)

    c) Marketing materials

    d) Documentation (texts, manuals, etc.).

    e) Office equipment (computers, copier, fax, telephones, etc.).

    f) Other(s)?

Include these costs under "Other Expenses" in your budget.

Step Three – Identify Revenue

Be conservative in your estimates; otherwise, undue optimism will very likely put your nonprofit in a tight bind for money, once it starts its operations. Obviously, you will not likely have all the grants that you would like to receive either. Still, consider the grants that you are going to pursue and depict those on your budget.

To include revenue on your budget, estimate:

1.   Fees from services to clients or dues from membership

2.   Grants from foundations

3.   Grants from corporations

4.   Grants from government

5.   Individual contributions

6.   Government contracts

7.   In-kind donations (donated services and materials)

8.   Investment income

Now you need to make a minor adjustment regarding any in-kind donations. In-kind donations must be recorded as both revenue and expense. For example, if you receive $25,000 of in-kind donations from a corporation in the form of $15,000 of furniture and $10,000 of computers, then you must include $25,000 as revenue and $15,000 and $10,000 as two separate expenses, one for furniture and one for computers. Include budget commentary that explains the in-kind donations.

Step Four – Balance Your Budget

Balancing your budget means making sure that the total of your expected expenses at least equals the total of your expected revenues. Otherwise, your nonprofit will suddenly stop operating when your revenue is all spent. While you might expect more expenses than revenues, you certainly must make plans for how you will address the difference between the expenses and revenues, for example, by fundraising.

To balance your budget:

1.   Add up your total revenues.

2.   Add up your total expenses.

3.   Subtract your total expenses from the total revenues.

If the result is a positive number (more than 0) then you are expecting a surplus.

If the result is less than 0, then you are expecting a deficit, and if you expect a deficit, then you must decide how you will address the deficit. Nonprofits can address expected deficits either by:

- Reducing expenses and/or

- Increasing revenues

Update your strategic plans based on the results of having balanced your budget. For example, to get more revenue, you may need to increase your marketing activities. These activities, in turn, might cause increased marketing expenses.

Step Five – Obtain Review and Approval of Budget

As with other major plans in your organization, your Board of Directors should review the budget, including the major expenses and forms of revenue. Any changes that Board members might recommend should be carefully considered and made, if appropriate. Then Board members should officially approve the budget. Often, Board members approve the budget by approving the strategic plan, when the plan includes the budget. Include mention of the approval in the official Board meeting minutes. (Minutes are the official written description of the major actions conducted during the Board meeting)

The table on the following page depicts an example of a basic operating budget. In the example, the budget is for fiscal year 2008 (in this case, January 1, 2008 to December 31, 2008). A strategic plan might include amounts (and separate columns of numbers) for each of the years during the time span of your strategic plan.

Sample Operating Budget Format

Revenue:	
Earned Income:	$
Fees from services to clients	$
Dues from membership	$
Government contracts	$
Investment income	$
Total Earned Income:	$
Contributions:	$
Grants from foundations	$
Grants from corporations	$
Grants from government	$
Individual contributions	$
In-kind donations	$
Total Contributions:	$
Total Revenue:	$
Expenses:	$
Personnel:	$
Chief Executive Officer	$
Program Director	$
Secretary	$
Training	$
Membership dues to professional associations	$
Total Personnel:	$
Facilities:	$
Rent	$
Utilities	$
Cleaning and janitorial	$
Insurance	$
Maintenance	$
Total Facilities:	$
Other Expenses:	$
Office supplies	$
Manuals	$
Marketing materials	$
Tools	$
Total Other Expenses:	$
Total Expenses:	$

Phase 5: Develop Strategic Plan Document

Now planners are ready to start "packaging" their accomplishments to communicate to others both inside and outside the organization. This effort should be quite straightforward if planners have been completing the various worksheets in this guidebook.

Draft Strategic Plan Document

Most planners decide to document the results of their strategic planning in a strategic plan document. Without clear documentation, results of the planning can get lost into the day-to-day details of running the nonprofit. Documentation also serves a useful purpose during marketing, when trying to get the word out about the nonprofit and its programs. Funders usually want to see a strategic plan, as do potential new members of the Board and management. At this point in planning, it is usually not much effort at all to assemble a plan, get it reviewed by key internal and external stakeholders, and then approved by members of the Board.

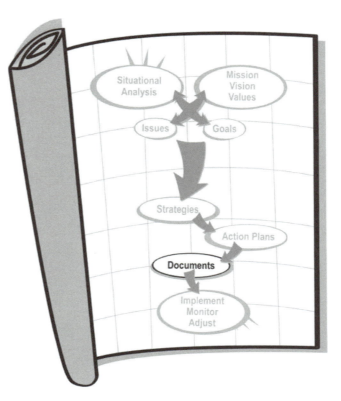

What Should Be in Strategic Plan Document?

The most important consideration when designing the format of the strategic plan is "What audiences will get the plan?" Various audiences might get different versions of the plan, depending on the use that the audience will have for the plan. The most popular uses of the strategic plan are to 1) provide direction to members of the Board and staff, and 2) educate key, external stakeholders, especially potential donors. The plan might be a different format for each of these two uses. A very effective strategic plan document might be as little as 5-7 pages, in addition to various attachments. Consider the following major sections:

1. **Title page**
   Include the name of the nonprofit, indication that it is a strategic plan, the scope of the plan (organization and/or programs), time span of the plan and indication if it is official (has been approved by the Board – if it is not official, then include the word "draft"). Include the date that the plan was drafted or approved.

2. **Cover letter**
   The Chief Executive (and Board Chair, if possible) should include a cover letter, noting his or her complete support of the plan and intentions to ensure the plan is implemented and evaluated on a regular basis.

3. **Executive summary**

   This is one of the most important parts of the plan. (More is explained about the Executive Summary in the topic immediately below.)

4. **Authorization page**

   Some organizations prefer to include an authorization page that designates whether the plan document is the official version of the plan. This page might include lines on which each of the members of the Board signs his or her name, indicating his or her approval of the plan. There might be a paragraph at the top of the page describing authorization, such as, "This plan is subject to approval by the Board of Directors as recommended by the Board Program Committee. Approval is indicated by the Board member signatures below."

5. **Description of nonprofit**

   Include the beginnings and history, major programs and services. Include any recent highlights, for example, moving to a new facility.

6. **Description of how the plan was developed**

   This description can be particularly useful for others to understand how the plan was produced. Future planners for the organization will appreciate this description as well. This description might be included as an appendix.

7. **Key strategic issues and/or goals and strategies**

   Along with the Executive Summary, this information is one of the most important parts of the plan. Planners might choose not to include any proprietary information in versions of the plan that will go to any external stakeholders.

8. **Action plans**

   Some planners might prefer to include those in a separate document and refer to them from the Strategic Plan document.

9. **Staffing plans**

   Some planners might prefer to include those in a separate document and refer to them from the Strategic Plan document.

10. **Any performance plans**

    Include plans, especially in regard to the organization and specific program plans.

11. **Financial plans**

    These plans usually include at least an operating plan for each of the years addressed in the time span of the strategic plan. These might be included as an appendix.

12. **Reference to related plans or documents**

    There might be reference to other related plans and documents, for example, program plans, marketing analysis and program evaluation plans.

13. **Appendices**

    The appendices are often reserved for information used to derive the body of the plan, for example, SWOT analysis data and names of planners.

Occasionally, planners want certain parts of the plan to be confidential, or proprietary to certain people. In that case, they should either separate out those parts or mark the pages as "confidential" or "proprietary". These parts might be about, for example, analysis of competitors and competitive strategies of the nonprofit.

Executive Summary

The Executive Summary is sometimes misunderstood to be similar to the Table of Contents, which is in error. The Executive Summary should not be merely a summary listing of the contents of the plan, but rather a summary of what the plan will accomplish and how. The Summary should include information such that Board members, executive management (and sometimes external stakeholders, such as funders) can quickly scan the Summary to grasp:

- The purpose of the plan, including how the plan will be used and any overall results expected from implementing the plan

- When implementation of the plan will be started and completed

- The most recent mission of the organization

- Most important strategic goals and strategies that were identified during the planning

- Any key highlights or issues discovered during planning and recommendations to address the issues

- How implementation of the plan will be monitored

The Executive Summary should usually be no more than 1-2 pages in length.

Who Should Write Strategic Plan?

The writer of the plan might have been identified when designing the plan for a plan. That person might have already been collecting information to include in the plan. Regardless of the ultimate format of the plan:

1. Have a small number of people write the first draft of the plan, ideally one or two people.

2. Do not worry about having every last detail in the first draft.

3. Include the word "draft" on each of the pages of the drafted plan until the Board approves the plan later on.

4. Include the latest revision date on each page of the drafted strategic plan.

5. Write the plan in a format that is easily understood and referenced by outside parties.

6. Rarely, should an external facilitator write the plan. The activity of writing brings writers in very close contact with all of the detail generated from the strategic plan and, thus, makes them very aware of the contents of the plan. The plan is the nonprofit's – not the facilitator's – to manage and implement. Therefore, members of the nonprofit should write it.

7. Review and authorize the strategic plan.

Coordinate Reviews and Approval of Document

Arrange Internal Review

Schedule an allotted time for internal review, for example, two weeks. Do not extend this time unless there is very good reason. Design some guidelines for review, including key questions or aspects of the plan that reviewers should address. During the review period, ask for reviewers' comments about the following aspects of the document:

- **Coherency of the organization of contents**
  Are the major contents arranged in an understandable manner?

- **Completeness**
  Is the plan complete? Are all necessary aspects of the planning process and results included in the plan?

- **Clarity**
  Do the format and wording make sense?

- **Direction**
  Is it clear what the plan requires to be done and in what order?

- **Practicality**
  Can the plan be implemented in a reasonable fashion?

- **Accountability**
  Is it clear who is to implement the plan? Is it clear how the implementation of the plan will be tracked? Is it clear who is ultimately responsible for the implementation of the plan?

Arrange Review Among External Stakeholders

Have the updated plan reviewed by at least some stakeholders outside of the planning group for understanding, completeness and accuracy. Again, be sure the plan is marked as "draft".

Limit the time allowed for review, for example, two weeks. Do not extend this time unless there is very good reason.

Design some guidelines or review, including key questions that external reviewers should address. For example, ask for reviewers' comments about:

- Any input to the goals and strategies?

- Any ideas about the future of the nonprofit organization?

- Any involvement that they might like to have?

- Who should receive the plan?

Coordinate Approval of Plan

Have the plan, along with any recent updates, authorized by the Board members. After their approval, indicated by a vote among members of the Board and inclusion of their decision in the Board meeting minutes, then attend to the following:

1.   Complete the authorization page.

2.   Develop the title page.

3.   Write the cover letter.

4.   Finalize the Executive Summary.

5.   Take off the word "draft" from the document.

6.   Finalize the date on each page of the plan.

Distribute and Communicate Strategic Plan

Consider distributing the strategic plan to everyone in the organization. It is amazing how even the newest staff member gains quick context, appreciation and meaning from review of the strategic plan.

1.   Widely distribute the mission, vision and/or values statements, including posting them on the walls in the facilities, placing them on stationery, placing them on Web sites, etc. Ensure they are posted in conference rooms where they can be visible during meetings among members of the Board and staff.

2.   Widely distribute the goals and strategies among members of the Board and management among staff.

3.   Slogans should be placed at the top of stationery and in as many marketing tools as possible, for example, brochures and e-mail signatures.

4.   Consider providing the plan (at least the statements and goals) to key stakeholders, for example, past and current funders, and community leaders, especially if they took part in your strategic planning.

Celebrate Completion of Plan

Research shows that cynicism is on the rise in organizations. One of the likely reasons is that organizations tend to herald in new initiatives (such as strategic planning), focus a great deal of effort on developing them, and then to start new initiatives without having ever mentioned whether the previous ones were ever successful or not. Members of these organizations begin to feel as is they are on a treadmill, running harder and harder, but never really getting anywhere.

One of the best ways to address this cynicism is to acknowledge when something has been accomplished. Let people feel good about it. Put the accomplishment in perspective in order to help people stay real about what has been done and what has not been done.

At this point, planners have achieved some major accomplishments in the strategic planning process. It is very likely that they have:

- Customized their own approach to strategic planning for their nonprofit.

- Gained strong understanding of the external and internal environments of their nonprofits.

- Identified the most important strategic issues facing their organization.

- Established meaningful strategic goals for the nonprofit to achieve.

- Identified targeted strategies to achieve goals and/or address strategic issues, and that provide focus and align activities in the nonprofit.

- Specified specific objectives and timelines to ensure that the strategies are implemented in a highly effective fashion.

Recognize these accomplishments with the group of planners!

Develop some suitable means to thank the planners. Include their organizations if external stakeholders took part in the planning. Remind them that strategic planning is an ongoing cycle of activities – it is a cycle of good leadership and management. Thank them for playing their part!

Phase 6: Monitor Implementation and Adjust Plans

Sometimes, the topics of implementation and monitoring of plans can seem overwhelming to planners. It can seem like there is a great deal of work to do and with a large amount of detail. However, at this point in their process, planners should remember that they have already come very far in the process, having sorted through a large amount deal of detail about their organization and the environment around it. Planners have already accomplished a lot, mostly by conducting the strategic planning process one step at a time. The same approach is needed when implementing the plan, monitoring the implementation of the plan and making any necessary adjustments to the plans.

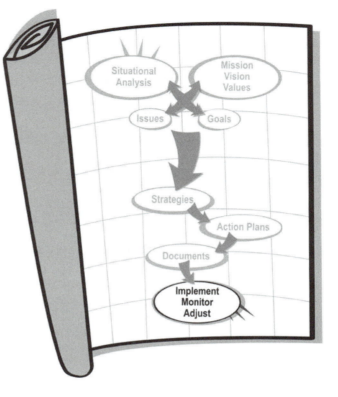

Monitor Implementation of Plans

The primary questions to consider regarding the monitoring of implementation of plans are:

1. What approaches can we use to ensure implementation of strategic plan?

2. What practical tools can we use to track status of the implementation?

3. Who will monitor the status?

These are important questions for the implementation of any key plan in an organization, including strategic plans, program plans, fundraising plans, marketing plans, etc.

Leadership, Supervision and Delegation

Leadership and Supervision

Leadership is setting direction and influencing others to follow that direction. Supervision is guiding the development and productivity of people in the organization. There simply is no substitute for the roles that leadership and supervision play in ensuring and monitoring the implementation of plans. Thus, leaders and supervisors in the nonprofit organization should carefully consider – and enact – the guidelines in this section about implementation and monitoring of plans. In particular, leaders and supervisors should monitor the application of certain tools that provide status about the implementation of plans. The tools are described later on in this section.

It is extremely important that leaders and supervisors in the organization have strong understanding of basic principles of successful change in organizations.

See "Tool #5: Guidelines for Successful Organizational Change" on page 269 in Appendix H for principles.

Note that supervisors exist throughout a nonprofit organization, depending on the particular structure of the Board and staff. For example, the Board of Directors supervises the Chief Executive Officer (CEO). The CEO supervises program directors or executive assistants. Program directors supervise other program staff, etc.

Delegation

The hallmark of good supervision is effective delegation. Delegation is when supervisors give responsibility and authority to subordinates to complete a task by a certain date, and let the subordinates figure out how the task can be accomplished.

Effective delegation develops people who are ultimately more fulfilled and productive. Managers become more fulfilled and productive themselves as they learn to count on their staffs and are freed up to attend to more strategic issues.

Delegation is often very difficult for new supervisors, particularly if they have had to scramble to start the organization or start a major new product or service by themselves. Many managers want to remain comfortable, making the same decisions they have always made. They believe they can do a better job themselves. They do not want to risk losing any of their power and stature (ironically, they do lose these if they do not learn to delegate effectively). Often, they do not want to risk giving authority to subordinates in case they fail and impair the organization.

However, there are basic approaches to delegation that, with practice, become the backbone of effective supervision and development. Thomas R. Horton, in *Delegation and Team Building: No Solo Acts Please* (Management Review, September 1992, pp. 58-61) suggests the following general steps to accomplish delegation:

1. **Delegate the whole action plan to one person.**
   This gives the person a sense of responsibility and increases his or her motivation to oversee the plan. In the case of action plans, even if the plan is to be implemented by a group, there still should be one person who ultimately is responsible for the action plan.

2. **Select the right people to conduct the activities to accomplish the objectives.**
   Assess the skills and capabilities of members of the staff and then assign the plans, and activities to accomplish its objectives, to the most appropriate people.

3. **Clearly specify your preferred results (performance targets).**
   Delegation might best be explained as conveying information on what, why, when, who and where regarding a task or assignment; but then leave the "how" up to the person to whom the responsibility is being delegated.

4. **Delegate responsibility and authority – assign the responsibility, not the method to accomplish it.**
   Let the person attend to the responsibility in the manner in which they choose, as long as the preferred results are accomplished. Let the person have strong input as to the completion date of the objective. Note that you may not even know how to accomplish the objective yourself – this is often the case with higher levels of management. Make sure that others in the organization understand that the person has both the responsibility and the authority to accomplish the objective.

5. **Ask the person to summarize back to you his or her impressions of the objective and the results you prefer.**

6. **Get ongoing non-intrusive feedback about progress on the action plan.**
   This is a good reason to continue to get weekly, written status reports from the person. Reports should cover what they did last week, plan to do next week and any potential issues. Regular meetings with the person should provide this ongoing feedback, as well.

7. **Maintain open lines of communication with the person.**
   Do not hover over him or her, but do try to get a sense for what he or she is doing and do support his or her regularly checking in with you.

8. **If you are not satisfied with the progress, do not take the project back.**
   Continue to work with the person to ensure that they perceive the action plan, or objective, as being his or her responsibility. Look for the cause of your dissatisfaction. For example, is it lack of communication, training, resources or commitment of the employee? Share your concern with them and convey what you were seeing or hearing that led to your concern.

9. **Evaluate and reward performance.**
   Evaluate results more than methods. Address insufficient performance and reward successes.

For additional information, see *Field Guide to Leadership and Supervision for Nonprofit Staff,* by this author.

Specific Approaches To Ensure Implementation of Plans

One of the most important approaches that can be used to ensure the implementation of the strategic plan is to develop a plan that is realistic, relevant and flexible – the three priorities of the guidelines in this guidebook. Members of the nonprofit can consider several other approaches, as well.

Authorization of Strategic Plan Document

The authorization of the document by the members of the Board indicates that they officially are in support of the implementation of the plan and will work to ensure that the plan is implemented. In fact, they are responsible to be sure that it is implemented. That is one of the most important responsibilities of a member of a Board.

Allocation of Resources

One of the most visible gestures to the ensure implementation of the strategic plan is to allocate the resources necessary to implement the plan. Often, that official allocation comes in the form of the Board's approval of an operating budget.

Board Work Plans

Work plans are specifications of the goals to be accomplished by the Board, in total or by various committees on the Board. Work plans should be updated soon after completion of the strategic plan. The following table represents one format and content of a work plan. Note that the following work plan is really an action plan for the Board or for a specific Board committee or task force.

Year 2008 Actions	Jan	Feb	Mar	Apr	May	Jun
Strategy 3.1: Develop Strategic Plan						
3.1.1. Recruit consultant help	---					
3.1.2 Plan for a plan		---				
3.1.3 Strategic planning			---	---		
3.1.4 Board review of plan				---		
3.1.5 Obtain Board approval of plan					---	

Policies and Procedures

Policies and procedures should be developed, or updated, to guide activities toward implementing the strategies and action plans produced from strategic planning. For example, goals or issues might indicate that the Board needs to be developed, staff needs to be hired and financial management needs to be improved.

Policies are broad guidelines that can be referenced by members of the Board or staff in order to make decisions. The most prominent examples are Board policies, personnel policies and fiscal policies. Board policies are in regard to how Board members want to interact with each other when governing the nonprofit organization. Personnel policies are in regard to how staff are recruited, hired, supervised, guided, rewarded and fired. The policies also help to ensure that management practices conform to important employment laws and regulations. Fiscal policies are in regard to how the organization should manage its financial information and processes.

Procedures are step-by-step directions regarding how to accomplish a certain activity. For example, there are often procedures regarding specifically how to use a computer system, ensure that facilities are locked and safe and use kitchen facilities.

Job Descriptions

A job description is a written description of the responsibilities of a certain position, or job, in the organization. Management should draft a job description for each job in the organization. The description should specify the general responsibilities of the position along with some of the specific duties to be conducted by the person in that role, the title for the position, and any special skills, training or credentials required. The responsibilities should be updated on a regular basis, particularly to reflect any responsibilities that are necessary to implement strategies from the strategic plan.

Performance Goals

Probably the best example of performance goals is the list of goals that a Board of Directors might establish for the Chief Executive Officer in an organization. In addition to a job description, certain roles in the organization, especially management roles, often have an associated list of specific accomplishments that they are to accomplish by a certain time in the organization.

Specific Tools To Track Status and Who Should Use Them

Verbal Commentary

This is probably the most frequent form of getting information about the status of an activity in the workplace. Although it is the most frequent, it is usually the least reliable because information is usually incomplete or about a small aspect of an overall activity needed to implement a strategy from the strategic plan. Verbal commentary should be used primarily to clarify information from other, written tools of communicating status. However, supervisors should remain highly accessible to their direct reports to continue to exchange commentary as much as possible.

"To-do" Lists

To-do lists are probably the most frequent means by which people manage what they need to do in the workplace. The list usually includes brief mention, or listing, of the tasks to attend to, and the status toward completion of the tasks. Supervisors sometimes request to-do lists from each of their subordinates.

Status Reports

Status reports are (usually) written descriptions of an individual's work activities. The reports are usually provided on a regular basis, perhaps weekly or biweekly. They should be dated and describe:

1.   What activities were done over the past time period

2.   Any current actions or issues that must be addressed by management

3.   Plans for activities on the next time period

Some supervisors might prefer written status reports, rather than to-do lists. Status reports are usually more complete. The time to prepare these is about 15 minutes if done weekly.

Staff Meetings

Staff meetings are regular meetings among members of the staff in order to exchange information about activities in the organization, often including status of what each member is doing and will be doing. Staff meetings should be held with supervisors and their direct reports at least once a month. Ideally, they are held with all members of the organization at least once a month or quarterly if in larger organizations.

Action Plans

The action plans are a handy means by which status can be reported, especially regarding progress toward accomplishing specific objectives from the strategic plan.

 See "Phase 4: Develop Action and Financial Plans" on page 96 for a description of Action Plans.

Action plans should be updated and provided to senior managers or members of the Board of Directors, usually once a month.

Chief Executive Officer Report

These written reports usually come from the Chief Executive to members of the Board, and are provided at each Board meeting. Usually, the reports briefly describe the highlights from activities since the last Board meeting and highlights of any future activities that are expected before the next Board meeting.

"Planned Versus Actual" Budget Reports

These reports can be extremely useful, particularly to members of the Board and management team. The reports can give a very quick impression regarding the status of financial activities. The reports usually include specification of:

1.   Some categories of expenses (or expense account), for example, employee training

2.   The amount of money planned for each month in that account category

3.   The amount of money actually spent for each month in the account category

The reports should be reviewed at least once a month by senior management and members of the Board of Directors.

Program Reviews

Reviews are regular examination of the activities to assess how well they are being conducted. Reviewers examine if activities are following the original plan. Usually, there are key indicators about the status of activities, such as:

1.   What major problems exist and what is needed to address them?

2.   How are the actual costs compared to the planned costs?

3.   Are any actions needed to avoid financial problems?

4.   What would you do differently about the program if you could do anything?

5.   What limitations are holding you back from what you would ideally do if you could?

6.	What are you learning from the program implementation so far?

7.	How are you acknowledging and celebrating the accomplishments?

Program reviews usually occur on an irregular basis. Usually, they are scheduled for a particular type of major activity, for example, program development and construction of a facility. Reviewers look for major milestones or deliverables that are specified on a project plan.

Adjust Plans As Needed

Strategic plans are rarely implemented as expected. It is acceptable to change the strategic plan. However, there are valid reasons and invalid reasons for changing the plan. Valid reasons are usually in regard to changes in the organization's external environment and/or changes in the availability of resources necessary to implement the plan. Valid changes are usually in regard to the extent of achievement of goals and objectives, and not to changes in the overall strategies themselves.

Invalid reasons are usually in regard to ineffective leadership, for example, members of the staff were left to do whatever they wanted and, later on, leadership realized that the plan was not getting implemented – so they simply changed the plan.

The plan is only a guideline – not a strict roadmap, which must be followed exactly as specified when first written. The most important aspects of deviating from the plan are:

1.	Recognizing the need for a deviation from the plan.

2.	Understanding the reason for the deviation.

3.	Deciding what the change should be.

4.	Communicating the need for the change to the plan and what the change should be (before making the change to the plan).

5.	Obtaining approval to make the change.

6.	Making the change.

7.	Updating the version of the plan, for example, changing the date on each of the pages and including commentary that explained the change.

8.	Updating tools to track the status of the plan.

PART III:

FOUNDATIONS FOR

EFFECTIVE

FACILITATION

Getting Started As Facilitator

NOTE: This major section refers to the "client" as the person or organization for whom the facilitator is working (for example, for the planners), rather than as the person or organization served by the nonprofit and its programs.

This part of the guide is intended for the person who will be facilitating the strategic planning process. The rest of the guidebook includes guidelines, tools and techniques that will be useful to facilitating strategic planning, as well. That information will be referenced by the facilitator when needed, as he or she facilitates the process with the planners from the nonprofit organization.

While information in this section is focused on the role of the facilitator, it can be useful to the planners as well. Planners might choose to help the facilitator by becoming familiar with the techniques provided here.

The facilitator might be someone internal to the organization, such as a member of the Board or staff, or someone who is external to the organization. Note that the CEO should typically *not* be the strategic planning facilitator (see the subsection, "Who Will Be Involved from Nonprofit? How? When?," in the section, "Phase 1: Design Plan for Plan," in PART II).

Crossroads: Read About Planning and Nonprofits First?

The Introduction of this guidebook includes a subtopic, "Reading Guidebook To Facilitate Strategic Planning?," that provides general advice for the facilitator regarding how to use this guidebook. The facilitator is advised to read PART I to learn about the strategic planning process, then PART III to learn about facilitation, and then PART II to guide planners through the process of developing their strategic plan. Also, if you are not familiar with the nature of nonprofits organization, then you are advised to read Appendix F on page 199. If you have not yet followed that advice, then you should do so now and then return here to PART III. Otherwise, proceed with the rest of the guidelines in PART III.

Understand What Strategic Planning Facilitator Does

The job of any facilitator is to work with a group of people to help them identify what they want to accomplish together and the process that they want to use. The focus for the facilitator is primarily on the process, not on the content. The process is in regard to *how* the group members work together, not on *what* they produce together. Usually, the facilitator helps the group primarily with how they solve problems and make decisions together. The facilitator is not singularly responsible for the process, the entire group is. The facilitator usually is not considered a member of the group.

A strategic planning facilitator helps the group of planners to customize their approach to strategic planning and then carry out that process to produce a highly relevant, realistic and flexible strategic plan. The facilitator might use any of a variety of techniques with members of the group and the group as a whole. These techniques might include careful design of an agenda, group discussion, various ground rules, methods of decision making, brainstorming, etc. (These techniques are explained later on in this part of the guidebook.)

A facilitator can carry out his or her role in various ways. For example, the facilitator might take a strong, directive approach to working with the group. Or, the facilitator might work rather indirectly to gently guide the group according to the wishes of the members of the group. The latter approach usually works best when facilitating strategic planning because it tends to cultivate members' strong participation and ownership in the process. This participation and ownership helps to ensure that the strategic plan is useful and actually gets implemented in their nonprofit.

Understand Yourself As Facilitator

Feedback from experienced facilitators and nonprofit planners indicates that many of the problems that occur between the facilitator and planners could have been avoided if they had taken the time to really understand each other even before starting their strategic planning process. Even though this understanding is very important in the process, it often is the most overlooked part of the process.

First, facilitators must understand their own style, including their overall goals in facilitation and basic assumptions about working with planners. They must recognize their own philosophy of planning, which ultimately determines their own priorities and personal biases during planning.

Suggested Overall Goals for Facilitators

Block (2000) suggests that the following goals be primary for those working to help groups of people, including facilitators helping an organization to conduct strategic planning. Facilitators should consider the following goals, decide their own and then mention them when first starting to work with the planners.

1. **Establish a collaborative relationship with planners**.
   This means working as an equal to the planners, rather than as a know-it-all "expert" who directs how everything must be done all the time. However, it also means not working as a mindless "pair of hands."

2. **Solve problems so that clients can solve the problems later on themselves**.
   That means always involving the planners in designing the process and making decisions about the process as well. That way, they will have a good understanding of the strategic planning process, thereby, making them more effective leaders and managers, as well.

3. **Ensure equal attention to the planning process and to the relationships**.
   The focus of the facilitator is on the process of the planning, at least as much, if not more, than the content of the plan.

Suggested Working Assumptions for Facilitators

Block (2000) also suggests the following working assumptions for those who are working with groups of people. Facilitators should clarify their own working assumptions and then mention them to the planners when the facilitator first starts working with the planners.

1. **Problem solving requires information that is as accurate as possible**.
   Strategic planning is about solving problems and/or achieving overall goals. The more accurate the information about them, the more accurate the methods in the plan to solve the problems or achieve the goals.

2. **Effective decision-making requires free and open choice among participants**. Strategic planning is also about decision-making. The more free and open the participants in the

planning process, the more effective their decision making during the process. Thus, the approach to facilitation must allow planners to freely consider, and to make, their own decisions during their strategic planning process.

3. **Effective implementation requires the internal commitment of participants.**
    A person's strong, internal commitment to implement a strategic plan comes from his or her belief that he or she had strong, influential participation in developing that plan.

Suggested Principles for Facilitators of Strategic Planning

Principles are basic beliefs. They represent one's "philosophy" of something, whether of life, work or even of facilitating. As a facilitator, you might identify your principles in working with others by considering from among those on the following list. You might describe your principles to the planners early on in the planning process.

1. **Be authentic – completely honest in the here-and-now – with the planners.**
    Block (2000) suggests that in any situation with a client, always resort to being authentic, that is, being aware of what you are feeling and seeing, and fully sharing your perspectives with the client. This approach always sustains complete trust between you and the client. (This principle is often the most difficult for new facilitators to follow, but eventually becomes their most powerful principle.)

2. **Do not worry about picking the "perfect" technique for each situation.**
    There are usually several techniques of facilitation available to a facilitator at any given time during the planning process. When in doubt about a technique to use, tell the client that you are not sure. Offer them several options and then ask for their advice.

3. **Come to the planning project with a basic planning framework in mind.**
    This guidebook describes a complete strategic planning framework from which planners can customize their own approach to strategic planning. As the facilitator, take some time to read through PART II to understand the framework and variety of approaches available to the planners.

4. **Follow the "20-80 rule."**
    It may be better to expend the planners' first 20% of effort on the work needed to produce the first 80% of the plan. Then the planners can complete the remaining 20% of the plan during its implementation. Although this approach may seem incomplete, it is far better than dragging on the planning process in an illusory effort to accomplish the "100% complete plan."

5. **Facilitate via example.**
    Model the behavior that you prefer from the group of planners. For example, if you prefer your planners to be prompt and participate wholeheartedly in an honest fashion, then do so yourself.

6. **Your credibility is in the flow of the process, not in the details of the plan.**
    If you focus, as authentically as possible, on helping planners to customize and participate in their process to develop their own plan, you will have done a wonderful job of facilitating.

Know Your Biases As Facilitator

Your biases play a major role in how you facilitate. Your perceptions are your reality, whether they are the reality for someone else or not. Differences in perceptions between you and the planners can make the difference between a successful planning process and a complete disaster. So know your own biases!

1.   Do believe that leaders should "take charge" and lead from the front of the group? If so, you might encounter frustration and resistance when working with planners who believe that leaders should lead from the middle of the group. Resistance is direct or indirect actions to intentionally or unintentionally subvert the planning effort because of fear or disagreement about the process, for example, not attending or continually rescheduling planning meetings.

2.   Do you believe that, if an organization struggles for a year or so, it should just be shut down? If so, then you might struggle to accept a small nonprofit that is working hard to meet an unmet need in the community, but just cannot get enough resources.

3.   Do you believe that people should just "shut up and listen to you?" If so, then you will probably find that either planners will seem very glad that you are there (but then they will not do what you say) or they will kick you out of their offices.

4.   Do you believe that nonprofits should operate like for-profit businesses? If so, then you will be frustrated when they keep talking about mission and passion, rather than the "bottom line."

5.   Do you believe that everyone should come to a meeting on time and leave on time? If so, then you will certainly be a frustrated when members of certain cultures come in a little bit late, spend a lot of time in the meeting interacting loudly with each other and then drift out before the meeting is over.

6.   Do you believe that most problems would be solved if people just "sucked it up" and did what they were supposed to do? If so, then you probably should not be a facilitator.

Determine Your Style As Facilitator

Answer the following questions to discern your style. Describe your style to planners early on in the planning process.

1.   What do you interpret as facilitating?

2.   Do you like to question a lot?

3.   Do you like to resort to challenges or confrontations?

4.   Do you like a fast pace?

5.   Do you like a lot of humor?

6.   How can you ensure that your own style is always carried out in highly respectful fashion?

Learn to Work with Diversity

When reading about the effects of diversity, think about how those effects might play out when facilitating strategic planning with nonprofits.

Considerations About Diversity and Strategic Planning

There are a wide range of values, opinions and perspectives among members of nonprofits. The more that a facilitator can understand and accept that situation, the more effective they will be in facilitating the strategic planning process among members of nonprofits.

- **There are often major differences among people.**
  For example, Western business cultures tend to be highly rationale and value things that are handy in meeting a current need. They value rugged individualism and competition. Other cultures might value patience, a sense of community and getting along with others. Yet others might value direct authority and privacy.

- **Differences between cultures can lead to increased resistance.**
  You and the planners might not understand each other because you have very different values. Those differences can hamper the progress of the planning process, if not stop it altogether.

- **Some cultures may be overly deferential to the facilitator.**
  The nature of good facilitation can be highly indirect. That might confuse planners who consider the facilitator to be extremely powerful in a group. A good facilitator will help planners to count on each other as much as on the facilitator.

- **Some cultures are deeply guarded about private matters.**
  Thus, it can be extremely difficult for planners in these cultures to effectively analyze the internal environment of nonprofit organization. The facilitators will have to judge for themselves how much to encourage planners to probe into their organizations and their interactions with each other.

- **There are no universal laws to ensure conformity in each culture.**
  There are no clear, consistent techniques of facilitation that are guaranteed to work in every situation. The best approaches to facilitation accept that there are clear differences among various people, try to identify those differences, and then work with the people to identify a process that conforms to their own nature and needs.

Basic Guidelines To Facilitating in Highly Diverse Environments

1. **Become knowledgeable about the local culture.**
   Pay close attention to features that you think might affect the planning process, for example, language, power and conflict.

2. **Consider a mentor, or representative, from the other culture.**
   Try to get an internal representative to help you to be compatible with the nature and needs of the local culture.

3. **Pay very close attention to matters of interpersonal communication.**
   Especially seek approaches that retain the dignity of each person in the group.

4.   **Let members of the group know that you respect them and want to learn.**
        A little humility can go a long way toward being accepted by people who, otherwise, do not
        know much about you at all.

Develop Contract With Nonprofit Organization?

The facilitator and planners might benefit from clarifying how they will work together. Often, a
written contract is the best way to specify what all of the participants want from the relationship and
who is going to do what in order to get it.

See Appendix E on page 193 for guidelines to develop a mutually
acceptable contract.

Note that many of the specifics that facilitators usually want to know about a project will already
have been considered by planners in their plan for a plan, for example, the desired results from the
planning process, length of the planning process, likely number of meetings and location of
meetings. Thus, contracting activities might go quite smoothly between the facilitator and planners.

Understand Planners' Nonprofit Organization

"Plan for Plan" Done Yet?

Planners may have already involved the facilitator early on in their planning activities, possibly
including customization of their strategic planning process by following the guidelines in "Phase 1:
Design Plan for Plan," in PART II. If the plan for a plan was completed with the facilitator, then the
facilitator already knows a great deal about the planners and their organization. If the plan for a plan
was completed without involvement from the facilitator, then the facilitator can learn a great deal
about the planners and their nonprofit organization by reviewing parts of that plan for a plan,
including:

1.   The planning committee, if the planners chose to use a committee

2.   Why the nonprofit is doing strategic planning now

3.   The approach that planners want to take to develop their strategic plan

4.   The time span of the plan

5.   The scheduling that might be used

6.   What people and materials that they think might be used and how

7.   How they might get strong "buy in" from members of their organization

8.   Their thoughts regarding any planning about the strategic planning process

Learn Nature of Nonprofit Planners and Their Organization

Regardless of whether the facilitator has seen a plan for a plan or not, the facilitator should attend to the following guidelines.

Look at Documentation in Organization

Ask to see the nonprofit's previous strategic plans, budgets, policies, most recent annual report, organization charts and advertising/promotions/sales literature, if any of those are available. From the materials, get a sense of the overall priorities of the organization.

1. If there is a full range of these types of documents, then you can probably assume that the organization highly values careful documentation when making important decisions, and will likely prefer the same during their strategic planning activities.

2. If these documents appear to be very comprehensive and include a great deal of graphs, figures and numbers, you can probably assume the organization highly values careful research, analysis and conclusions, and will prefer the same during strategic planning.

3. Do they show strong considerations and documentation about sound fiscal management, expanding services, effectiveness of services, efficiency of services, etc.? They will probably show the same traits during strategic planning.

Observe People in Organization

A great deal can be learned by observing behaviors during conversations and meetings with the planners. They will likely carry out their planning in the same style.

1. Is there a high degree of participation among members?

2. Are ideas encouraged and clarified?

3. Is there closure about ideas; for example, are people taking notes to ensure completion of tasks?

4. Do people support each others comments, for example, are they highly team-oriented ("let's work together"), individualistic ("it is your problem"), task-oriented ("get things done!"), process-oriented ("let's do it the right way") or crisis managed ("we've got to do something now!")?

Interview People in Organization

Interview the Chief Executive Officer and/or Board Chair.

1. Attempt to detect if he or she is highly entrepreneurial, team-oriented, analytical, diverging, "organic," etc. Sensing the person's nature is important to effective communication with him or her.

2. You might consider using personality assessments if your client is willing. For example, the Myers-Briggs Type Indicator® Instrument (MBTI) is popular and some online versions are available. Be careful with this approach, as some clients might be rather skeptical about these kinds of assessments.

3. Ask if the organization prefers planning with highly focused meetings that closely follow an agenda, or meetings that provide time to do "whatever is necessary to come to consensus." The answer to this question may indicate the extent of meeting management needed by the facilitator.

Clarify Expectations Between You and Planners

Clarify Planners' Expectations of Planning Effort

It is critical for the facilitator to understand what planners expect from the planning effort. Interview the key planning members(s), including the Board Chair and Chief Executive, and ask them the following questions.

Did They Ever Do Strategic Planning Before?

If so, how did it go? If it worked well, why? If it failed, why?

Many nonprofits indicate that they have not had successful strategic planning experiences before. Reasons they often cite are that the plan ended up sitting on a shelf, the planning process took too much time, the plan ended up including too much to do in too short of time, and meeting attendance and/or planning participation dropped significantly. If the nonprofit has not had a successful planning effort before, then it is critical to understand the reasons why and, in particular, what planners could have done before to have a better planning experience.

What Do They Want from Strategic Planning Now?

Do they have a preferred planning process? Have the nonprofit planning members describe in detail what they want out of the planning process, including outcomes, documents, services, etc. (That information might be in the plan for a plan, if completed.)

You might start by having the planners envision a successful planning process and describe it to you. Ideally, they want strategic planning to get more focus, direction and cohesion in their organization.

While asking the above questions, attempt to sense who is the implicit authority among the clients, that is, the person who is listened to the most when they speak to others, even though they may not have formal authority via his or her role. This understanding comes in handy when ensuring that leadership completely supports the planning process. Support of leadership is critical if the plan is to be implemented.

Clarify Your Expectations in Planning Effort

As a facilitator, reflect on what would you like from the planners and discuss your preferences with the planners. For example, you might ask for:

- Their full participation in meetings

- Timely scheduling of meetings

- Provision of meeting facilities

- Access to certain personnel or resources

- Their evaluation feedback about the overall planning effort and your role in it, etc.

Asserting these expectations may seem somewhat unnatural for inexperienced facilitators, but often becomes one of the most important requirements for developing a useful working relationship with the planners.

Clarify Your Roles to Planners

What You Will Do

Clarify your expectations to the planners and what activities or roles you will conduct, such as:

1. Help planners develop and implement a planning process.

2. Train planners on planning fundamentals.

3. Help their meeting processes along.

4. Intervene when the group is experiencing difficulty.

Explain to the planners that you may have several different roles with them, including:

1. Facilitator

2. Trainer

3. Expert on any certain subject

You might provide some basic descriptions of roles, including that trainers "convey specific information about basics of a process, often by lecturing" and facilitators "help group members to develop a process and move along in the process."

What You Will Not Do

Clarify what you will not do, for example:

1. Environmental scanning about the nonprofit's services and people served by the nonprofit

2. Market analysis about how the nonprofit should meet needs in the community

3. Scheduling planning meetings

4. Writing meeting minutes

5. Providing ideas about specific services and approaches when identifying strategies (unless your expertise is in the organization's service area)

6. Writing and implementing the plan

Establish Criteria to Evaluate Planning Effort

The project should be evaluated regularly, including briefly at the end of each meeting (about the process used in that meeting), at mid-point in the planning effort and at its end. Ideally, the efforts could be evaluated at three months and six months after completion of the planning document, particularly about whether the plan is being implemented or not.

Establish criteria early on from which the overall planning effort can be evaluated at mid-point and at end. Establish criteria by having planners specify what constitutes a successful planning process. Get descriptions to be as detailed as possible now in order to know, later on, if the planning process was clearly a success or not.

One of the biggest mistakes when planning how to evaluate an effort is to have planners make evaluations based on their feelings. Avoid this mistake by having planners, as much as possible, specify *behaviors* they would like to see from the facilitator and *specific aspects* they would like to see in a successful planning process.

As a facilitator, include your own terms in the criteria for success of the effort.

The extent of planners' willingness to participate in planning the evaluation activity is often an indicator of how much they see themselves responsible for the overall quality of the planning effort.

Common Techniques in Facilitation

The guidelines in PART II usually recommend which facilitation technique to use and when during the strategic planning process. However, the particular technique that is used should depend on the nature and needs of the planners and the facilitator. Thus, it is helpful for a facilitator to have at least a basic understanding of the most common techniques.

Overview of Common Techniques and Their Applications

The following table might be useful for facilitators when deciding what technique that they want to use in various situations in strategic planning. The procedures associated with the following techniques are described more fully later on in this section.

Common Techniques	Application in Strategic Planning ("the technique is used to:")
Brainstorming	Generate a broad range of new and creative ideas, for example, in a group to identify: ▪ Opportunities, threats, strengths and weaknesses (SWOT) ▪ Strategic issues ▪ Strategic goals ▪ Strategies ▪ Objectives
Consensus	Make a group decision in a highly participative, egalitarian fashion, and that everyone can "live with," for example, to: ▪ Select the most important or desired item from a list of items (by ranking) ▪ Select a range of the most important or desired items from a list of items (by rating)
Discussion	To ensure interaction between group members to identify, clarify, analyze and/or select an item, for example: ▪ Opportunities, threats, strengths and weaknesses (SWOT) ▪ Strategic issues ▪ Strategic goals ▪ Strategies ▪ Objectives
Facilitator intervention	Bring the group members back to focus and/or behaviors that are most effective for the group process, for example, if: ▪ The ground rules are being broken ▪ The group seems stalled or stuck ▪ There are prolonged conflicts among members ▪ Some members are not participating

Ground rules	Guide and scope the group members to certain, desired behaviors in meetings, for example, to ensure: • Members do not interrupt each other • Meetings start and stop on time • Everyone participates
Meeting agendas	Ensure meetings are highly focused and results-oriented around certain topics
Meeting management	Ensure processes in meetings are highly effective and efficient.
Nominal Group Technique[1]	Collect a wide range of ideas from among members of the group, organize the ideas into categories, and make a decision about which idea, or range of ideas, are most desired, for example, to identify, collect, organize and select: • Opportunities, threats, strengths and weaknesses (SWOT) information • Strategic issues • Strategic goals • Strategies • Objectives
Parking Lots	Postpone addressing, or even ignore, a certain topic or issue, for example: • Operational, or day-to-day, issues that can be dealt with later because the group is dealing with strategic issues now
Round-Robin	Ensure complete collection of all ideas from all participants, for example, to collect every one of the group member's ideas about: • Opportunities, threats, strengths and weaknesses (SWOT) information • Strategic issues • Strategic goals • Strategies • Objectives
Stories	Focus individuals and groups of stakeholders on positive and holistic considerations about: • Vision • Values • Action plans
Voting	Make a selection from various alternatives, for example: • Select the most important or desired item from a list of items (by ranking) • Select a range of the most important or desired items from a list of items (by rating)

Note 1: The nominal group technique (NGT) can be a very powerful and versatile technique in the strategic planning process. The NGT can include a wide range of other techniques, as well, including all of the techniques listed in the previous table. This guidebook suggests various different approaches to the NGT, each to be used at different times in the planning process. Each time, a specific procedure for the NGT is provided, for ease of use.

Procedures for Common Techniques in Facilitation

The purposes, or applications, for any of the following techniques are specified in the preceding table, "Overview of Common Techniques and Their Applications." Note that some techniques are applied by using various other techniques, as well.

Brainstorming Technique

1.   Specify the facilitation topic or goal to the planning group (if possible, do this step as pre-work before the next meeting).

2.   Ask for free-for-all generation of ideas from among members of the group.

3.   List all the ideas on a flipchart, holding back any reactions and/or discussion from any members of the group until all ideas are collected. (Members might ask a quick question about an idea, but only to understand the meaning of the idea, not to make a decision about the idea.)

Optional:

4.   Combine the ideas into common categories. This can be done by using the discussion, voting (ranking or rating) and/or consensus techniques.

5.   Select the most preferred categories and/or ideas. This can be done by using the discussion, voting (ranking or rating) and/or consensus techniques.

Consensus Technique

Often, there is confusion around the term consensus. Consensus means that every member of the group can live with the group's final decision. It does not mean that every member completely agrees with the decision. Consensus is often the means by which highly participative groups members reach their decisions, especially if they favor a highly egalitarian approach to decision making.

There are several approaches to the technique of reaching consensus. One quick approach to consensus is to just ask for a quick conclusion from the group by 1) suggesting a specific answer to the decision that must be made by the group and 2) asking if everyone in the group can live with that suggestion. Although that approach might save a lot of time, it certainly does not support the kind of strategic discussion and thinking that is so important in strategic planning. Therefore, planners might consider the following, more thoughtful approach to reaching consensus.

Before Meeting

Members receive information that:

1.   Clarifies the decision to be made.
It is often best if the decision is written in the form of a "yes/no" question or a choice from among alternatives, for example, "Should we approve ___?" or "Should we hire ___?".

2.   Is sufficient for each member to come to some conclusion on his or her own.

Ground Rules During Consensus Activities

The facilitator explains ground rules to other members of the group, for example:

1.   Members do not interrupt each other.

2.   Members can disagree with each other.

3.   Members do not engage in side discussions.

4.   Silence is considered agreement with the decision to be made.

5.   If decision is reached by consensus, then all members act as a united front to support decision.

Consensus Process in Meeting

The facilitator guides the procedure.

1.   The facilitator specifies a deadline by which to reach consensus in the meeting.

2.   In a roundtable fashion, each member:

   a) Gets equal time to voice his or her preferences and reasons in regard to the question.

   b) Focuses perspectives on what is *doable.*

   c) Does not mention other members' names.

   d) The most senior leader or manager in the group voices his or her opinion last.

3.   At the end of each person's time slot, all members take a quiet minute to:

   a) Collect his or her own thoughts in response to the last speaker's preferences.

   b) Decide what he or she would be willing to compromise or have in common with the last speaker.

4.   At the deadline:

   a) The facilitator poses what seems to be the most common perspective voiced by members.

   b) Asks all members if they can support that perspective.

5.   If no consensus is reached, members might choose one of following options:

   a) Consider further research until a specified future time. Decide what additional information is needed and maybe appoint a committee to do research. The committee researches and provides recommendations, preferably in writing to each member of the group before the next meeting. At the next meeting, members hear the committee's recommendations and initiate the consensus process again.

b) Consider using a vote to decide (via rating or ranking). Some people would assert that voting is not consensus, but it sure is handy if the consensus process has not reached a conclusion by an absolute deadline. See the Voting Technique, later on below, for a description of the rating and ranking approaches to voting.

Discussion Technique

1. Specify the discussion topic and the goal to the planning group (if possible, do this step as pre-work before the next meeting). The goal is usually to identify, clarify, analyze and/or select an item.

2. It is often best if the topic is described in the form of a "yes/no" question or a choice from among alternatives, for example, "Should we approve ___?" or "Should we hire ___?".

3. Specify when the discussion is to start and stop.

4. Allow for open, unassigned exchange of information, including, for example, questions, suggestions and general comments, until it is time stop the discussion.

5. Facilitate to focus the discussion around the topic.

6. Attempt to capture key points on a flipchart.

Optional:

7. Attempt to summarize the discussion by identifying conclusions or decisions from the discussion.

8. The group can make selections from the results using voting (ranking or rating) and/or consensus techniques.

Facilitator Intervention Technique

The nature of the intervention depends on the nature of the problem in the group.

1. If the group seems stuck, then it is appropriate to point this out to the entire group. (Ideas about how to handle this situation are included in the next subsection.)

2. If there is prolonged conflict between certain members, then it may be more appropriate to invite the members out of the group and to conduct an intervention among those members. (Ideas about how to handle this situation are included in the next subsection.)

3. If a ground rule is being broken, then it may be appropriate to point this out to the entire group.

There are a wide variety of intervention techniques, for example, summarizing, confronting, making suggestions, asking questions, providing other perspectives, asking for clarity, reminding the group about their ground rules and structuring activities.

Whenever intervening in a group, try to give the group an opportunity to take responsibility for recognizing the situation and deciding what to do about it. If an intervention is to the entire group, consider:

1.　Briefly describe what you are seeing or hearing (in the here and now) that leads you to conclude that there is a problem. Do not just report what you feel or sense – try to be more specific.

2.　Ask the group what they want to do.

3.　Be silent while group members react and discuss the situation.

4.　Focus the discussion on the problem at hand.

5.　Ask them for a decision.

Ground Rules Technique

Ground rules can be identified before the group meeting and then proposed to the group for their review, modification and/or approval. Or, the ground rules can be developed by members of the group in a group meeting. Common ground rules for strategic planning are:

1.　Meetings start and stop on time.

2.　Focus on priorities, not on personalities.

3.　Everyone participates.

4.　All opinions are honored.

5.　No interruptions.

6.　No sidebars (or conversations not involving the main group).

Meeting Agendas Technique

1.　Design the agenda together with the organization's leadership – do not design it yourself. Ensure an effective meeting by first reflecting on the goals for the meeting and then the activities to meet those goals.

2.　Think about how you label an event so that people come in with that mindset. It may pay to have a short dialogue around the label to develop a common mindset among attendees, particularly if they include representatives from various cultures.

3.　Always include introductions or some type of "check in" early on so that all members get involved early in the meeting.

4.　Be sure to dedicate time to reviewing status of actions assigned in previous meetings.

5.　Allow time for brief evaluations, or "satisfaction checks," among the members.

6. Next to each major topic, include the type of action needed, the type of output expected, and time estimates for addressing each topic.

7. Review the agenda at the beginning of each meeting, giving participants a chance to understand all proposed major topics, change them and accept them.

8. Ask participants if they will commit to the agenda.

9. Keep the agenda posted at all times.

10. Ensure a meeting recorder (or documenter) who documents major activities during the meeting and actions to be conducted after the meeting. This person should issue meeting minutes shortly after the meeting (although meeting minutes may seem the most perfunctory duty from a meeting, the minutes can end up being the most useful part of the meeting by ensuring all actions are completed).

11. In general, do not over design the meeting. Be willing to adapt the meeting agenda if members are making progress in the planning process.

Meeting Management Technique

Meeting management tends to be a set of skills often overlooked by facilitators and planners. The following suggestions for facilitators apply to most planning meetings, regardless of when they occur in the overall planning process.

Facilitator Preparation for Meetings

Remember that your behavior sets the tone for the meeting. Depending on your personality, you should become as comfortable as possible before each meeting. Regardless of your personality, it is important to acknowledge to yourself whatever you are feeling about the meeting.

Note what might be the best and worst outcomes of the meeting, and realize the meeting will probably be somewhere in between.

Developing Agendas

The agenda is the "roadmap" for the entire meeting, so it is very important to design the agenda carefully. See the above-listed "Meeting Agendas Technique."

Opening Meetings

1. Start on time. This respects those who showed up on time and reminds any late-comers that the meeting and its scheduling are serious.

2. Ask if anyone is missing who should be present. If there is anyone who should be there and is not, visit the reason for the absence and address how to get him or her involved.

3. Model the kind of energy and participation needed by the facilitator and meeting participants.

4. Clarify your roles for that meeting, that is, note when you will be doing any training, facilitating, recording, etc.

Establishing Ground Rules for Meetings

The ground rules establish the overall "personality" of the meeting, so they are very important to establish early on when working with a group. See the previous subsection, "Ground Rules Technique."

Time Management

One of the most difficult facilitation tasks is time management. In a highly energized meeting, time seems to run out before tasks are completed. Therefore, the biggest challenge is keeping momentum to keep the process moving.

1. Consider asking the group for a volunteer to help monitor and remind the group about the time.

2. If the planned time on the agenda is getting out of hand, present it to the group members and ask for their input as to a resolution.

3. Adjourn a meeting when scheduled – rarely deter from this guideline. It is far better to adjourn a meeting even if members feel work is incomplete than to drag a meeting on and on with the illusion that everyone should leave the meeting with a strong sense of closure. Adjourning a meeting on time ensures that all members feel their time is respected and they can continue to count on sound meeting management.

Evaluations During Meeting Process

Evaluation of the quality of a meeting is a critical, but often overlooked, requirement for effective meetings. Avoiding evaluations in an effort to "get more work done" in meetings is a good example of working harder, rather than smarter. Perhaps the most critical element of any successful meeting is each member's complete and responsible participation. Round-Robin evaluation is a useful technique for ensuring meetings include this full participation.

If the meeting is a long one, for example, more than 1.5 hours, then every hour or so, conduct a 5-minute "satisfaction check." Have each member visit his or her "internal weather" and report his or her evaluation so that each person is involved (have the senior management provide their evaluations last). Far too many meetings end up with members going out of the room, remarking to each other that the meeting was not useful. Get this impression *during* the meeting so you can do something about it.

Evaluating Overall Meeting

Leave 10 minutes near the end to evaluate the quality of the meeting. Do not skip this portion of the meeting. The facilitator and planners can quickly learn a great deal about what is working and what is not.

1. Have each member rate the meeting from 1-5, with 1 as the lowest.

2. Have the member explain his or her rating.

3. Finally, have the member explain what he or she could have done *in that meeting* to now be rating the meeting a 5.

Have the senior management provide their evaluations last.

Closing Meetings

At the end of a meeting, review actions and assignments, establish the time and location for the next meeting, and ask group members if they can make it or not (to get their commitment). Deciding membership in meetings is extremely important, but often overlooked. Ask who should be at the next meeting and ensure that someone is assigned to invite them.

Nominal Group Technique

There are many versions of the overall nominal group technique (NGT), which, in any form, is a combination of various other techniques. One version of the NGT is used for various applications in this guidebook, for example, to finalize information about SWOT, strategic issues, goals and strategies. Each application of the NGT is customized somewhat, so the procedure for each application is included elsewhere in the guidebook, rather than below.

The technique usually includes various phases, including:

1.   Facilitator clarifies the topic or goal to be addressed by the group, for example, to select the most important items from a list.

2.   Ideas are collected from members of the group.

   a) The Round-Robin technique is often used to compile an initial list of ideas.

   b) Brainstorming is used to expand the compiled list of ideas.

3.   The overall list is organized and analyzed.

   a) The discussion technique is often used.

   b) The list is analyzed for overlaps, duplications, conflict, interdependences, etc.

4.   Ideas are selected from the overall list, using any of the following techniques.

   ▪ The discussion technique can be applied, depending on the nature of the members of the group.

   ▪ The consensus technique can be applied if the group highly values strong participation and egalitarian approaches to decision making.

   ▪ The voting technique can be used to make a final selection.

Parking Lot Technique

1.   One or more members of the group mentions that a matter before the group is not directly related to the established topic or goal that the group wants to address.

2.   The facilitator or a group member suggests that the matter go on the "parking lot."

3.   If group members agree with the suggestion, the matter is listed on a "parking lot," which is usually a flipchart sheet posted off to the side in the meeting room.

4. Before the end of the meeting, members agree how the "parking lot" matters will be addressed later on, if at all.

Round-Robin Technique

1. The facilitator clarifies the topic or goal to be addressed by the group, for example, to generate ideas about a topic or goal.

2. Members get quiet time before the group meeting, or early in the group meeting, to identify ideas on their own.

3. In the meeting, the facilitator collects a list of ideas by getting one idea from one person at a time, going around the table, until all members have shared all of the ideas from their list.

4. Members do not analyze or discuss any of the ideas until all ideas have been collected. Members can ask a question during the Round-Robin, only to get clarification on a suggested idea.

5. The facilitator and members avoid duplication of ideas on the list.

Optional:

6. Combine the ideas into common categories. This can be done by using the discussion, voting (ranking or rating) and/or consensus techniques.

7. Select the most preferred categories and/or ideas. This can be done by using the discussion, voting (ranking or rating) and/or consensus techniques.

Stories Technique

This technique borrows from the field of appreciative inquiry. For information about appreciative inquiry, go to http://appreciativeinquiry.case.edu/

Facilitator explains that the focus of this technique is on the positive by building on the strengths and opportunities of the organization and its stakeholders. Facilitator clarifies goal of technique, for example, to establish vision, values and/or action plans.

1. Each member quietly reflects on his or her best experience with the organization and the people it serves.

2. In pairs, members interview each other (each interview is 10 minutes long) about their best experience, including about:

    a) What made it the best experience? What were they doing? Who was involved?

    b) What do they value about the organization and whom it serves now?

    c) What would they like to be core value in the organization?

d) Three wishes for the organization and the people it serves?

3.   The interviewer documents the top 5-8 major themes in what the other person talked about, for example, "helping other people, " "feeling of fulfillment" and "working in a team". The interviewer mentions the themes to the other person to get his or her agreement, disagreement or modifications to the themes.

4.   Use the Round-Robin technique in the group to collect all of the themes. Also, use brainstorming technique to expand the list of themes if the group prefers.

5.   Use the voting technique (rating) to select the top 5-8 themes to include in the vision and/or reflect in the values.

6.   Use the Round-Robin technique for each person to identify his or her action plans to enact the vision and/or values.

Voting Technique

There are a variety of approaches to the voting technique.

Show of Hands

The most common approach to the technique is simply to ask for a show of hands regarding each item on a list, one at a time, and the item that gets the most show of hands is the item that is selected from the list.

Ranking

Ranking is assigning one distinct value to each item in order to select the single, most important item from a list. For example, a ranked list would have one item ranked as 1, three as 2 and four as 3.

Rating

Rating is associating a value with each item in order to select a range of items from a list. Some items can have the same value associated with them. For example, a rated list might have several items rated as high, medium or low or as 1, 2 or 3.

Dot-Voting

A common approach to using the technique is as follows.

1.   Each member gets a certain number of votes that he or she can use regarding items on a list. The number of dots that they get is usually equal to the number of choices that are to be made from a list. For example, if three items are to be selected, then each person gets three dots.

2.   Each member walks up to the overall list of items and places his or her dots next to the items that the member recommends be selected from the list.

3.   After all members have cast their votes, the items that received the most votes get selected from the list.

The dot-voting technique has variations. Different colored dots can represent more than one vote, or even a negative vote. Sometimes, each participant is given one vote of each weight and required to apply each vote to a different item. In some cases, a member is allowed to cast multiple votes for one item.

Challenges in Facilitating Strategic Planning

Many facilitators continue to struggle about whether to intervene in the group's process or to let the members of the group find their own path through a particular activity or major issue in the group. This section includes guidelines to address the following situations for facilitators:

1.   The members of the Board are not ready for strategic planning.

2.   Participation is uneven or too low.

3.   There is prolonged conflict among group members.

4.   The group appears to be stuck.

5.   Some members of the group continue to resist the process.

What if Board Is Not Ready for Planning?

Primary responsibilities of a nonprofit Board of Directors are to:

1.   Establish the direction of the organization in accordance with the needs of the community and expectations of the people whom it serves, and

2.   Regularly examine the nonprofit's services in order to ensure that they fulfill the mission of the agency and achieve its overall goals.

Therefore, Board members should be highly involved in strategic planning. In order to conduct effective strategic planning, the Board should show strong interest and participation in the planning process, and commitment to working together towards agreement. If Board members are not involved in the planning, they will be impaired from carrying out their role as Board members.

Some Signs the Board Is Not Ready for Strategic Planning

1.   Board members are not involved in planning the process.

2.   Chief Executive specifies that the Board will not be involved.

3.   Board members chronically disagree about the nonprofit's mission and/or vision.

4.   There is inconsistent involvement from Board members in the planning process.

5.   Board members lack understanding of their role as Board members.

6.   Board members assert they want a planning document primarily to show funders so they can get more funding.

If Board Is Not Developed Enough for Strategic Planning

If, as a facilitator, you suspect that the Board is not ready for strategic planning, then consider the following:

1.   Acknowledge the problem and your concerns to the members of the Board.

2.   If Board members appear not to be interested in strategic planning at all, then ask Board members some hard questions, such as "What would you do if your largest donor pulled away" or "What if your Executive Director is hit by a large truck tomorrow?" This may spawn them to additional considerations in the form of strategic planning.

3.   Suggest Board development activities, including Board self-assessment/inventory, Board training with clarification of Board roles, and responsibilities prior to planning.

4.   Suggest the nonprofit recruit new Board members who have experience in strategic planning.

5.   Recognize that Board development is probably needed and should be included as a goal and/or strategy in the strategic plan.

6.   If the Board still is highly skeptical about the value of strategic planning, the best service the facilitator might provide is to explain his or her concern and then try to guide the planners toward a prompt decision about how to enhance Board involvement. It is up to the facilitator as to whether he or she should continue the strategic planning effort without the Board involvement or not. It is very difficult, though, to accept that a Board can effectively carry out its governance role without having strong involvement in strategic planning. .

Guidelines for enhancing a Board of Directors are not included in this guidebook. However, step-by-step guidelines are included in the guidebook, *Field Guide to Developing and Operating Your Nonprofit Board of Directors,* by this author.

How To Enhance Group Participation

One of the overall goals of this guidebook is to help ensure that the strategic planning process includes the strong participation of members of the Board and staff. Much of what supports the active participation of group members lies in how the meeting is designed and managed.

Meeting Preparation and Opening

1.   Meet offsite. This minimizes interruptions and members' preoccupation with their day-to-day activities.

2.   At the beginning of each meeting, get them involved early, for example, include introductions or do a brief "check in" from each member.

3.   Have people share information about them. This is usually easier to talk about and initially they may be more motivated to talk about themselves than planning.

4.   Have each person state what he or she wants from the meeting. Ask each member of the group to help others achieve their goals for the meeting. Post a sheet of each person's wants. Review this list at end of meeting.

5.   If a member is gone from a meeting, the Chief Executive Officer should acknowledge who is missing and find out why.

6.   Review ground rules, including the ground rule that "everyone participates."

During Meeting Process

The group of planners should include members of the organization who are most vested in the planning process and implementation of the plan. Consider some or all of the following:

1.   Use an "inner circle, outer circle" approach where the inner circle is comprised of planners and the outer circle includes experts who provide critical information and/or review this information at various times, as invited by members of the inner circle.

2.   Use break-out groups, or small groups, to increase attention and participation among members. Be sure to provide very specific directions about what the groups are to accomplish and by when. Be sure to have a spokesperson for the small group.

3.   If the facilitator feels the group is in a lull, then he or she should say so, and then ask the group if they agree and what they can do to get out of the lull.

4.   Allow time for individual thinking and taking notes.

5.   Build in physical movement periodically throughout the meeting.

6.   Bring in some jokes, cartoons, etc., and share them at different times. Be careful about not to offend members who might misinterpret the humor as being insensitive.

7.   Post the mission, vision and/or values statements on the walls where the meeting is held in order to remind people of why they are there.

8.   Do a Round-Robin about the current topic, asking each person what he or she thinks about the current activity or topic.

9.   Specifically address the quiet people, for example, mention, "We have not heard from you yet."

10.   For some groups, it might help to have each person bring an object and share it with the group during an initial icebreaker. This can increases personal involvement, trust and confidentiality.

11.   Ask lots of questions.

12.   Use a variety of aids to ensure all learning styles are considered, including verbal, visual and kinesthetic. This is important to keep members with varying styles equally engaged.

13.   Share facilitation roles, including letting someone else facilitate as you take the time to record, organize and prepare information.

During Meeting Closure

1.   Be sure that the meeting process includes recognizing and documenting results in each meeting. This shows progress, promotes satisfaction and cultivates fulfillment among members of the group.

2.   Within a week after the end of the meeting, have the meeting recorder (documenter) issue meeting minutes, including major actions and assignments from the meeting.

How To Manage Group Conflict and Come to Decisions

If the facilitator detects prolonged conflict among two or more members of the group, then consider the following guidelines. Sometimes the conflict is consistently between certain members. In that case, you might consider off-line conversations (or conversations outside the planning group) with the conflicting members.

Otherwise, consider the following general process:

1.   Acknowledge to the group that the group seems to be stuck in conflict.

2.   Name or describe what behaviors you are seeing that indicate that the group seems to be in conflict.

3.   Explain that conflict is a natural occurrence, especially in healthy groups, and is not to be avoided, but should be managed.

4.   Ask the group for any reactions about the current situation, and listen while you remain quiet.

These comments often help members of the group to get to their "real" needs and assumptions behind disagreements.

Also, consider some or all of the following specific suggestions:

1.   Explore if differences really appear to exist, or if the problem is poor communication techniques, for example, people are cross-talking.

2.   Organize ideas, for example, use Post-It® Notes – this is often the best way to quickly record, present and reorganize ideas. (Post-It notes is a registered trademark of the 3M Corporation.)

3.   Propose a majority vote if the discussion or consensus techniques are not useful.

4.   Focus on what the group agrees on, including posting the mission, vision and/or values statements in order to remind people of why they are there.

5.   Have members restate their position. If it will take longer than three minutes, then allow opportunities for others to confirm or question, for understanding not disagreement.

6.   Resort to prioritizing alternatives, rather than excluding all alternatives but one.

7.   If two or three people strongly disagree, try a role reversal, that is, if person/group A and B disagree, then have A assume B's point of view and try to defend it, and B assume A's point of view and try to defend it.

8.   Draw structures, for example, process flowcharts and wheel diagrams to fill in and portray different viewpoints.

9.   Use the Nominal Group Technique to record and discuss ideas on a flipchart.

10.   Propose an "agree to disagree" disposition.

11.   If disagreement or lack of consensus persists around an issue, have a committee break-out to select options and then report back to the larger group.

12.   With the group's permission, bring in a neutral outside speaker. Have the speaker talk about the issue that is dividing the group.

13.   Tell stories of successes and failures in strategic planning, including how planners got past their differences and reached agreement.

14.   Ask the group, "If this disagreement continues, where will we be?"

15.   Have one or two of the people whom the organization serves to come in and remind the group of how important their work really is.

How Do We Get Unstuck?

Sometimes, even if there is a lot of participation from members and no prolonged conflicts, a group might seem not to be making any progress on particular planning activities. They may simply be stuck. Block (2000) suggests that you know you are stuck if you find that you are explaining something for the third time. The first two times should be good faith efforts to address a situation. The third time suggests that things are stuck.

Consider the same general process as when a group seems in prolonged conflict. Consider the following general process:

1.   Acknowledge to the group that the group seems to be stuck.

2.   Name or describe what behaviors you are seeing that indicate that the group seems to be stuck.

3.   Ask the group for any reactions about the current situation, and listen while you remain quiet.

Also, consider some or all of the following specific suggestions:

1.   Take a five-minute break to let members do whatever they want.

2.   Resort to some movement and stretching.

3.   Ask for five examples of "out of the box" thinking.

4.   Resort to thinking and talking about activities in which resources do not matter.

5.   Play games that stimulate creative thinking.

6.   Use metaphors (stories, myths, archetypal images, etc.), for example, ask each person to take five minutes and draw or write a metaphor that describes where they are at in the meeting.

7.   Have a 5-minute period of silence, with no suggested tasks to do in this time.

8.   Take 5-10 minutes and in groups of two, each person shares with the other what they are confused or irritated about. The other person in the pair helps the speaker to articulate his or her views to the larger group.

9.   Have each or some of the planners tell a story and include some humor.

10.   Use visualization techniques, for example, visualize reading an article about the organization's success some years into the future. What does the article say about how the success came about?

11.   Play reflective or energizing music (depending on the situation).

12.   Restructure the group to smaller groups or move members around in the large group.

13.   Have a period of asking question after question after question (without answering necessarily). Repetition of questions, "why?" in particular, can help to move planners into deeper levels of reflection and analysis, especially if they do not have to carefully respond to each question.

14.   Establish a "parking lot" for outstanding or unresolved issues, and then move on to something else. Later, go back to stuck issue. (The parking lot technique is explained earlier in PART III.)

15.   Turn the problem around by reframing the topic and/or issue. Usually questions work to make this reframing happen.

16.   Ask key questions, for example, "How can we make it happen? How can we avoid it happening?"

17.   Remember different learning styles, for example, the group may get more clarity by using visual aids.

18.   Focus on what the group agrees on, including posting the mission, vision and/or values statements to remind people of why they are there.

19.   Ask the group, "If we continue to be stuck, where will we be?"

20.   Have one or two of the people whom the organization serves to come in and remind the group of how important their work really is.

How Do We Deal With Resistance?

Dealing with resistance is one of the most important aspects of the facilitator's role. Some forms of resistance from the client may include, for example, getting items sent to you far too late for adequate preparation in an upcoming meeting, negativism, canceled/rescheduled meetings, coming late, not doing pre-work, silence, intellectualizing, extended analysis or passive compliance.

Realize that the resistance is the members' reactions to the process, not to you. Do not take it personally. Also, remember that resistance is seldom managed with sound logic and arguments.

Consider the following general process:

1.   Acknowledge the resistance, name what behaviors you believe indicate the resistance.

2.   Use language that is simple, specific and brief.

3.   Explain that resistance is often an indirect expression of some strong emotion and typically happens in a planning group.

4.   Ask the group members for their reaction, and listen while you remain quiet.

Also, consider some or all of the following specific suggestions.

1.   Use a Round-Robin technique to get all views out in the open.

2.   Be sensitive to ethnic/cultural differences. These differences are likely to become apparent only after the members who are resisting begin to communicate. Ask group members if the resistance might be based on cultural differences, for example, around language, group norms and styles.

3.   Remind members of the difference between either/or and both/and perspective. Is the resistance from the perception of a win-lose situation?

4.   Focus on what the group agrees on, including posting the mission, vision and/or values statements to remind people of why they are there.

5.   If resistance persists, consider off-line conversations with the resisting planners.

APPENDICES

Appendix A: Glossary

The following list includes many of the most common terms used in strategic planning. Note that many planners might have a different interpretation of a particular term, especially if they prefer a specific approach to strategic planning (goals-based, issues-based, organic, etc.). The most important requirement around the use of strategic planning terms and concepts is that the facilitator and planners share common interpretations, at least during the planning process. Therefore, the facilitator and planners should discuss the meaning of terms before they use them. A good starting point for this useful discussion is to conduct a brief training about strategic planning before the planning process gets underway. Usually the facilitator can guide this training. Perhaps the most useful role of a definition is to provide the facilitator and planners a common point of reference around which to select their own interpretations.

Action plan

The action plan lists the specific actions that must be taken, by whom and by when in order to achieve an overall goal or implement a strategy. Some people include the costs of each action in the action plans, resulting in budget information being included in the action plans, as well. (Action plans for Board Committees or top management are sometimes called work plans.)

Board of Directors

A Board is the group of people who are legally charged to oversee the operations of a corporation, whether for-profit or nonprofit.

Chief Executive Officer (CEO)

The Chief Executive Officer reports to the Board of Directors, and is the staff position to whom all other staff (non-Board members) report. Some nonprofit organizations include the CEO as a member of the Board.

Clients

Clients are the people who directly receive the benefits from the services of a nonprofit. They might include, for example, attendees to an art show, members of an association, citizens attending a civic event, grantees of a foundation, patients in a hospital, members of a congregation, students in a school, participants in social service programs or patrons to a library. Primary clients are the people who directly benefit from the services of the nonprofit. Secondary, or supporting, clients are people who indirectly benefit from the services.

Driving forces

These are various, major influences, usually external to the organization, that must be considered when conducting an external analysis, especially environmental scan activity. There are numerous driving forces, and are usually organized into categories, including political, economic, societal, technological and environmental.

Environmental scan

(See external analysis)

External analysis

This form of analysis includes examining the opportunities and threats that might affect the organization, often by using various assessment tools to assess, for example, various potential changes to driving forces, stakeholders, competitors and collaborators. External factors are those outside the control of the organization. The external analysis and internal analysis comprise the situational analysis. The external analysis, especially analysis of various driving forces, is sometimes called the environmental scan.

Facilitator

The facilitator helps planners to develop their strategic planning process and move them along in that process. The facilitator also intervenes when the group seems to be deviating from the process, for example, breaking one of their ground rules.

Goals

A goal is a specific accomplishment to be achieved at some point in the future. Planners often distinguish between several types of goals in the strategic planning process.

An outcomes goal is in regard to accomplishments of clients who participate in a particular program. Outcomes are changes in knowledge, skills and/or conditions for the clients.

An activities goal is in contrast to an outcomes goal and is in regard to actions to be accomplished by the organization.

An organization-wide goal is an overall accomplishment in regard to actions across the organization and often involves more than one program.

A program goal is an overall accomplishment in regard to actions in a specific program. The goal can be an activities goal or outcomes goal.

Goals-based strategic planning

This form of strategic planning places heavy emphasis on identifying clear, overall goals that the organization must address in its strategic planning. Goals are usually identified in reference to the organization's mission, vision and/or values, and results of the situational analysis. Goals-based strategic planning is in contrast to issues-based strategic planning in which planners place heave emphasis on addressing strategic issues.

Governance

This term refers to the nature of the activities conducted by the Board of Directors, including clarifying the overall purpose of the organization; optionally the vision and/or values of the organization; establishing broad policies and plans for how the organization operates to that purpose; and monitoring the implementation of those policies and plans.

Internal analysis

This includes examining the strengths and weaknesses of the organization, often by using various assessment tools to examine the quality of internal aspects of the organization, for example, the Board, strategic planning, program planning, financial management, fundraising, human resources management and evaluations. Internal factors are generally those considered to be under the control of the organization. The external analysis and internal analysis comprise the situational analysis.

Issues (strategic)

Strategic issues are very important challenges that the organization must face, often in the forms of weaknesses of the organization and pending threats to the organization. Identification of strategic issues often results from external and internal analyses, which, together, comprise the situational analysis.

Issues-based strategic planning

This form of strategic planning places heavy emphasis on identifying overall issues, or priorities, that the organization must address in its strategic planning. Issues-based strategic planning is in contrast to goals-based strategic planning in which planners place heavy emphasis on addressing strategic goals.

Mission (statement)

The mission statement describes the overall purpose of the organization. It should concisely describe the type of services provided by the nonprofit, the groups of clients served by the nonprofit and sometimes how the nonprofit generally provides those services. Some planners refer to the vision and/or values statements as part of the mission statement as well.

Nonprofit

A nonprofit organization exists primarily to meet a community need. An informal nonprofit is a group of people who gather to work on usually a short-term need in the community, for example, to clean up the neighborhood streets. A "chartered," or incorporated, nonprofit has filed with the appropriate government agency to be a legal entity separate from the members of the organization. A tax-exempt nonprofit has attained status from the appropriate government agency that allows the nonprofit to refrain from paying certain federal, state (provincial in Canada) and/or local taxes. A tax-deductible nonprofit has attained status from the appropriate government agency enabling it to receive donations and allowing donors to reduce their tax liabilities based on the amount of their donations.

Operating plan (annual plan)

The operating plan is focused on the goals, strategies, action plans and budgets of the organization, specifically over the next year (either 12-month period of fiscal year period). A strategic plan often spans several years, and the first year of the strategic plan period is planned and described in more detail than the other years in the strategic plan. The detailed first year is often included in a plan document called an operating (or annual) plan that is separate from the strategic plan. Some planners refer to the operating plan as the set of action plans, but this usually is not the case in nonprofit planning.

Operational

Operational activities are focused on the day-to-day, or short-term, activities. This is in contrast to strategic matters (see "strategic"). In reality, the continuum between strategic and operational can become quite blurred.

Operational plan

An operational plan is usually in regard to the first year of a mult-year strategic plan and includes another level of detail than the strategic plan. For example, organizations that utilize operational plans often include broad goals in the multi-year strategic plan, but include more specific objectives, responsibilities and deadlines (to accomplish the broad goals) in the operational plan.

Organic strategic planning

This form of strategic planning places heavy emphasis on meeting regularly with stakeholders to establish mission, vision and/or values statements and then identifying short-term actions that can be taken in order to adhere to the statements.

Outcomes (results)

Outcomes are changes in clients that result from participating in a nonprofit program. Outcomes can be short-term (usually changes in knowledge), intermediate (changes in skills) and long-term (changes in conditions). Outcomes are the real results that nonprofits aim to accomplish and that the community expects from their nonprofits.

Planners

These are members of the nonprofit organization who are directly involved in conducting the strategic planning process. Occasionally, planners include others outside of the organization, such as funders, community leaders and program experts. Facilitators help the planners to develop and follow their own planning process.

Planning Committee

The Committee is a group of people, often 5-8 in number, who work together to oversee the development of the strategic plan. The Committee does not conduct all of the activities to develop the plan; usually other personnel become involved in the planning process during various stages.

Program

A program is a set of highly related products and/or services provided by a nonprofit in order to meet certain common needs among certain groups of clients. Nonprofits usually provide major services in the form of programs.

Scenario (planning technique)

A scenario is depiction of an organization, its clients and certain significant conditions in society at some point in the future. Scenario technique can be used to ensure rigorous strategic thinking in any approach to strategic planning. The manner in which the technique is applied depends on the approach to strategic planning that is selected by the planners.

Situational analysis

The situational analysis includes conducting analyses of the environments that are external and internal to the organization, in order to identify strategic issues or goals to be addressed during the strategic planning.

Staff

This includes all of the personnel who work in the nonprofit organization and are other than the members of the Board of Directors. This usually includes the Chief Executive Officer (if this role is not a member of the Board, as well) and all of the people who report to the Chief Executive Officer.

Stakeholders

Stakeholders are those people or groups of people who have a stake, or strong interest, in the operations, or affects of operations, of the nonprofit. Usually the term is in reference to people outside the organization, for example, clients, community members, funders, collaborators and suppliers. However, Board members and staff members also are stakeholders.

Strategic

A matter is considered to be strategic if it: involves strong input and support from leaders in the organization; was produced from careful consideration of the effects of potential changes in the external and internal environments of the organization; is based on the future of the organization; will have significant impact on the governance, leadership and operations of the organization; and will involve extensive use of the organization's resources during implementation of the plan. Strategic matters are in contrast to operational activities (see "operational").

Strategy

A strategy is a major approach that uses the internal strengths of an organization to take advantage of external opportunities, while shoring up internal weaknesses to ward off external threats. Strategies are often major approaches to achieve strategic goal or address strategic issues. Strategies are usually long-term in nature. ("External," in this sense, means something that the organization cannot directly control, as opposed to "internal", which is something that the organization usually can control.)

Strategic planning

Basically, this is assessing what is going on in the organization's external and internal environments, identifying what needs to be done as a result in order to better meet client needs, how it will be done, who will do it and by when. Note that the strategic plan is the top-level, sometimes multi-year, plan for the organization. For some organizations, annual operating plans are developed (or plans that specify what will be done over the year). Some planners clearly distinguish strategic planning from long-range planning, where the former establishes unique approaches to address changes in the external and internal environments, and the latter could merely imply a plan that spans several years.

Strategic thinking

Strategic thinking is the nature of activities in and among planners as they conduct the various analyses, make the necessary considerations and come to the appropriate conclusions regarding the future actions of their organization, particularly to ensure an effective fit between the organization's external and internal environments.

Tactic

A tactic is a series of activities, usually short-term and small in scale, intended to achieve some accomplishment (goal or objective). This is compared to a strategy, which is a series of activities, usually long-term and large in scale, intended to address a strategic goal or strategic issue.

Values (statement)

The values statement describes the overall, top-level priorities for how a nonprofit chooses to conduct its activities and to be viewed by the public, for example, integrity, efficiency and reliability. Some planners distinguish between preferred values and actual values. Preferred values are those that the nonprofit hopes to adhere to in its activities. Actual values reflect the behaviors that are actually occurring in the workplace.

Vision (statement)

The vision is a vivid and compelling description of the organization and its clients at some time in the future, sometimes at the point at which the organization has implemented all strategies in the strategic plan. Some planners refer to the mission statement as also including the vision and/or values statements as well.

Work Plan

Action plans for Board Committees or top management are sometimes called work plans. (See Action Plan.)

Appendix B: Resources for Nonprofits

Free Management Library^{SM}

The Library includes extensive free materials about personal, professional and organization development. The Library includes over 675 topics that are organized into the following popular categories. The list of topics is located at http://www.managementhelp.org/ on the Web.

Advertising and Promotion	Benefits and Compensation	Boards of Directors
Career Development	Chief Executive Role	Communications (Interprsnl)
Communications (Writing)	Computers, Internet & Web	Consultants (using)
Coordinating Activities	Creativity and Innovation	Crisis Management
Customer Satisfaction	Customer Service	E-Commerce
Employee Performance	Employee Wellness Programs	Ethics - Practical Toolkit
Evaluations (many kinds)	Facilities Management	Finances (For-Profit)
Finances (Nonprofit)	Fundraising (Nonprofit)	General Resources
Group Performance	Group Skills	Guiding Skills
Human Resources Mgmnt	Insurance (Business)	Interpersonal Skills
Interviewing (all kinds)	Jobs	Leadership (Introduction)
Leadership Development	Legal Information	Management (Introduction)
Management Development	Marketing	Operations Management
Organizational Alliances	Organizational Change	Org'l Communications
Organizational Performance	Organizations (Introduction)	Organizing (many kinds)
Performance Management	Personal Development	Personal Productivity
Personal Wellness	Planning (many kinds)	Policies (Personnel)
Product Selection & Dev.	Program Management	Project Management
Public and Media Relations	Quality Management	Research Methods
Risk Management	Sales	Social Entrepreneurship
Staffing	Starting an Organization	Supervision (Introduction)
Supervisory Development	Systems Thinking	Taxation
Training Basics	Volunteers	———————

Free Nonprofit Micro-eMBA^{SM}
Organization Development Program

This state-of-the-art, on-line training program includes 12 highly integrated courses that can be taken free by anyone, anywhere at any time. At the end of the program, each learner will have all of the basic systems and processes needed to start and operate a nonprofit. Learners are encouraged to work with their Boards of Directors while going through the program. Participants going through the program together can share plans, policies and procedures.

Any of the 12 courses in the program can be taken separately. The courses and their learning objectives are located at http://www.managementhelp.org/np_progs/org_dev.htm on the World Wide Web, in the "Course Catalog." (Your organization may also have a wide range of materials around which you could organize courses.) Courses include the following:

1. Preparatory Workshop (skills in reading, studying, getting help, etc.)

2. Starting and Understanding Your Nonprofit

3. Overview of Role of Chief Executive

4. Basic Skills in Management and Leadership

5. Building and Maintaining an Effective Board of Directors

6. Developing Your Strategic Plan

7. Designing and Marketing Your Programs

8. Managing Your Finances and Taxes

9. Developing Your Fundraising Plan

10. Staffing and Supervision of Employees and Volunteers

11. Evaluating Your Programs

12. Organizational "Fitness Test"

Organizations Assisting Nonprofits

In the USA:

1.   Contact your Secretary of State and/or state's Attorney General's office and ask for a list of resources.

2.   Executive Service Corps (ESC) provides experienced consultation in the areas of technical and management.

3.   National Council of Nonprofit Associations (NCNA) has chapters in almost all of the states.

In Canada:

1.   The Voluntary Sector Knowledge Network provides information, assistance and tools regarding a wide range of functions in nonprofits (http://www.vskn.ca/).

2.   United Way Canada provides information, publications and funding to Canada voluntary sector organizations (http://www.unitedway.ca/english/).

3.   The Canadian Centre for Philanthropy provides programs, resources, tools and information for the benefit of Canadian communities (http://www.ccp.ca/).

General Resources:

1.   Contact the local volunteer recruitment organization in your community and ask for assistance.

2.   Look in the Yellow Pages of your local telephone directory for professional associations. Look for networks or associations of organization development practitioners, facilitators or trainers.

3.   Look in the Yellow Pages of your local telephone directory under the categories "Consultant" and "Volunteering".

4.   Contact local large corporations. They often have community service programs and can provide a wide range of management and technical expertise. Speak to the head of the Human Resources Department.

5.   Call a local university or college and speak to someone in the college of Human Resources, Training and Development, or Business Administration.

6.   Ask other nonprofits (particularly those that have similar services and number of staff,) or current clients for ideas, contacts and references.

7.   Ask a retired business person (from a for-profit or nonprofit organization). Often, they have facilitated a wide variety of meetings.

Free, On-Line Newsletters and Forums

1. **CharityChannel forums**
   CharityChannel provides a wide array of forums, including forums on Canada-specific topics. Go to http://www.charitychannel.com/ on the Web.

2. **PULSE**
   on-line newsletter published by the Support Centers of America and the Nonprofit Management Association. To subscribe, send an e-mail message to "sca@supportcenter.org" and, in the body of the message, type "SUBSCRIBE PULSE!". Or, call (415) 541-7708.

3. **Board Cafe**
   is a free on-line newsletter for nonprofit Boards of Directors, published by CompassPoint Nonprofit Services. To subscribe, send a blank e-mail message to "boardcafe-subscribe@lists.compasspoint.org".

Additional newsletters and forums are listed in the Free Management Library under the topic "General Resources."

Major Sources of Trends Information About Nonprofits

There are a wide variety of sources of available information that can be useful during an external analysis. For example:

1. Find out what trade journals publish information about the types of clients that your programs serve and/or how the programs might better serve those clients. Sign up for at least two of them.

2. Contact educators about nonprofits. Their job is to stay up-to-date on nonprofit matters. Take them to lunch and interview them.

3. Take a course on nonprofit management.

4. Attend conferences on nonprofit matters. You can find out about many of the conferences by contacting the organizations that assist nonprofits (a list is provided, above).

5. Contact nonprofit alliances and councils and ask where you can get information regarding trends in services similar to those provided by your nonprofit.

6. The planning office of the city or state (or province) often has a vast array of information about trends in the area.

7. Interview some funders and examine their annual reports. Funders often have a good understanding of community needs and what is being done to address the needs.

8. Program evaluations are some of the best forms of information about how your nonprofit and its programs are doing! Probably your most important stakeholders are your clients. Nonprofits should have clear impressions of clients' impressions of those programs. The

above-mentioned guidebook by this author also includes practical guidelines for designing and conducting useful program evaluations.

9.   Conduct your own market research. Market research is collecting information about "markets" or groups of potential clients whose needs might be might by your nonprofit's programs, now or in the future. The next subsection, "Major Sources of Trends Information About People," will be useful to you.

(The guidebook, *Field Guide to Nonprofit Program Design, Marketing and Evaluation,* by this author, includes extensive, practical guidelines to carry out market research.)

Major Sources of Trends Information About People

The following list conveys some of the major sources that nonprofits can reference to get information about markets, clients, trends, etc. The way that you use the following sources depends on the purpose of the information that you are seeking, for example, to understand more about your clients, a certain industry, a certain market, market trends or competition.

1.   **Census Bureau (in the USA)**
There is a vast amount of information available to you, and much of this is on-line at http://www.census.gov/ or call 301-763-INFO (4636).

Statistics Canada (in Canada)
There is a vast amount of information about Canadian society and commerce. Go to http://www.statcan.ca/start.html

2.   **Chamber of Commerce (in the USA)**
Get to know the people in your local office. Offices usually have a wealth of information about localities, sources of networking, community resources to help your business, etc. Go to http://www.uschamber.com/default.htm or call 202-659-6000.

Chamber of Commerce (in Canada)
Similar to Chambers in the USA. Go to http://www.chamber.ca/newpages/main.html

Board of Trade (in Canada)
Various cities in Canada have a Board of Trade, for example, the Toronto Board of Trade, that supports local organizations by providing information and resources and also supporting networking among members. Reference the Yellow Pages telephone directories in Canada.

3.   **Department of Commerce (in the USA)**
The Department has offices in various regions across the country and publishes a wide range of information about industries, products and services. Go to http://www.doc.gov/ or call 202-501-0666.

4.   **Libraries**
One of the richest and most helpful sources of information is your local library! Let the Librarian help you. For example, in the USA, see:
a) *Directory of Associations*
b) *Sales and Marketing Management magazine*
c) *American Statistics Index (ASI)*

d) *Encyclopedia Of Business Information Book*
e) *Standard & Poor's Industry Survey's and Consumer's Index*

5. **Trade and Professional Organizations**
Organizations often produce highly useful newsletters for members, along with services for networking, answering questions, etc. For example, in the USA, you can start by contacting the National Council of Nonprofit Associations. Go to http://www.ncna.org/ or call 202-962-0322. Also, contact the United Ways of America or Canada, which publish a variety of directories for nonprofits. Go to http://national.unitedway.org/index.cfm for the United Way America or to http://www.unitedway.ca/english/ for the United Way Canada.

6. **Trade Publications**
Publications are becoming much more useful as various trades become more specialized and their expectations are increasing for timely and useful information. The type of trade publication that will be useful to you depends on the nature of your product or service, for example, health care, arts and education.

Appendix C: Nonprofit Management Indicators

This organizational assessment tool is also online at
http://www.surveymonkey.com/s.asp?u=3754722401

Description

The following checklist is a resource developed by staff and volunteers of the Greater Twin Cities United Way for internal use by nonprofit organizations. Management can use the checklist to identify their organization's administrative strengths and weaknesses. It is believed that widespread use of the checklist ultimately results in a more effective and efficient nonprofit community. The checklist is not intended to be used as a tool for external evaluation, or by grant makers in making funding decisions. This tool will be used to assist nonprofit organizations to gain a better understanding of their management needs and/or make improvements to management operations.

Note that the following checklist, or assessment tool, originally developed by the Greater Twin Cities United Way of Minnesota (USA), has been slightly modified by the author in order to make it relevant to organizations outside the United States.

This checklist includes the following sections:

- How To Use the Tool
- Disclaimers
- Legal Indicators
- Governance (Board) Indicators
- Human Resources Indicators
- Planning Indicators
- Financial Indicators
- Fundraising Indicators

How To Use the Tool

The checklist indicators represent what is needed to have a healthy, well-managed organization. Since it is a self-assessment tool, organizations should evaluate themselves honestly against each issue and use the response to change or strengthen its administrative operations.

Ratings: Each indicator is rated based on its importance to the operation and effectiveness of any nonprofit organization. The ratings are:
E: Indicators with an "E" are essential or basic requirements to the operations of all nonprofit organizations. Organizations which do not meet the requirements of these indicators could place their organizations in jeopardy.
R: An "R" rating signifies that these indicators are recommended as standard practice for effective nonprofit organizations.
A: Additional indicators which organizations can implement to enhance and strengthen their management operations and activities are rated with an "A".

Checklist Responses:

Organizations can respond in one of three ways to each indicator used:

1. *Needs Work* - An indicator that is marked as "Needs Work" implies that work has been done towards achieving this goal. The organization is aware of the need for this indicator, and is working towards attaining it.

2. *Met* - All indicators marked as "Met" demonstrate that the organization has fulfilled that essential management need. However, the organization should review these indicators in the future to be sure that their management remains healthy in view of the many internal and external changes which constantly occur in all organizations.

3. *N/A* - Indicators marked as "N/A" can mean several things, including:

- the indicator is not applicable to the management operations of this organization
- the organization is not sure of the need to meet the requirements of this indicator
- the organization has not met, nor is working on this indicator presently, but may address it in the future.

All organizations should take note:

All responses to indicators should be reviewed carefully to see if they could improve management operations. Indicators checked "N/A" due to uncertain applicability to the organization must be further reviewed to determine if they should become a part of "doing business." If the assessors simply do not know what the indicator means, further information may be needed to accurately assess the feasibility of its application. Indicators may require immediate attention is they were marked "N/A" because they have not been met but still apply to the organization. Technical assistance, consulting, or training may be required to implement these indicators.

The indicators in this checklist should be informative and thought provoking. The checklist can be used to not only achieve a beginning level of good management, but also improve existing management to provide the organization with greater stability, reliability and success in the nonprofit community. If an organization is experiencing management problems, the checklist can be useful to help pinpoint any weaknesses where action can be taken or assistance sought to improve the organization's health. All organizations should use the checklist to re-assess themselves periodically to ensure compliance with established rules and regulations and to continue improving administrative health through the indicator's helpful suggestions.

Disclaimer

This checklist is designed to provide accurate and authoritative information regarding the topics covered. Legal requirements and non-legal administrative practice standards reflected herein are capable of change due to new legislation, regulatory and judicial pronouncements, and updated and evolving guidelines. The same are utilized with the understanding that the provision of this checklist does not constitute the rendering of legal, tax or other professional services.

If the organization requires professional assistance on these or other nonprofit tax, management, or accounting issues, please contact your own professional advisors.

Legal Activities

Rating *	Indicator	Met	Needs Work	N/A
E	1. All relevant legal filings are current and have been made according to the laws and regulations of the nonprofit's country. (For example, in the USA, requirements might include: Annual Registration, Articles of Incorporation with all amendments, Change of Corporate Name or Address.)			
E	2. The organization is registered with and has filed its annual report with the appropriate governmental agency. (For example, in the USA, the report might be filed with the state's Attorney General's office.)			
E	3. For organizations operating on a tax-exempt basis, the organization has filed the necessary government form to obtain tax-exempt status. (For example, in the USA, IRS form 1023 was filed and the IRS provided a letter of determination. If the Form 1023 was filed after 7/15/87 or was in the nonprofit's possession on this date, it is available for public inspection.)			
E	4. Tax reports are filed on a regular basis. (For tax-exempt organizations in the USA, the IRS form 990 and 990T for unrelated business income, if required, have been filed and copies of the 990 are available to the public.)			
E	5. Federal and state (or provincial) payroll taxes withholding payments are current. (This requirement applies to organizations with employees.)			
E	6. Quarterly and annual payroll report filings are current. (This requirement applies to organizations with employees.)			
E	7. If the organization has qualified employee health, welfare and/or retirement benefit plans, they meet with all the federal and state/provincial laws. (For example, in the USA, COBRA; initial IRS registration; plan documents; annuals filings of the 5500 C/R with copies available to employees.) This requirement applies to organizations with employees.			
E	8. Organization acknowledges and discloses to their Board and auditor any lawsuits or pending legislation which may have a significant impact on the organization's finances and/or operating effectiveness.			
E	9. When the Board of Directors makes decisions, a quorum is present and minutes are maintained.			
E	10. If the organization is subject to sales tax(es), then federal, state/provincial and/or city filings and payments are current.			
E	11. Organizations that participate in grassroots or direct lobbying have complied with all necessary filings and government regulations.			
E	12. Organizations that conduct charitable gambling have complied with government regulations.			
E	13. Organizations with employees represented by a union must have copies of the union contracts on file.			
E	14. Organizations that operate in a fiscal or host-organization relationship with another organization or group have a written agreement on file.			

Indicators ratings: E=essential; R=recommended; A=additional to strengthen organizational activities

Governance / Boards

Rating *	Indicator	Met	Needs Work	N/A
E	1. The roles of the Board and the Chief Executive Officer (if applicable) are defined and respected, with the Chief Executive Officer delegated as the manager of the organization's operations and the Board focused on policy and planning.			
R	2. The Chief Executive Officer is recruited, selected, and employed by the Board of Directors. The Board provides clearly written expectations and qualifications for the position, as well as reasonable compensation.			
R	3. The Board of Directors acts as governing trustees of the organization, on behalf of the community at large and as contributors, while carrying out the organization's mission and goals. To fully meet this goal, the Board of Directors must actively participate in the planning process as outlined in planning sections of this checklist.			
R	4. The Board's nominating process ensures that the Board remains appropriately diverse with respect to gender, ethnicity, culture, economic status, disabilities, skills and/or expertise.			
E	5. The Board members receive regular training and information about their responsibilities.			
E	6. New Board members are oriented to the organization: the organization's mission, bylaws, policies and programs, as well as their roles and responsibilities as Board members.			
A	7. Board organization is documented with a description of the Board and Board committee (if applicable) responsibilities.			
A	8. Each Board member has a Board operations manual.			
E	9. If the organization has any related party transactions between Board members or their family, they are disclosed to the Board of Directors (the Internal Revenue Service in the USA) and the auditor.			
E	10. The organization has at least the minimum number of members on the Board of Directors as required by their bylaws, federal statute and/or state/provincial statute.			
R	11. If the organization has adopted bylaws, they conform to federal and/or state/provincial statutes and have been reviewed by legal counsel.			
R	12. The bylaws should describe: a) how and when notices for Board meetings are made; b) how members are elected/appointed by the Board; c) what the terms of office are for officers/members; d) how Board members are rotated; e) how ineffective Board members are removed from the Board; and f) a stated number of Board members to make up a quorum which is required for all policy decisions.			
R	13. The Board of Directors reviews the bylaws annually.			
A	14. The Board has a process for handling urgent matters between meetings.			
E	15. Board members serve without payment unless the agency has a policy identifying reimbursable out-of-pocket expenses.			
Indicators ratings: E=essential; R=recommended; A=additional to strengthen organizational activities				

Governance (Cont.)

Rating *	Indicator	Met	Needs Work	N/A
R	16. The organization maintains a conflict-of-interest policy and all Board members and executive staff review and/or sign to acknowledge and comply with the policy.			
R	17. The Board has an annual calendar of meetings. The Board also has an attendance policy which requires that a quorum of the organization's Board meets at least quarterly.			
A	18. Each Board meeting has a written agenda and the materials relating to significant decisions are given to the Board members in advance of the meeting.			
A	19. The Board has a written policy prohibiting employees and members of employees' immediate families from serving as Board Chair or treasurer.			
Indicators ratings: E=essential; R=recommended; A=additional to strengthen organizational activities				

Human Resources: Staff and Volunteers

Staff

Rating *	Indicator	Met	Needs Work	N/A
E	1. The organization has a written personnel handbook/policy that is regularly reviewed, updated and approved by Board: a) to describe the recruitment, hiring, termination and standard work rules for all staff and b) to maintain compliance with government employment laws and regulations. (For example, in the USA, this includes: Fair Labor Standards Act, Equal Employment Opportunity Act, Americans with Disabilities Act, Occupational Health and Safety Act, Family Leave Act, Affirmative Action Plan if required, etc.)			
R	2. The organization follows nondiscriminatory hiring practices.			
R	3. The organization provides a copy of or access to the written personnel policy to all members of the Board, the Chief Executive Officer (if applicable) and all staff members. All staff members acknowledge in writing that they have read and have access to the personnel handbook/policies.			
R	4. The organization has job descriptions including qualifications, duties, reporting relationships and key indicators.			
R	5. The organization's Board of Directors conducts an annual review/evaluation of its Chief Executive Officer in relationship to a previously determined set of expectations.			
R	6. The Chief Executive Officer's salary is set by the Board of Directors in a reasonable process and is in compliance with the organization's compensation plan.			
R	7. The organization requires employee performance appraisals to be conducted and documented at least annually.			
A	8. The organization has a compensation plan and a periodic review of salary ranges and benefits is conducted.			
A	9. The organization has a timely process for filling vacant positions to prevent an interruption of program services or disruption to organization operations.			
A	10. The organization has a process for reviewing and responding to ideas, suggestions, comments and perceptions from all staff members.			
A	11. The organization provides opportunities for employees' professional development and training with their job skill area and also in such areas as cultural sensitivity and personal development.			
A	12. The organization maintains contemporaneous records documenting staff time in program allocations.			
Indicators ratings: E=essential; R=recommended; A=additional to strengthen organizational activities				

Human Resources: Staff and Volunteers (Cont.)

Volunteer HR Management

Rating *	Indicator	Met	Needs Work	N/A
E	1. The organization has a clearly defined purpose of the role that volunteers have within the organization.			
E	2. Job descriptions exist for all volunteer positions in the organization.			
R	3. The organization has a well-defined and communicated volunteer management plan that includes a recruitment policy, description of all volunteer jobs, an application and interview process, possible stipend and reimbursement policies, statement of which staff has supervisory responsibilities over what volunteers, and any other volunteer personnel policy information.			
E	4. The organization follows a recruitment policy that does not discriminate, but respects, encourages and represents the diversity of the community.			
E	5. The organization provides appropriate training and orientation to the agency to assist the volunteer in the performance of their volunteer activities. Volunteers are offered training with staff in such areas as cultural sensitivity.			
R	6. The organization is respectful of the volunteer's abilities and time commitment and has various job duties to meet these needs. Jobs should not be given to volunteers simply because the jobs are considered inferior for paid staff.			
R	7. The organization does volunteer performance appraisals periodically and communicates to the volunteers how well they are doing, or where additional attention is needed. At the same time, volunteers are requested to review and evaluate their involvement in the organization and the people they work with and suggest areas for improvement.			
R	8. The organization does some type of volunteer recognition or commendation periodically and staff continuously demonstrates their appreciation towards the volunteers and their efforts.			
A	9. The organization has a process for reviewing and responding to ideas, suggestions, comments and perceptions from volunteers.			
A	10. The organization provides opportunities for program participants to volunteer.			
A	11. The organization maintains contemporaneous records documenting volunteer time in program allocations. Financial records can be maintained for the volunteer time spent on programs and recorded as in-kind contributions.			
Indicators ratings: E=essential; R=recommended; A=additional to strengthen organizational activities				

Planning (Strategic and Programs)

Strategic Planning

Rating *	Indicator	Met	Needs Work	N/A
E	1. The organization's purpose and activities meet community needs.			
R	2. The organization frequently evaluates, by soliciting community input, whether its mission and activities provide benefit to the community.			
R	3. The organization has a value statement that is reflected in the agency's activities and is communicated by its constituents.			
A	4. The value statement includes standards of ethical behavior and respect for other's interests.			
E	5. The organization has a clear, meaningful written mission statement which reflects its purpose, values and people served.			
R	6. The Board and staff periodically review the mission statement and modify it to reflect changes in the environment.			
E	7. The Board and staff developed and adopted a written strategic plan to achieve its mission.			
A	8. Board, staff, service recipients, volunteers, key constituents and general members of the community participate in the planning process.			
E	9. The plan was developed by researching the internal and external environment.			
R	10. The plan identifies the changing community needs including the agency's strengths, weaknesses, opportunities and threats.			
R	11. The planning process identifies the critical issues facing the organization.			
R	12. The plan sets goals and measurable objectives that address these critical issues.			
E	13. The plan integrates all the organization's activities around a focused mission.			
R	14. The plan prioritizes the agency goals and develops timelines for their accomplishments.			
A	15. The plan establishes an evaluation process and performance indicators to measure the progress toward the achievement of goals and objectives.			
R	16. Through work plans, human and financial resources are allocated to insure the accomplishment of the goals in a timely fashion.			
A	17. The plan is communicated to all stakeholders of the agency – service recipients, Board, staff, volunteers and the general community.			
Indicators ratings: E=essential; R=recommended; A=additional to strengthen organizational activities				

Planning (Cont.)

Planning Regarding the Organization's Programs

Rating *	Indicator	Met	Needs Work	N/A
E	1. Programs are congruent with the agency's mission and strategic plan.			
A	2. The organization actively informs the public about its programs and services.			
A	3. Clients and potential clients have the opportunity to participate in program development.			
R	4. Sufficient resources are allocated to ensure each program can achieve the established goals and objectives.			
R	5. Staff has sufficient training and skill levels to produce the program.			
A	6. Programs within the organization are integrated to provide more complete services to clients.			
R	7. Each program has performance indicators to insure that the program meets its goals and objectives.			
R	8. Performance indicators are reviewed annually.			
A	9. The agency networks and/or collaborates with other organizations to produce the most comprehensive and effective services to clients.			
Indicators ratings: E=essential; R=recommended; A=additional to strengthen organizational activities				

Planning Regarding the Organization's Evaluations

Rating *	Indicator	Met	Needs Work	N/A
R	1. Every year, the organization evaluates its activities to determine progress toward goal accomplishment.			
A	2. Stakeholders are involved in the evaluation process.			
R	3. The evaluation includes a review of organizational programs and systems to insure that they comply with the organization's mission, values and goals.			
R	4. The results of the evaluation are reflected in the revised plan.			
A	5. Periodically, the organization conducts a comprehensive evaluation of its programs. This evaluation measures program outcomes (impacts on clients).			
Indicators ratings: E=essential; R=recommended; A=additional to strengthen organizational activities				

Financial Activities

Rating *	Indicator	Met	Needs Work	N/A
E	1. The organization follows accounting practices which conform to generally accepted standards.			
E	2. The organization has systems in place to provide the appropriate information needed by staff and Board to make sound financial decisions and to fulfill government requirements (for example, the requirements of the Internal Revenue Service in the USA).			
R	3. The organization prepares timely financial statements including the balance sheet, income statement and cash flow statement which are clearly stated and useful for the Board and staff. (Note that these statements might be referred to by different names in various countries.)			
R	4. The organization prepares financial statements on a budget versus actual (comparative basis) to achieve a better understanding of their finances.			
E	5. The organization develops an annual comprehensive operating budget which includes costs for all programs, management and fundraising and all sources of funding. This budget is reviewed and approved by the Board of Directors.			
R	6. The organization monitors unit costs of programs and services through the documentation of staff time and direct expenses and using a process for allocation of management, general and fundraising expenses.			
E	7. The organization prepares cash flow projections.			
R	8. The organization periodically forecasts year-end revenues and expenses to assist in making sound management decisions during the year.			
E	9. The organization reconciles all cash accounts monthly.			
E	10. The organization has a review process to monitor that they are receiving appropriate and accurate financial information, whether from a contracted service or internal processing.			
E	11. If the organization has billable contracts or other service income, procedures are established for the periodic billing, follow-up and collection of all accounts, with documentation to substantiate all billings.			
E	12. Government contracts, purchase of service agreements and grant agreements are in writing and are reviewed by a staff member of the organization to monitor compliance with all stated conditions.			
E	13. Payroll is prepared following appropriate federal and state/provincial regulations and organizational policy.			
E	14. Persons employed on a contract basis meet all federal and state/provincial requirements for this form of employment. (In the USA, disbursement records are kept so 1099's can be issued at year end.)			
E	15. Organizations that purchase and sell merchandise take periodic inventories to monitor the inventory against theft, to reconcile general ledger inventory information and to maintain an adequate inventory level.			
R	16. The organization has a written fiscal policy and procedures manual and follows it.			
Indicators ratings: E=essential; R=recommended; A=additional to strengthen organizational activities				

Financial Activities (Cont.)

Rating *	Indicator	Met	Needs Work	N/A
E	17. The organization has documented a set of internal controls, including handling of cash and deposits and approval over spending and disbursements.			
E	18. The organization has a policy identifying authorized check signers and the number of signatures required on checks in excess of specified dollar amounts.			
E	19. All expenses of the organization are approved by a designated person before payment is made.			
R	20. The organization has a written policy related to investments.			
R	21. Capital needs are reviewed annually and priorities established.			
R	22. The organization has established a plan identifying actions to take in the event of a reduction or loss in funding.			
R	23. The organization has established, or is actively trying to develop, a reserve of funds to cover at least three months of operating expenses.			
E	24. The organization has suitable insurance coverage which is periodically reviewed to ensure the appropriate levels and types of coverage are in place.			
E	25. Employees, Board members and volunteers who handle cash and investments are bonded to help assure the safeguarding of assets.			
E	26. The organization files forms in regard to tax-exempt and/or tax-deductible (charity) status in a timely basis within prescribed time lines.			
R	27. The organization reviews income annually to determine and report unrelated business income to the necessary government agency (for example, to the IRS in the USA).			
R	28. The organization has an annual, independent audit of their financial statements, prepared by a certified public accountant.			
R	29. In addition to the audit, the auditor prepares a management letter containing recommendations for improvements in the financial operations of the organization.			
R	30. The Board of Directors, or an appropriate committee, is responsible for soliciting bids, interviewing auditors and hiring an auditor for the organization.			
R	31. The Board of Directors, or an appropriate committee, reviews and approves the audit report and management letter and with staff input and support, institutes any necessary changes.			
E	32. The audit, or an organization-prepared annual report which includes financial statements, is made available to service recipients, volunteers, contributors, funders and other interested parties.			
A	33. Training is made available for Board and appropriate staff on relevant accounting topics and all appropriate persons are encouraged to participate in various training opportunities.			
Indicators ratings: E=essential; R=recommended; A=additional to strengthen organizational activities				

Fundraising Activities

General Fundraising

Rating *	Indicator	Met	Needs Work	N/A
E	1. Funds are raised in an ethical manner for activities consistent with the organization's mission and plan.			
E	2. The Board of Directors and organization staff are knowledgeable about the fundraising process and the roles in the organization.			
E	3. The organization's Board of Directors has established a committee charged with developing, evaluating and reviewing fundraising policies, practices and goals.			
E	4. The committee is actively involved in the fundraising process and works to involve others in these activities.			
R	5. The Board of Directors, Chief Executive Officer (if applicable) and committees support and participate in the total fundraising process, including project identification, cultivation, solicitation and recognition.			
R	6. The fundraising program is staffed and funded at a level consistent with fundraising expectations.			
A	7. There are direct communications and relationships between information services or marketing, accounting and other administration support functions to assist in the fundraising needs and efforts.			
E	8. The organization is accountable to donors and other key constituencies and demonstrates its stewardship through annual reports.			
Indicators ratings: E=essential; R=recommended; A=additional to strengthen organizational activities				

Fundraising (Cont.)

Using an Outside Fundraiser

Rating *	Indicator	Met	Needs Work	N/A
A	1. The organization meets the nonprofit standards of the state/provincial charities review council, if one exists.			
R	2. If the organization chooses to use outside professional fundraisers, several competitive bids are solicited. Each prospective outside fundraiser's background and references are checked.			
E	3. The organization makes legal, mutual agreed upon, signed statements with outside professional fundraisers, outline each parties' responsibilities and duties, specifying how the contributed funds will be physically handled, and to guarantee that the fees to be paid are reasonable and fair.			
E	4. The organization has verified that the contracted fundraiser is registered as a professional fundraiser with the appropriate government agency and all filings necessary have been made before the work commences.			
E	5. The fundraising committee or appropriate representatives from the Board of Directors reviews all prospective proposals with outside professional fundraiser and reviews and accepts all agreements before they are signed.			
R	6. If the outside professional fundraiser plans to contact potential donors directly, the organization must review the fundraising materials (e.g., public service announcements, print or broadcast advertisements, telemarketing scripts, pledge statements, brochures, letters, etc.) to verify their accuracy and to ensure that the public disclosure requirements have been met.			
E	7. The organization properly reports all required information regarding use of outside professional fundraisers, amount of funds raised and the related fundraising expenses as required by federal and state/provincial governments. The gross amount of funds raised by the contracted fundraiser is reported on the organization's financial statement. The fees and costs of the campaign must be reported on the statement of functional expenses.			
Indicators ratings: E=essential; R=recommended; A=additional to strengthen organizational activities				

Appendix D: Data Collection Guidelines

Conducting Interviews

Interviews are useful during the situational analyses portion of strategic planning, for example, interviewing external stakeholders (funders, clients, community leaders, etc.) or internal stakeholders (Board members, staff, etc.). The interviewer can pursue in-depth information around a topic. Interviews may be useful as follow-up with certain respondents to questionnaires in order to further investigate their responses.

Before you start to design your interview questions and process, clearly articulate to yourself what problem or need is to be addressed by using the information to be gathered by the interviews. This helps you keep clear focus on the intent of each question.

NOTE: Much of the information herein was adapted from Michael Patton's book, *Qualitative Evaluation and Research Methods* (Sage Publications, Newbury Park, CA, 1990).

Preparation for Interview

1. **Choose a setting with little distraction.**
   Avoid loud lights or noise. Ensure the interviewee is comfortable (you might ask them if they are), etc. Often, they may feel more comfortable at their own places of work or homes. Keep in mind that it may be more difficult to control interruptions there.

2. **Explain the purpose of the interview.**

3. **Address terms of confidentiality.**
   Note any terms of confidentiality. (Be careful here. Rarely can you absolutely promise complete confidentiality. Courts may get access to information, in certain circumstances.) Explain who will get access to their answers and how their answers will be analyzed. If their comments are to be used as quotes, then get their written permission to do so.

4. **Explain the format of the interview.**
   Explain the type of interview you are conducting and its nature. If you want them to ask questions, specify if they are ask them as they have them or wait until the end of the interview.

5. **Indicate how long the interview usually takes.**

6. **Tell them how to get in touch with you later if they want to.**

7. **Ask them if they have any questions before you get started with the interview.**

8. **Do not count on your memory to recall their answers.**
   Ask for permission to record the interview or bring along someone to take notes.

Types of Interviews

1.   **Informal, conversational interview**
     No predetermined questions are asked, in order for the interviewer to remain as open and adaptable as possible to the interviewee's nature and priorities. During the interview, the interviewer "goes with the flow."

2.   **General interview guide approach**
     The interview guide approach is intended to ensure that the same general areas of information are collected from each interviewee. This provides more focus than the conversational approach, but still allows a degree of freedom and adaptability in getting information from the interviewee.

3.   **Standardized, open-ended interview**
     The same open-ended questions are asked to all interviewees (an open-ended question is where respondents are free to choose how to answer the question, that is, they do not select "yes" or "no" or provide a numeric rating, etc.). This approach facilitates faster interviews that can be more easily analyzed and compared.

4.   **Closed, fixed-response interview**
     All interviewees are asked the same questions and asked to choose answers from among the same set of alternatives. This format is useful for those who are not practiced in interviewing.

Types of Topics in Questions

Patton (1990) mentions six kinds of questions. One can ask questions about:

1.   **Behaviors**
     Regarding what a person has done or is doing.

2.   **Opinions/values**
     Regarding what a person thinks about a topic.

3.   **Feelings**
     Regarding what a person feels about something. Note that respondents sometimes respond with "I think ..." so be careful to note that you are looking for feelings.

4.   **Knowledge**
     Regarding what a person knows about a topic.

5.   **Sensory**
     Regarding what a person has seen, touched, heard, tasted or smelled.

6.   **Background/demographics**
     Standard background questions, such as age, education, etc.

Note that the above questions can be asked in terms of past, present or future.

Sequence of Questions

1.   **Get the respondents involved in the interview as soon as possible.**

2.   **Before asking about controversial matters (such as feelings and conclusions), first ask about some facts.**
With this approach, respondents can more easily engage in the interview while warming up to more personal matters.

3.   **Intersperse fact-based questions throughout the interview**
to avoid long lists of fact-based questions, which tends to leave respondents disengaged.

4.   **Ask questions about the present before questions about the past or future.**
It is usually easier for them to talk about the present and then work into the past or future.

5.   **The last questions might be to allow respondents to provide any other information they prefer to add and their impressions of the interview.**

Wording of Questions

1.   **Wording should be open-ended.**
Respondents should be able to choose their own terms when answering questions.

2.   **Questions should be as neutral as possible.**
Avoid wording that might influence answers, for example, evocative or judgmental words.

3.   **Questions should be asked one at a time.**

4.   **Questions should be worded clearly.**
This includes knowing any terms particular to the program or the respondents' culture.

5.   **Be careful asking "why" questions.**
This type of question infers a cause-effect relationship that may not truly exist. These questions may also cause respondents to feel defensive, that they have to justify their response, which may inhibit their responses to this and future questions.

Carrying Out Interview

1.   **Occasionally verify the tape recorder (if used) is working.**

2.   **Ask one question at a time.**

3.   **Attempt to remain as neutral as possible.**
That is, do not show strong emotional reactions to their responses. Patton suggests acting as if "you've heard it all before."

4.   **Encourage responses with occasional nods of the head, "uh huh"s, etc.**

5.   **Be careful about the appearance when note taking.**
That is, if you jump to take a note, it may appear as if you are surprised or very pleased about an answer, which may influence answers to future questions.

6. **Provide transition between major topics.**
    For example, "we have been talking about [some topic] and now I would like to move on to [another topic]."

7. **Do not lose control of the interview.**
    This can occur when respondents stray to another topic, take so long to answer a question that times begins to run out, or even begin asking questions to the interviewer.

Immediately After Interview

1. **Verify if the tape recorder, if used, worked throughout the interview**.

2. **Make any notes on your written notes.**
    For example, to clarify any scratchings, ensure pages are numbered and fill out any notes that do not make sense.

3. **Write down any observations made during the interview.** For example, where did the interview occur and when, and was the respondent particularly nervous at any time? Were there any surprises during the interview? Did the tape recorder break?

For Additional Information

See the topic "General Guidelines for Conducting Interviews" in our Free Management Library[SM] at
http://www.managementhelp.org/evaluatn/intrview.htm

Conducting Focus Groups

Focus groups can be powerful means to efficiently collect peoples' feedback during the situational analyses portion of strategic planning, for example, with groups of external stakeholders (funders, clients, community leaders, etc.) or of internal stakeholders (Board members, staff, etc.).

Preparing for Session

1. **Identify the major objective of the meeting.**

2. **Carefully develop 5-6 questions (see below).**

3. **Plan your session (see below).**

4. **Call potential members to invite them to the meeting.**
    Send them a follow-up invitation with a proposed agenda, session time and list of questions the group will discuss. Plan to provide the final report from the session to each member and let him or her know when to expect a copy.

5. **About three days before the session, call members to remind them to attend.**

Developing Questions

1. **Develop 5-6 questions**.
    The meeting should last one to 1.5 hours. In this time, you can usually ask at most five or six questions.

2. **Always first, ask yourself what problem or need will be addressed by the information.**
    For example, do you need to examine if a new service or idea will work, or further understand how a program is failing?

3. **Focus groups are basically multiple interviews.**
    Therefore, many of the same guidelines for conducting focus groups are similar to conducting interviews.

Session Planning

1. **Scheduling**
    Meetings are usually one to 1.5 hours long. Over lunch seems to be a very good time for others to find time to attend.

2. **Setting and refreshments**
    Hold sessions in a conference room or other setting with adequate air flow and lighting. Configure chairs so that all members can see each other. Provide name tags for members, as well. Provide refreshments, especially boxed lunches if the session is held over lunch.

3. **Ground rules**
    It is critical that all members participate as much as possible, yet also to move along while generating useful information. Because the meeting is often a one-time occurrence, it is useful to have a few, short ground rules that sustain participation, yet do so with focus.

Consider the following three ground rules: a) keep focused, b) maintain momentum and c) get closure on questions.

4. **Agenda**
Consider the following agenda: welcome, review of agenda, review of goal of the meeting, review of ground rules, introductions, questions and answers, wrap up.

5. **Membership**
Focus groups are usually conducted with 6-10 members who have some similar nature, for example, similar age group or status in a program. Select members who are likely to be participative and reflective. Attempt to select members who do not know each other.

6. **Recording**
Plan to record the meeting with either an audio or an audio-video recorder. Do not count on your memory. If this is not practical, involve a co-facilitator who is there to take notes.

Session Facilitation

1. **Major goal of facilitation is collecting useful information to meet goal of meeting.**

2. **Introduce yourself, and the co-facilitator, if used.**

3. **Explain the means to record the session.**

4. **Verify that the tape recorder (or other recording device) is working throughout the session.**

5. **Carry out the agenda.** (See "agenda" above.)

6. **Carefully ask each question before that question is addressed by the group.**
Allow the group a few minutes for each member to carefully record his or her answers. Then, facilitate discussion around the answers to each question, one at a time.

7. **After each question is answered, carefully reflect back to all of them a summary of what you heard all of them say** (the note taker may do this).

8. **Ensure even participation.**
If one or two people are dominating the meeting, then call on others. Consider using a round-table approach, including going in one direction around the table, giving each person a minute to answer the question. If the domination persists, note it to the group and ask for ideas about how the participation can be increased.

9. **Close the session.**
Tell members that they will receive a copy of the report generated from their answers, thank them for coming and adjourn the meeting.

Immediately After Session

1. **Make any notes about the recording or flipcharts.**
For example, clarify any scratching, ensure pages are numbered and to fill out any notes that do not make sense.

2.   **Write down any observations made during the session.**
For example, where did the meeting occur and when, what was the nature of participation in the group? Were there any surprises during the meeting? Did the tape recorder break?

For Additional Information

See the topic "Conducting Focus Groups" in our Free Management Library[SM] at http://www.managementhelp.org/evaluatn/focusgrp.htm

Basic Methods To Assess Client Needs

Program staff can often get a good sense of the needs among various groups of clients by conducting the following standard activities.

1.   **Analyze client needs during strategic planning.**
During the SWOT analysis of strategic planning, identify what threats might exist to the various client groups because of trends in government programs, economy, society and technology. You might stop by the library and ask the librarian for sources of information about these trends.

2.   **Listen to your staff members.**
They often have a good sense about the needs of various groups of clients. Be careful not to just count on these sources within your organization, though – make sure that your research includes sources outside of your organization, as well.

3.   **Observe and listen to your clients.**
Where do they seem to struggle? What are they interested in? For example, are they having difficulty getting to your facility? What do they complain about? What do they ask for?

4.   **Conduct at least basic client satisfaction surveys by using simple questionnaires.**
These will help you to conclude if your current program(s) are meeting their needs or not. On the questionnaire, ask what other needs they have that are not being met.

5.   **Include a few questions in your newsletter.**
Ask clients to call a phone number to report their unmet needs.

6.   **On a yearly basis, do a few focus groups.**
This appendix includes guidelines to conduct focus groups.

7.   **Study the results of your program evaluations.**
Evaluations can be wonderful means to help clients to really think about their unmet needs.

8.   **Network among clients and other nonprofits with missions similar to yours.**
Interview some of them. Over time, you will begin to hear about the same unmet needs among clients and organizations.

9.   **Read the newspaper.**
Notice current problems in the community. Notice "hot topics" that people might be interested in.

10. **Ask your Board members for ideas about new clients and their needs.**
    Note that if you have been selective in recruiting Board members to your organization, then you probably have Board members who represent a good cross section of the types of clients that your organization serves or wants to serve. Board members often know a lot about the clients that an organization wants to serve. Some of them may even be past clients.

Appendix E: Getting and Working With Consultants

Situations When Consultant Is Useful

Typical applications for consultants in nonprofits include fundraisers, strategic planning facilitators, marketing consultants, computer consultants, Board trainers and organization development consultants. The following are typical reasons for a nonprofit organization to use a consultant.

1.   The organization has no expertise in the area of need.

2.   The time of need is considered short-term, for example, less than a year, with a general start and stop time.

3.   The organization's previous attempts to meet their own needs were not successful.

4.   Organization members continue to disagree about how to meet the need and bring in a consultant to provide expertise or facilitation skills to come to consensus.

5.   Leaders want an objective perspective, that is, someone without strong biases about the organization's past and current issues.

6.   A consultant can do work that no one else wants to do.

7.   An outside organization demands that a consultant be brought in, for example, a funder wants to ensure the organization is well suited to spend the funder's money.

8.   The organization wants a consultant to lend credibility to a decision that has already been made (this situation would be looked at by many experienced consultants as highly unethical).

Where To Get Consultants

1.   Contact professional associations, for example, networks of organization development practitioners, facilitators, trainers, fundraisers, accountants, lawyers or computer users.

2.   Contact local large corporations; they often have community service programs and can provide a wide range of management and technical expertise.

3.   Consult the local telephone company's Yellow Pages under the category "Consultant" and "Volunteering".

4.   Call a local university or college and speak to someone in the college of Human Resources, Training and Development, or Business Administration.

5.   Ask other organizations for ideas, particularly those that have similar services and head-count size, for contacts and references.

Nonprofits can often get consultants to provide services on a pro bono basis. It is worth asking the consultant, especially if the consultant is in strong agreement with the community's need for the nonprofit's services.

How You Can Make Consultancy As Productive As Possible

1. Know what you want before you get a consultant. Imagine what you would have if the consultancy worked out perfect. Keep that vision when you start to look for a consultant.

2. Get Board agreement on the hiring of the consultant. Ideally, (if your Board uses committees) appoint a committee such as the Personnel Committee or Project Committee to oversee the consultant progress.

3. Do not become dependent on a consultant. Be sure that the project has a start and stop point.

4. If possible, do not limit the consultant to recommending action. Get the consultant involved in implementing recommendations.

5. Fix causes, not symptoms. Do assessments, look closely at what you see and hear, then figure out the cause. Appendix C on page 171 of this guidebook includes assessments you could use. It is often not what you see or hear that is the root cause of problems, rather it is the nonprofit's structures, roles, plans, etc., that cause the problems.

Getting and Hiring Best Consultant

(This section includes advice graciously provided by Barbara Davis, Consultant, St. Paul, Minnesota.)

1. Give interested people the information they need to understand your needs by using a "request for proposal" (RFP) or "request for quote" (RFQ) or through direct conversation.

2. Get a written proposal from every interested party. Do not just talk to one consultant.

3. Get a bid on the fee and reimbursable expenses.

4. Look at more than one proposal and examine them all carefully.

5. Interview the best prospects and check their references. Consider their extent of expertise, listening skills, ability to adapt to the nature of your organization, ability to coach to ensure the organization can address the problem in the future, etc.

6. Do not pick someone based only on price.

7. Be sure there is no conflict of interest with the consultant that you want to hire. That is, the consultant should not be faced with conflicting roles if working for your organization. For example, the consultant should not also be on your Board of Directors or be a member of your staff.

8. Write a good contract including:

    a) Start and stop date of the agreement.

    b) List of specific, tangible "deliverables" that will be produced by the consultant.

    c) Project completion date, including date for deliverables.

d) Payment schedule (consider making partial payments based on provision of each deliverable or project phase).

e) Checkpoints at which you can evaluate programs, for example, have a Phase I, Phase II and Phase III.

f) "Bail-out" clause, ideally that you can immediately bail out by providing notice in writing.

g) Name of person in your agency who has the authority to agree to expenditures or approve work.

h) Agreement on reimbursable expenses.

i) Understanding on who will do the actual consulting.

j) Specification of the roles and responsibilities of the consultant and of your organization.

k) Confidentiality about sharing any information regarding your organization and its activities.

l) Ownership of any materials used and/or produced during the project.

m) Scope of the agreement, that is, that it supercedes any other agreements that you have with the consultant regarding that project

Additional Advice

Help Consultants Understand Your Organization

A few basic techniques can greatly help the consultant to understand your organization, particularly if they are brought in to work organization-wide and non-technical issues.

1. **Help them understand your service(s), market(s) and stakeholder(s).**
   For example, provide them with copies of your strategic plans, budgets, policies, most recent annual report, organization charts, and advertising/promotions/sales literature. If there is a full range of these types of documents, your organization probably values careful documentation when making important decisions, and will likely prefer the same from the consulting project. If these documents appear to be very comprehensive and include a great deal of graphs, figures, and numbers, your organization probably highly values careful research, analysis, and conclusions, and will prefer the same in the consultation project.

2. **Give them a sense for the overall nature of your organization.**
   Are staff highly independent and work alone or do they prefer working in teams? Do you go for consensus on decisions even if it takes a long time to get or do you want timely closure on decisions? Are their strong traditions you require based on the diversity of your workforce? How does the staff feel about using consultants?

3. **Give them a sense for the overall priorities of your organization.**
   For example, you might attempt to identify the general life stage of your nonprofit, such as start-up, developing/building, stabilizing and declining. The stage will indicate your overall

priorities, as well, for example, getting any help you can get, grabbing more market share and/or more clients and/or more revenue, developing a wide range of careful documentation, or divesting resources while ensuring client needs are met.

Include Frequent Evaluations, Including Project Follow-Up

The extent of the consultant's and clients' participation in evaluating the project is often an indicator of how much they really see themselves responsible for the overall, long-term quality of the consulting project.

1. **The consulting project should be evaluated regularly.**
   For example, include a brief evaluation at the end of each meeting (about the process used in that meeting), at mid-point in the planning effort and at its end. Specify in the contract that certain deliverables, for example, tangible products, such as reports, presentations and project reviews be delivered during the project. Ideally, the project is evaluated at three months and six months after completion of the project, particularly about whether the consultant's recommendations were implemented or not and whether the project's goals were reached or not.

2. **Establish criteria early on from which the consulting effort will be evaluated.**
   Establish criteria by having you and the consultant specify what constitutes a successful consulting project and process. Get descriptions to be as detailed as possible to later know if the project was clearly a success or not.

3. **Do not base evaluations mostly on feelings.**
   Avoid this mistake by specifying, as much as possible, behaviors that will reflect a successful consulting project.

Be Sure You Enter Into "Independent Contractor" Relationship

A major, recent issue with some government agencies is what they perceive as some organizations arranging to use what the organizations consider to be "independent contractors," but what the agencies conclude are really "employees". In these cases, the agencies demand that the organizations pay employees' taxes and penalties. Consequently, a nonprofit must be very careful when entering into a relationship with a consultant in order to ensure that government agencies will not deem the relationship an "independent contractor" relationship.

For example, in the USA, the Internal Revenue Service (IRS) is diligent about this matter and has issued guidelines about how to discern if a relationship is really more of an employee relationship than an independent contractor relationship. The IRS guidelines are similar to guidelines in Canada. Whether someone is deemed by the IRS to be an employee or an independent contractor depends primarily on the extent of control the nonprofit has over the person: the less control in the relationship, the less likely the IRS will deem the person to be an employee. Consider the following actions when attempting to define the relationship with an independent contractor:

1. Carefully specify your relationship with the person in a written contract.

2. The terms of the relationship (specific services, fees, project start and stop dates, etc.) should all be specified in the contract.

3. Attempt to arrange fees to be based on results or tasks, rather than on time.

4.   In the contract, specify the relationship to be with an "independent contractor" who is responsible to pay his or her own taxes.

5.   The person doing the work should have all or considerable discretion in how services are carried out, including the process and scheduling.

6.   The person doing the work should be responsible to obtain and pay for his or her own training to carry out the services.

7.   The person should not be required to carry out his or her services at the offices of the client.

8.   The person should have or be making obvious efforts to advertise and retain business with other clients.

9.   The person should have his or her own place of business.

The more a person appears as a manager in the organization (that is, makes operating decisions, supervises people, is responsible for resource allocations, etc.), the more likely that a government agency will deem the service provider an "employee", and not an independent contractor.

In the USA, the IRS uses a set of questions to help determine which status (employee or independent contractors) best fits the role. To see these questions, go to http://www.mnwfc.org/tax/87-41.htm on the Web.

Appendix F: Nature of Typical Nonprofit Organizations

A successful strategic planning process for a large corporation simply will not work for a small nonprofit. Therefore, it is critical that facilitators and planners understand the nature of the typical nonprofit organization before they design and conduct their strategic planning process.

Unique Culture

The culture of a typical nonprofit tends to be a rather tight-knit group of people, each of whom is very dedicated to the mission of the organization. They will chip in to help wherever and whenever they can. Often, they are like a small family.

(Adapted with permission from Sandra Larson, previous Executive Director of The Management Assistance Program for Nonprofits, St. Paul, Minnesota.)

- **The heart of the matter is leadership and management.**
  At the heart of any successful nonprofit is an effective Chief Executive Officer and Board of Directors, assuming the organization is even big enough to warrant having a Chief Executive. These leaders must work as a team with vision, skill and sufficient resources to accomplish the organization's mission. While the leadership is shared, critical management skills must rest with the Chief Executive Officer. However, the Board must also be sufficiently skilled in management to assess the work of this Chief Executive Officer and assist in strategic decision-making.

- **Values are the bottom line.**
  Values are the driving force in a nonprofit. The bottom line is the realization of a social mission, not profits. This poses complex problems for the leadership team. For example, how are programs agreed upon, progress monitored and success measured? How are priorities set and consensus reached? How are staff rewarded and what control systems are applicable? Skilled consultants may be needed from time to time to assist the team in answering these qualitative, value-laden questions and focus on appropriate management systems.

- **Nonprofit personnel are often highly diverse.**
  Diversity is reflected, not only by different races and ethnic groups, but ultimately by different values, opinions and perspectives. This strong diversity is a major benefit to the nonprofit because input from a wide variety of perspectives usually ensures complete consideration of situations and new ideas. Thus, nonprofit personnel must ensure they cultivate, and remain open to, all of their various values and perspective in their organizations.

- **Problems are especially complex for the small nonprofit.**
  The majority of nonprofits have small staffs and small budgets, for example, less than $500,000, which compounds the leadership and management problems they face, especially given their charters and the magnitude of community needs with which they deal. Those new to nonprofits may react that, because nonprofits tend to be small in size, issues in nonprofits should be small, as well. On the contrary, the vast majority of organizations (regardless of size) experience similar range and complexity of issues, for example, in

planning, organizing, motivating and guiding. However, when these issues are focused in a small organization, the nature of the issues in the organization can become very dynamic and complex.

- **Sufficient resources to pay leadership may be lacking**.
  With lack of sufficient money, attracting and retaining paid management also can be problematic. Hard work with little career development opportunity encourages turnover of Chief Executives and staff. This can stall the organization's work. Expertise that is brought in to advise the management may be lost once that leadership leaves.

- **Lack of managerial training is problematic for the nonprofit**.
  Many nonprofit managers have been promoted primarily out of non-management disciplines and do not have the managerial skills needed to run a nonprofit organization. Training and consultation can do much to help these new leaders and managers to gain the skills they seek and help them up the myriad of learning curves that rainbow out in front of them.

- **Chief Executives wear too many hats.**
  A nonprofit Chief Executive has to be a current expert in planning, marketing, information management, telecommunications, property management, personnel, finance, systems design, fundraising and program evaluation. Obviously, this is not possible, regardless of the size of the organization. A larger organization may be able to hire some internal experts, but this is certainly not the case for the smaller organization. Furthermore, the technology of management progresses far too rapidly today for the non-specialist to keep abreast of new thinking and expertise, whatever the size of the organization. Outside expertise therefore is often a must for both the large and small organization.

- **Nonprofit often is too small to justify or pay for expensive outside advice.**
  Most nonprofits, even larger ones, often hesitate to spend money on administrative "overhead", such as consultants or other outside experts because this is seen as diverting valuable dollars from direct service. Of course, most nonprofits have no choice. They do not have enough money to even consider hiring consultants at for-profit rates. Low-cost, volunteer-based assistance is often is a more appropriate solution.

- **One-shot assistance often is not enough**.
  While most consultant organizations want to teach managers "how to fish," rather than give them a "fish", "fishing" (management skills) is not something that often can be learned in one consultation. Especially in technical arenas, such as computerization, learning comes while grappling with an issue or management problem over a period. Building internal management capacity takes more time than a one-shot consultation. Repeat help therefore is not a sign of failure but of growth – a new need to know has surfaced.

- **Networks are lacking.**
  Many people outside the nonprofit sector observe, "Why do not those Chief Executives get together more, share more ideas, undertake cooperative ventures?" There are many reasons. First of all, running a successful organization (delivering the quality service that fulfills the organization's mission) is not enough. Most nonprofit Chief Executives run a second business – raising money to support the first. Both are complex and very time-consuming activities, especially when the Chief Executive Officer wears all the management hats. Second, developing networks or researching joint ventures is time-consuming, expensive and risky.

- **Nonprofits usually have little time and money.**
  Funders do not seem to think that research and development activity justifies new expenditures; at least many are hesitant to fund what might not succeed. While nonprofits may be more entrepreneurial than funders, they also have little capital at risk. Collaborative planning will be enhanced by computerization and telecommunications, but these investments also are difficult to fund. In some ways, affordable consultants can substitute for expensive, up-front research and development costs, at least at the feasibility level. In many cases, they can carry an organization through the needed planning to actually develop a new system of collaboration, merger or automation.

- **Nonprofits need low-cost management and technical assistance.**
  Nonprofits are valuable community assets that must be effectively managed. The need to provide affordable, accessible management and technical assistance to nonprofit organizations is clear for all the reasons stated above: the complexity of the task, the lack of Board and internal expertise, the lack of time and money, changing needs, the learning curve, and, finally the importance of the results to the community. What is well done is based on what is well run.

- **Typical nature of planning in nonprofits is on current issues.**
  Many nonprofits do not have a lot of time, money or resources for sophisticated, comprehensive strategic planning. The focus is usually on the major issues facing the nonprofit and quickly addressing them. Typical major challenges for the facilitator are basic training of personnel about planning concepts and processes, helping the nonprofit to focus and sustain its limited resources on planning, ensuring strategies are really strategic rather than operational/efficiency measures, and helping design small and focused planning meetings that produce realistic plans that actually get implemented.

Organization Chart of Typical Start-Up Nonprofit

It is common that a start-up nonprofit organization has one major program that is carried out by a hands-on group of volunteers, some of whom act as the Board of Directors and others who act as staff. Both groups might be involved in providing services to clients.

Note that, unlike a for-profit corporation in which the stockholders own the organization, the nonprofit Board of Directors "reports" to the public, at large, which "owns" the nonprofit.

A new nonprofit often does not include the role of Chief Executive (or Executive Director).

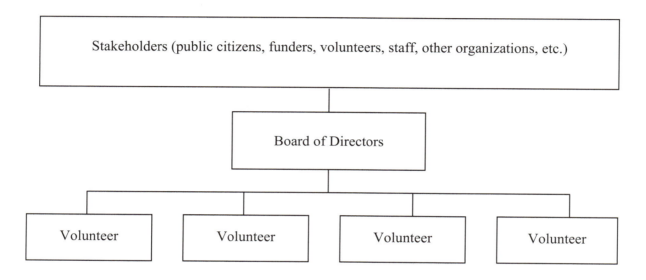

Organization Chart of Typical Small Nonprofit With CEO

A nonprofit might have a part-time or full-time Chief Executive Officer (CEO) role that is a paid or volunteer position. If the nonprofit has staff other than the CEO (the CEO is a staff member), then the CEO supervises the other staff members, who also might be part-time or full-time and in paid or volunteer positions. The CEO reports to a Board of Directors.

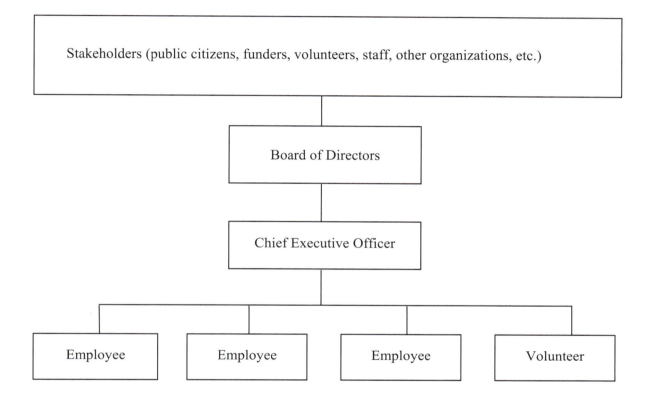

Organization Chart of Typical Medium-Sized Nonprofit

This design might be called a medium-sized nonprofit, although there really is no standard delineation of sizes of nonprofits. This size of nonprofit might have more than one program.

This design usually includes the role of a full-time or part-time, paid CEO who supervises various staff members, all or most of whom are on a full-time or part-time basis. Staff might be paid or on a volunteer basis.

The CEO reports to a Board of Directors.

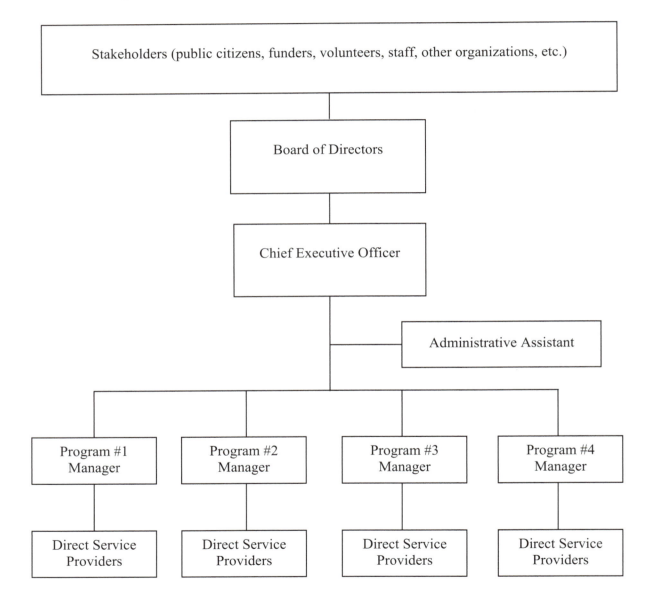

Diversity of Board Structures

The particular design of the Board can be a major consideration when conducting strategic planning, especially when organizing and assigning Board and/or staff to implement strategies and action plans. Therefore, it is very important to realize that Board members can choose from a variety of options for how to structure their Board. There is no one "perfect" Board structure for all types of nonprofits. The type of structure depends on the preference of the members of the Board.

Working Governing Board (Administrative Governing Board)

In a "working" Board, Board members attend to the top-level strategic matters of the organization, but at the same time, attend to the day-to-day matters of the organization, as well. This structure arises usually because the organization is just getting started, cannot afford staff, or members prefer to operate completely on a volunteer basis. The nature of this Board structure is usually rather flexible and informal. Board members and staff (if the nonprofit has staff) work together to do whatever they can to help wherever they can. Ideally, Board members remember that they are responsible for the governance of the organization and to develop the organization's plans and policies. They might conduct Board operations in the form of Board committees. Many times, there is no Chief Executive Officer role in the organization.

Policy Governing Board

A "policy" Board is often viewed as a more "mature" Board that has passed through the "working" Board stage. For example, on a policy Board, paid and/or volunteer staff members have been recruited and organized. Thus, Board members can often attend primarily to strategic matters, while staff attends to day-to-day matters. Often, the definitive characteristic of a policy Board is the presence of a variety of Board committees and a Chief Executive Officer who reports to the Board.

Policy Governance® Board

The structure of the Policy Governance® Board is designed particularly to help Board members to always operate in a fashion that maintains strong, strategic focus for the organization. Members of this Board structure focus as much as possible on policies that determine the "ends" (results) for the organization to achieve and then leave the "means" (procedures) to achieve the results up to the Chief Executive Officer and other staff to decide. Board members set limits within which the Chief Executive Officer operates. This structure is characterized by few, if any, distinct officer roles or Board committees. ("Policy Governance" is a registered trademark of Carver Governance Design, Inc.)

Collective Board

The "collective" Board is the epitome of a team effort. Board members and staff act as if they share equal responsibility in deciding strategic matters and carrying them out, as well. This type of Board is often popular among cultures that highly value equality and power sharing for the good of the community.

Other Board Structures

There are other structures, too. For example, church Boards tend to be organized and operate according to the regulations of its particular church law. School Boards are often highly structured

Boards that resemble policy Boards, but not always. Other local community Boards, for example, Chambers of Commerce, can have their own way of structuring themselves, as well.

 For more information about Boards, obtain the guidebook, *Field Guide to Developing and Operating Your Nonprofit Board of Directors,* by this author.

Typical Cycle of Operations in Nonprofits

Ideally, activities in a nonprofit organization should follow a certain, overall cycle. An understanding of the cycle can be very useful during strategic planning, particularly when conducting an internal analysis of the organization and when examining the effects of certain potential strategies and action plans. Nonprofits carry out the cycle either formally and explicitly or informally and implicitly. The activities in the cycle are usually highly integrated and not always sequential. Their order depends on whether the organization is just getting started, is starting a new program or is experiencing no major changes.

1. **Boards of Directors**
   The nonprofit is equipped with Board members who provide the necessary skills to govern the nonprofit organization. Thus, the role of the Board is critical to the success of strategic planning.

2. **Strategic Planning**
   The Board and staff conduct strategic planning to determine the overall purpose (mission), direction (vision, values and goals) and methods (strategies and action plans) for the nonprofit.

3. **Program Planning (and Inbound Marketing)**
   Program development occurs to build and operate programs that are organized as means to implement the strategies. Early program marketing activities are conducted to fully understand clients, their needs and how those needs can be met.

4. **Financial Management**
   Finances must be managed as the strategic plan is implemented, monitored and adjusted. This financial activity includes developing budgets for major, new initiatives. It also includes developing and implementing policies and procedures for ongoing activities, bookkeeping (administrating transactions, generating reports), analyzing finances, making decisions about spending, etc.

5. **Fundraising**

By now, the nonprofit has some overall plans about programs, including how much money they might make (revenue), how much money they might cost (expenses) and if there are any deficits (expenses exceed revenue). The deficits are addressed usually by fundraising.

6. **Staffing and Supervision**

To effectively implement the strategic plan, the nonprofit must develop and implement plans for staffing (obtaining, training and organizing human resources) and supervising employees, which might include the role of a Chief Executive Officer.

7. **Facilities management**

Often, there are a large number of various kinds of resources, such as facilities, materials and equipment that must be obtained and managed on an ongoing basis. Management activities can include tracking purchases, labeling equipment, replacing materials, etc.

8. **Advertising, Promotions and Public Relations (Outbound Marketing)**

These activities are geared to inform stakeholders (clients, funders, community leaders, etc.) about the nonprofit's programs and services, and keep those programs and services in the minds of stakeholders.

9. **Program services**

Programs provide services to clients on an ongoing basis. Supervision, training, policies and procedures help guide staff when working with clients. Clients benefit from services, including accomplishing certain outcomes, or changes in knowledge, skills and conditions in their lives.

10. **Evaluations**

Evaluations are focused on assessing the extent and effectiveness of implementation of all or parts of the strategic plan. Evaluation is systematically collecting information about various roles and activities in the nonprofit in order to make decisions about them. For example, nonprofits might evaluate the quality of the Board, CEO's performance, staff and programs.

Nonprofits Programs, Configurations and Types

Role of Programs in Nonprofit Strategic Planning

A nonprofit program is a set of related products and/or services provided by a nonprofit organization in order to meet certain needs among certain groups of clients. Programs are usually the primary means by which nonprofits implement the major strategies to work toward their missions. Nonprofits often design or refine their programs during strategic planning. Therefore, it is very important for facilitators and planners to have some sense about what a nonprofit program is.

Types of Program Services

There are a wide variety of types of programs, or services, offered by nonprofit organizations. For example, nonprofits provide services in the areas of:

- Advocacy and lobbying

- Arts

- Associations (business leagues, labor organizations, social clubs, associations of specific types of professions, etc.)

- Civic or community services

- Foundations

- Hospitals

- Literary

- Religious

- Schools

- Scientific

- Social services

- Others?

Program Configurations

Programs have two major types of configurations, including a:

1. Free-standing program, where the program's services are delivered completely within the context of the program.

2. Multi-program effort, where two or more programs are tightly integrated to provide a set of services.

The organizations that provide programs can be:

1. Free-standing, where a program, or multi-program effort, is provided completely within the context of one organization.

2. Multi-organization (or collaborative) effort, where a program, or integration of programs, is provided by two or more organizations that work closely together.

 For more information about nonprofit programs, see the guidebook, *Field Guide to Nonprofit Program Design, Marketing and Evaluation,* by this author.

Appendix G: Worksheets

1. **Plan for Plan**

    1.1   Is Nonprofit Ready for Strategic Planning?

    1.2   Organize Planning Committee?

    1.3   Why Do Strategic Planning Now?

    1.4   What Is Organizational Scope of Plan?

    1.5   What Strategic Planning Approach Might Be Used?

    1.6   How Might Strategic Planning Approach Be Followed?

    1.7   What Time Span Will Be Used?

    1.8   What Schedule Might Be Used?

    1.9   Who Will Be Involved from Nonprofit? How? When?

    1.10   Outside Help Needed? How? When? How To Get It?

    1.11   What Materials Are Needed? When? How To Get Them?

    1.12   Any Conventions for Use of Terms?

    1.13   Provide Planning Guide to Planners?

    1.14   Develop Organizational Profile

    1.15   How Will You Get "Buy-In" When Announcing Process?

    1.16   How Will Planners Be Trained About Strategic Planning?

2. **Primary Client Analysis**

3. **Stakeholder Analysis**

4. **Environmental Scan**

5. **Collaborator Analysis**

6. **Competitor Analysis**

7. **Opportunities and Threats**

8. **Strengths and Weaknesses**

9. **Strategic Issues**

10. **Mission, Vision and Values**

11. **Strategic Goals**

12. **Strategies**

13. **Action Planning**

Worksheet #1: Plan for Plan

1.1 – Is Nonprofit Ready for Strategic Planning?

Before you start on your "plan for a plan," you should determine whether your nonprofit organization is ready to begin strategic planning. There are several questions to guide you in this decision. Check off whether you think your organization is ready, based on each question. Make notes near each question to discuss with key individuals, such as the Board Chair and Chief Executive Officer. If you realize you are not ready based on one or more of these questions, use the considerations in the last column to determine how to get ready and when you might be able to begin strategic planning.

Readiness Questions	Yes – Ready!	Not Ready	Considerations if not ready
Does nonprofit have enough money to pay bills over next six months?			How can your nonprofit get enough money? By when? Start strategic planning when?
Does nonprofit have history of being able to plan and implement its plans?			What can be done to address this issue? Leadership development? Other ideas? Start strategic planning when?
Do Board members get along? Do staff members get along?			Problem in Board? Problem with staff? What can be done? Start strategic planning when?
Are Board members willing to be involved in top-level planning?			What can be done? Start strategic planning when?
Can Board members and staff find the time to do the planning?			What can be done to help them free up more time? Start strategic planning when?

1.1 – Is Nonprofit Ready for Strategic Planning? (Cont.)

No major changes expected in the next 1-2 months?			What changes? What can be done to get ready for strategic planning? By when?
Extensive cynicism about planning in our nonprofit? (You should not have.)			What can you do to address the cynicism? Start strategic planning when?
Are you doing strategic planning only because funder wants you to? (You should have other reasons.)			Yes? What should you do about this? Start strategic planning when?
Other considerations or concerns?			What are they? What can be done? Start strategic planning when?

If you have any checks in the "Not Ready" column, consider addressing the questions noted there before beginning strategic planning and to determine when you might be able to start.

Is your nonprofit ready to do strategic planning?

If you are ready, did you have any comments or concerns that you want to be sure to capture and share with the Planning Committee?

If you are not ready, create an action plan based on the answers to questions in the last column. Work with key individuals to execute that plan and set a schedule for getting back to strategic planning.

1.2 – Organize Planning Committee?

The Committee should include 5-8 highly committed individuals who oversee development of the strategic plan. If the number of planners, including members of the Board and staff, would total 10 people or less, then a Committee might not be needed. Otherwise, the membership of the Committee should be decided now.

	Name	Specific Role On Committee?
1.		Chair of Committee
2.		In charge of strategic planning
3.		Will "champion" the effort
4.		Will write draft of plan document
5.		
6.		
7.		
8.		
9.		
10.		

1.3 – Why Do Strategic Planning Now?

What reason(s) exist for the nonprofit to do strategic planning now?

For each reason, describe it and any evidence that led you to identify it.

Reason #1:

Reason #2:

Reason #3:

Reason #4:

Reason #5:

Reason #6:

Reason #7:

1.4 – What Is Organizational Scope of Plan?

Focus Primarily On Organization-Wide Strategic Planning?

Indicate which of the following is true and explain:

☐   It is that time of year to do organization-wide strategic planning again.

☐   Your nonprofit is quite new or the nonprofit has not established: a mission, vision and/or values; goals and strategies; and clear assignments regarding who will be doing what and by when.

☐   The environments of your nonprofit are changing rapidly.

☐   Your nonprofit is experiencing frequent, internal problems.

☐   Decision-making seems difficult to achieve and ineffective to follow.

☐   There is prolonged conflict among staff and/or Board members.

☐   Other reason(s)?

Is there significant reason to choose organization-wide strategic planning?

1.4 – What Is Organizational Scope of Plan? (Cont.)

Focus Planning Specifically On One or More Program(s)?

Planning is not likely to including organization-wide focus if one or more of the following is true. Indicate which of the following is true and explain:

☐   Overall organization is fairly stable and did organization-wide strategic planning within past year or two.

☐   The program is new.

☐   The program is expecting a major change in methods to deliver services to clients.

☐   Major changes are expected among the clients served by the program.

☐   The programs in the nonprofit are quite different from each other.

☐   The program is experiencing prolonged problems.

☐   Other reason(s)?

Will more focused program planning be done later on with, for example, more focus on inbound and outbound marketing, outcomes, program evaluations, etc.?

Yes? Reason(s)?

No? Reason(s)?

Is there significant reason to choose program-specific strategic planning?

1.5 – What Strategic Planning Approach Might Be Used?

Goals-Based Strategic Planning?

Indicate which of the following is true:

☐   Planners believe they can identify goals for the future.

☐   The environments of the nonprofit are fairly stable.

☐   Your nonprofit conducted strategic planning process before.

☐   Your nonprofit includes several, major programs, each of which might conduct its own focused planning and, thus, the program plans will need to be integrated into an overall organizational strategic plan? Goals-based planning makes this easier.

☐   Planners would like to accomplish a major change in direction for the organization over the next year or so. Goals-based planning makes this easier.

☐   Other reason(s)?

Is there significant reason to choose goals-based strategic planning?

1.5 – What Strategic Planning Approach Might Be Used? (Cont.)

Issues-Based Strategic Planning?

Indicate which of the following is true:

☐ Your nonprofit currently faces several, very critical issues.

☐ There are expected to be major changes in the environments of your nonprofit (external and/or internal) over the next year or so.

☐ The time span for your strategic plan can be one or two years, or at most three years out, rather than having to be for a longer term.

☐ Planners struggle to identify clear goals for the future.

☐ Other reason(s)?

Is there significant reason to choose issues-based strategic planning?

1.5 – What Strategic Planning Approach Might Be Used? (Cont.)

Organic Strategic Planning?

Indicate which of the following is true:

☐ The vision for your organization and its clients applies to a large group of people, and will take a long time to achieve.

☐ The culture of the organization is quite averse to conducting orderly, sequential activities.

☐ The roles of vision and values in your organization are extremely important.

☐ The culture of the organization highly values the telling of stories.

☐ If your organization expects funding from donors, it has confidence that it can obtain funding without having to present a conventional strategic plan document?

☐ Other reasons?

Is there significant reason to choose the organic approach to strategic planning?

1.5 – What Strategic Planning Approach Might Be Used? (Cont.)

Scenario Planning Technique?

Indicate which of the following is true:

☐   Planners have concerns that their planning might not effectively consider future trends and how those trends affect their nonprofit.

☐   Planners prefer to develop, and work from, a vision for their organization and its clients, but they struggle to create that vision.

☐   The culture of the organization highly values the telling of stories.

☐   Other reason(s)?

Is there significant reason to choose the scenario planning technique?

If so, plans for use of scenarios include to:

☐   Integrate with other strategic planning model? Which one?

☐   Use as complete strategic planning process?

☐   Number of years into future that scenarios will be developed?

☐   Do worst-case scenario?

☐   Do best-case scenario?

☐   Do nominal (most realistic) scenario?

☐   Focus scenarios on the nonprofit, programs and clients?

☐   Focus scenarios on broader elements of society?

☐   Other application(s) of scenarios?

1.5 – What Strategic Planning Approach Might Be Used? (Cont.)

Other Strategic Planning Model?

Description:

List the reasons you prefer to use this model.

☐   Reason #1

☐   Reason #2

☐   Reason #3

☐   Reason #4

Where will you find resources to help you to define and design the model?

What concerns might you have about this novel approach to strategic planning?

Other comments?

Is there significant reason to choose this approach to strategic planning?

1.6 – How Might Strategic Planning Approach Be Followed?

Develop a written strategic plan?

Indicate which of the following is true and explain:

☐ Your organization is very small and does not need any funding from donors.

☐ Your nonprofit conducted a very comprehensive strategic planning process within the past two years and the environments (external and internal) of your nonprofit are quite stable.

☐ Other reason(s)?

Is there sufficient reason to create a written strategic plan?

Mostly top-down planning?

Indicate which of the following is true and explain:

☐ Has an effective Board of Directors, including members who are very participative and representative of the stakeholders of the nonprofit.

☐ Has frequent turnover of staff.

☐ Is spread across a wide geographic area, so staff interaction is very difficult.

☐ Has a culture that highly values the power of its upper management.

☐ Other reason(s)?

Is there sufficient reason to choose top-down planning?

1.6 – How Might Strategic Planning Approach Be Followed? (Cont.)

Mostly Bottom-Up Planning?

Indicate which of the following is true and explain:

☐   Members of the Board of Directors are difficult to organize and/or engage.

☐   Planning will be focused mostly on one or more programs.

☐   Staff have strong expertise in the nonprofit's programs, including needs among clients and how those needs are met.

☐   Other reason(s)?

Is there sufficient reason to choose bottom-up planning?

Mostly Concurrent (Combined) Planning?

Indicate which of the following is true and explain:

☐   Members of Board of Directors are participative and aware of programs.

☐   Staff is participative and aware of programs.

☐   Organization highly values participation and teamwork.

☐   Other reason(s)?

Is there sufficient reason to choose concurrent planning?

1.6 – How Might Strategic Planning Approach Be Followed? (Cont.)

Extent of originality (incremental or fresh start)?

Will the new strategic plan be built mostly by fine-tuning an older strategic plan (incremental planning)?

Reason(s)?

Will the new strategic plan be built mostly from a fresh start?

Reason(s):

1.7 – What Time Span Will Be Used?

What time span will be considered for each aspect of the strategic plan?

	3 mos	6 mos	1 year	2 yrs	3 yrs	5 yrs	10 yrs
Goals-based planning, especially goals and strategies							
Issues-based planning, especially issues and strategies							
Organic planning, including short-term activities to conform to vision and/or values							
Scenarios for goals-based, critical-issues, other models, etc.							
Action planning, including who will be doing what and by when for goals-based, critical-issues, other models, etc.							
Budgets for any form of planning							
Other(s)?							

1.8 – What Schedule Might Be Used?

Set a tentative schedule for your planning activities. Depending on the strategic planning model chosen, include activities such as initial Board and/or staff discussion about planning; announcement to full Board and/or staff; scheduling meetings and locations; reviewing mission, vision and/or values; conducting external analysis; conducting internal analysis; identifying strategic issues; identifying goals; identifying strategies; identifying action plans; developing budgets; drafting a plan document; and gaining Board approval. Indicate which activities might include "homework" to be done before that meeting.

	Planning Activities	**Approximate Dates**	**Locations**	**Any Homework?**
1.				
2.				
3.				
4.				
5.				
6.				
7.				
8.				
9.				
10.				
11.				
12.				
13.				
14.				
15.				
16.				
17.				
18.				
19.				
20.				

1.9 – Who Will Be Involved from Nonprofit? How? When?

Focus on who will participate in developing the plan, not necessarily in overseeing the development of the plan. (The latter is the role of the Planning Committee, but you can disregard that involvement here). When thinking about how a person might be involved, consider the activities in Worksheet 1.8 about the scheduling your strategic planning. When thinking about "when", consider the major activities in the particular strategic planning model that you have selected, for example, developing the mission, vision and/or values; goals and strategies; and action planning.

Who?	Role in Org?	Their Value in Planning?	When?

1.10 – Outside Help Needed? How? When? How To Get It?

Who?	How To Use Them?	When?	How To Get Them?
Strategic planning facilitator (external)?			
Expert on nonprofit trends?			
Expert on program trends?			
Funder?			
Funder?			
Others?			

1.11 – What Materials Are Needed? When? How To Get Them?

What?	When?	How To Get Them?

1.12 – Any Conventions for Use of Terms?

The terms that you use will depend on the particular strategic planning model that you use and on the particular culture of your organization. You will finalize your conventions as you develop and implement your plans. For now, describe your preliminary thoughts.

Use?	Term	Definition	Level in Planning
Strategic planning			
Mission			
Vision			
Values			
External analysis			
Internal analysis			
Strategic issues			
Strategic goals			
Strategies			
Objectives			
Tactics			
Action planning			
Other term(s)?			

1.13 – Provide Planning Guide to Planners?

If you want to use a Planning Guide to provide information to your planners, complete the first set of questions. If you do not want to use a planning guide, proceed to the last block.

Select the information that will be in the guide:

☐ Cover sheet with title and date

☐ Brief explanation of the major reason for conducting strategic planning now

☐ Brief description of the strategic planning process designed by the Planning Committee, including any particular model and how that model will be applied

☐ Listing of who will be involved in the planning and when, including a planning schedule

☐ Brief description of the organizational scope of the plan

☐ Brief description of the time span of the plan

☐ Brief description of the role of the Planning Committee

☐ Listing of who can be contacted with any questions about the strategic planning process for the nonprofit

☐ Any other sources of information about strategic planning

☐ Other contents?

Who will be responsible to assemble the guide?

To whom will the guide be provided?

Who will provide it and how?

If you do not want to use a Planning Guide, how will planning information be provided to the planners?

1.14 – Develop Organizational Profile

Name of nonprofit organization:
Highlights from the history of the organization: a) When was it started?   b) Who started it and why?   c) What was/were the first program(s) and whom did they serve?
Any significant events during its history, for example: a) Major awards? b) Mergers? Collaborations? c) Grants or cuts in funding?
Any trends that planners should know about, for example: a) In funding? b) In staffing? c) Among clients?

1.14 – Develop Organizational Profile (Cont.)

Name of Program (current or expected)	Type of service provided	Whom program serves	Comments about program

Other information that planners should know about now? (Upcoming activities in the planning process will go into more detail about the opportunities, threats, strengths and weaknesses facing the organization.)

1.15 – How Will You Get "Buy-In" When Announcing Process?

Select methods that you prefer to use to get buy-in:

☐   Announce in meeting with the Board Chair present? If not, then how to show Board support?

☐   Announce in meeting with Chief Executive Officer (CEO) present. There are few reasons why the CEO would not be in the meeting.

☐   Explain reason(s) for planning, benefits of the process, when it will likely start and stop. Any concerns now?

☐   Do not overly "sell" the process. Any concerns?

☐   Accompany the announcement with an official memo?

☐   Mention any previous strategic planning activities, including successes, failures and what is being done to avoid failures this time around?

☐   Mention who will be on the Planning Committee?

☐   Provide time for staff reaction, including questions and suggestions?

☐   Provide the name of one person who can be contacted regarding any questions about the upcoming process?

☐   Mention when additional information will be available, including who will be involved in the process and when?

☐   Plan some quick successes in the strategic planning process? If so, what might those quick successes be?

☐   Other ideas?

1.16 – How Will Planners Be Trained About Strategic Planning?

If you want to train your planners on strategic planning, complete the first set of questions. If you do not want to provide training, proceed to the last block.

Consider the following questions about your strategic planning training:

1. Who will design the training?

2. What topics should be in the training? Consider:

   ☐   Explanation of the major reason for conducting strategic planning now

   ☐   Overview of the strategic planning process for the nonprofit, including the scope, time span and approach to planning

   ☐   Listing of who will be involved and how, during the process

   ☐   Discussion of the schedule for planning activities

   ☐   Listing of who can be contact

   ☐   Brief description of the time span of the plan

   ☐   Other topics?

3. Who will deliver the training?

4. When the training be delivered?

5. Who will attend the training?

6. Other considerations?

If you decide not to schedule a training session for your planners, how will information on the strategic planning approaches be provided to planners?

Worksheet #2: Primary Client Analysis

Primary clients are the people who you intend to directly benefit from your services now. Verify any assumptions about clients. Also, note that there is a difference between what clients want and what they need. Often, they will come to a service based on what they want (usually in regard how a service is packaged), but they will keep using the service, based on what they need (usually in regard to their well-being).

1.   What groups of primary clients do we serve now?

        For each group of clients:

a)   What do they want from us now? How do we know?

        Are we providing what they want? How do we know?

b)   What do they need from us now? (Think in terms of outcomes, that is, changes in their knowledge, skills and/or conditions.)

        Are we providing what they need? How do we know?

Worksheet #2: Primary Client Analysis (Cont.)

2.   Are there new groups of clients that we might serve? If so, what are the groups?

If so, for each new group:

a) How might we provide more of our current services to the new group?

b) How might we provide any new services to the new group?

3.   Might we do more in the future for our current groups of clients?

If so, for each group:

a) Might we provide more of our current services to current group?

b) Might we provide new services to the current group?

4.   In the future, how can our nonprofit more specifically identify and verify:

a) Whether our nonprofit is reliably meeting the needs of our current clients? (The answer to this question usually means conducting a marketing analysis.)

b) Identification of new groups of future clients, their needs and how our nonprofit can reliably meet those needs? (The answer to this question usually means conducting a marketing analysis.)

Worksheet #3: Stakeholder Analysis

The more influence that a group of stakeholders, or an individual stakeholder, might have on your nonprofit, the higher you might rate that stakeholder. Rate the stakeholders with the numbers 1, 2 and 3, with 1 indicating the most influential. (These stakeholders might be considered as secondary clients. Current and future clients are analyzed in "Worksheet 2: Primary Client Analysis.")

Stakeholder Group or Person	Rating of Influence On Our Nonprofit	Proponent, Opponent, Persuadable ?	Questions to Ask Them	How Might We Ask Them?	How Might We Involve Them in Our Nonprofit?
Past clients			What are their candid impressions of our nonprofit? What are their most important needs now? What might they appreciate from our nonprofit in the future?		
Current funders			What are their candid impressions of our nonprofit? What are their current priorities in funding? Future priorities? How might we work together in the future?		
Past funders			What are their candid impressions of our nonprofit? What are their current priorities in funding? Future priorities? How might we work together in the future?		
Potential funders			What are their current priorities in funding? Future priorities? How might we work together in the future?		

Worksheet #3: Stakeholder Analysis (Cont.)

Volunteers	What are their candid impressions of our nonprofit? Would they help us in the future, and why? How can we help them make an impact on the community?	
Nonprofit service providers	What trends do they see coming? What would they suggest for our nonprofit now? How might we work together in the future?	
Suppliers	What are their candid impressions of our nonprofit? What would they suggest for our nonprofit now? What would they suggest for our nonprofit in the future?	
Community leaders	What are their candid impressions of our nonprofit? What trends do they see coming in the community? What community needs might we help to meet? Any other nonprofits that we should talk to?	
Special interest groups	What are their candid impressions of our nonprofit? What trends do they see coming in the community? What community needs might we help to meet? Any other nonprofits that we should talk to?	
Unions	What are their candid impressions of our nonprofit? What would they like us to do for their members?	

Worksheet #4: Environmental Scan

The worksheet is useful for:

- Conducting a driving-force impacts analysis during the external analysis activities in strategic planning.

- Developing scenarios to use during various activities in strategic planning.

Planners might decide which approach to use by first reading the guidelines in this worksheet and then selecting their approach.

Note that planners' assumptions about the future will be most useful if some, or all, of the planners have utilized a variety of sources of information about external trends. A variety of sources are listed in the subsections, "Major Sources of Trends Information About Nonprofits" and "Major Sources of Trends Information About People," in Appendix B on page 165.

Using Worksheet for Driving Forces Impacts Analysis

A driving-forces impact analysis includes examination of a wide range of types of major influences (or driving forces) that might affect the nonprofit in the future, for example, political, social, economic, technological and environmental influences. Planners attempt to identify the most relevant and likely trends in the future and how those trends might affect their nonprofit and clients.

To use the worksheet for conducting this analysis, planners should follow these guidelines for each type of driving force (row of information), one at a time. Do not get bogged down in lots of detail in the various assumptions. Attempt to complete the entire analysis in four to six hours. Trust your gut instinct, too.

1.   Make assumptions regarding any future trends about that type of driving force (about each row of information in the worksheet). It might help to first think about trends for your region, state or province, and then country.

2.   Make assumptions about how that trend might affect the nonprofit and clients.

3.   After all rows have been addressed, then document the likely trends and effects in Column "C" of the worksheet.

Using Worksheet for Scenario Planning Technique

Scenario planning is a useful technique that can be used to provoke planners to really be strategic in their planning activities, especially when developing a vision statement, conducting an external analysis, identifying strategic issues and identifying strategic goals. (The scenario planning technique is described in the subsection, "What Strategic Planning Approach Might Be Used?," in the section, "Phase 1: Design Plan for Plan," in PART II.)

Planners might prefer to use a scenario planning technique if any of the following is true:

Worksheet #4: Environmental Scan (Cont.)

1.   Planners have concerns that their planning might not effectively consider future trends and how those trends affect their nonprofit.

2.   Planners prefer to develop, and work from, a clear vision for their organization and its clients, but they struggle to create that vision.

3.   The culture of the organization highly values the telling of stories.

4.   Planners believe they can make the time to utilize the technique, including generating assumptions and developing scenarios.

The following worksheet can be very useful in scenario planning. It includes three sets of assumptions. Assumptions in set "A" are in regard to the most optimistic outlook on trends that might occur for each driving force. Assumptions in set "B" are in regard to the most pessimistic outlook on trends that might occur for each driving force. Assumptions in set "C" are in regard to the most likely trends that might occur for each driving force.

To use the worksheet for scenario planning, planners should repeat the following steps for each set of assumptions, starting with set "A" and then doing set "B" and then set "C". Do not get bogged down in lots of detail in the various assumptions. Attempt to complete the entire analysis in four to six hours. Trust your gut instinct, too.

1.   Make assumptions regarding any future trends about that type of driving force (about each row of information in the worksheet). It might help to first think about trends for your region, state or province, and then country.

2.   Make assumptions about how that trend might affect the nonprofit and its clients.

3.   After all rows have been addressed for that set of assumptions (for example, A, B or C), then write a one- to three-page depiction of what conditions might be like for your nonprofit and, especially, for its clients, regarding that set of assumptions. Planners might also include depiction of broader elements of society in their scenarios, as well.

        When attending to the steps, select the specific number of years into the future for which your scenario applies, for example, 3, 5, 10 or 20 years out. Use the same number of years when writing the scenarios for A, B and C. Generally, the more rapid the change that you expect for your nonprofit and clients, the smaller the number of years into the future for which to apply your scenario.

Planners might update their scenarios after conducting various other external analyses, for example, analyses of primary clients, stakeholders, collaborators and competitors.

Refer to your scenarios, especially when developing a vision statement, conducting an external analysis, identifying strategic issues and identifying strategic goals. Planners might choose to refer mostly to the "A", "B" or "C" scenarios, during their strategic planning.

Worksheet #4: Environmental Scan (Cont.)

Note that a scenario is usually larger in size than a vision statement and includes a more complete depiction of the organization, its clients and often significant conditions in society at some point in the future.

(Reprinted with permission from Neil Gustafson, Instructor, University of St. Thomas' "Macrocontemporary Scene" course in its Executive MBA program.)

Types of Driving Forces That Could Affect Future of Your Organization	"A" Assumptions Best-Case Trends/Effects	"B" Assumptions Worst-Case Trends/Effects	"C" Assumptions Most Likely Trends/Effects
Business (types, vitality, location, capital availability, management, philosophy, etc.)			
Communications and access to information			
Economic conditions (for example, GNP, productivity, inflation, etc.)			
Education (elementary, secondary, higher, life-long, etc.)			
Employment and labor force characteristics			
Energy (for example, availability, types, uses, costs, etc.)			
Environmental conditions (air, water, soil)			
Equal opportunities (women, minorities)			
Food (production, distribution, consumption)			

Worksheet #4: Environmental Scan (Cont.)

Governance (structures and operations as a government)			
Health and human services			
Housing (types, location, conditions, costs, etc.)			
International relations (economic, social, political)			
Life-style conditions			
Natural resources (minerals, fuels, foreign products, etc.)			
Politics (voting, political parties, lobbying, methods of influence, etc.)			
Population (growth or decline, composition, distribution, etc.)			
Religion and ethics			
Security (personal, property, crime, law enforcement, etc.)			
Technology (communication, medical, military, robotics, artificial intelligence)			
Transportation (auto, rail, air, etc.)			
Other			

Worksheet #5: Collaborator Analysis

Name of the potential collaborator's organization.

Name of their program or service.

Compare and contrast your services and theirs.

What are the potential areas of collaboration?

What might be the advantages of collaboration with them?

What might be the potential disadvantages of collaboration?

Any additional activities that you believe should be carried out in order to complete your collaborator analysis?

Worksheet #6: Competitor Analysis

Name of the likely competitor's organization.

Describe their program(s) or service(s) that compete with yours.

Describe the groups of clients that both of your organizations serve.

What are the likely to be benefits of their service(s) to each group of their clients?

Compare their pricing and yours.

How do you know about how they advertise their services? What messages do they convey in their advertising and promotions?

Worksheet #6: Competitor Analysis (Cont.)

What do you know about how they package and provide their services? (Think of packaging as the overall design of a service or product to make it as convenient as possible for the client to access and use the service or product, for example, providing day-care when people are working or providing handicap access.)

What seem to be the strengths and weaknesses of their services?

How do your overall services(s) compare to theirs?

How will you compete? Lower prices? More convenient location? Better service?

Any additional activities that need to be carried out in order to complete the competitor analysis?

Worksheet #7: Opportunities and Threats

Consider this template when listing the opportunities and threats that you perceive after conducting the external analysis of your organization.

Opportunities	Relevant External Influence?

Threats	Relevant External Influence?

Worksheet #8: Strengths and Weaknesses

Consider this template when listing the strengths and weaknesses that you perceive from conducting your internal analysis of your organization.

Strengths	Relevant Aspect of Organization
Weaknesses	**Relevant Aspect of Organization**

Worksheet #9: Strategic Issues

Ranking of issue ("1" is high)	Description of strategic issue, including relationship to SWOT information	How is it strategically important, and not just urgent?	What if nothing is done about it?	Timing (short- or long-term)	Level (org. or program)

Worksheet #10: Mission, Vision and Values

Mission Statement

State your mission:

Is it clearly understandable by people internal and external to the organization (a strong requirement for a mission statement)? If not, then what changes might be needed to it?

Does it:

☐   Succinctly describe the purpose of the organization (strong requirement)

☐   Succinctly describe the overall type(s) of client served by the nonprofit (strong requirements)

☐   Provide sufficient focus and direction that members of the Board and staff can reference the mission when making major decisions (strong requirement)

☐   Succinctly describe the particular need(s) met by the nonprofit (recommended)

☐   Mention the particular results (new knowledge, skills and/or conditions) that the nonprofit tries to help its clients to achieve (recommended)

☐   Differentiate the nonprofit from other nonprofits in the area (recommended).

☐   Convey strong, public image (recommended)

☐   Mention the communities in which the nonprofit operates (optional)

☐   Mention any particular strengths and opportunities identified during the situational analysis (optional)

☐   Stay within any legal requirements of the nonprofit, for example, maintain charitable status, conform to church law, conform to national by-laws or maintain foundation status?

Worksheet #10: Mission, Vision and Values (Cont.)

What additional attention might be needed to developing the mission statement?

Does your nonprofit have a purpose statement? What is it?

[Our nonprofit exists:] "To _____."

What additional attention might be needed to developing the purpose statement?

Does your nonprofit have a slogan? What is it?

What additional attention might be needed to developing the slogan?

Worksheet #10: Mission, Vision and Values (Cont.)

Vision Statement

Why you are doing a vision statement?

What is the purpose of the statement?

How will it be used?

State your vision:

Is it clearly understandable by people internal and external to the organization (a strong requirement) for a vision statement)? If not, then what changes might be needed to it?

Does it:

☐   Depict the desired future state of the organization and its clients at some point in the future (strong requirement)?

☐   Inspire members of the organization and key stakeholders (strong requirement)?

☐   Depict the environment in which the nonprofit operates and how clients benefit from the nonprofit's services (strong requirement)?

☐   Depict the strengths and opportunities regarding the organization and as identified during the situational analysis (recommended)?

What additional attention might be needed to developing the vision statement?

Worksheet #10: Mission, Vision and Values (Cont.)

Values Statement

Why you are doing a values statement?

What is the purpose of the statement?

How will it be used?

Draft your values statement:

Is it clearly understandable by people internal and external to the organization (a strong requirement for a values statement)? No? Then what changes might be needed to it?

Does it:

☐ Depict the top priorities in the nature of how the nonprofit wants to operate in order to meet the needs of clients and other stakeholders?

☐ Depict the top priorities in how the nonprofit wants to operate in order to address current challenges in the workplace?

☐ Depict how the nonprofit wants to be viewed by staff and external stakeholders?

Will be adhered to, as much as possible, by all members of the Board and staff?

What additional attention might be needed to developing the vision statement?

Worksheet #11: Strategic Goals

Complete this worksheet for each strategic goal.

Describe the strategic goal (see checklist below):

How is this goal a strategic goal?

Validate this goal using these criteria:

☐ Is the description of the goal understandable and explainable?

☐ Is the goal within the legal charter of the organization?

☐ Is the goal in accordance to mission, vision and/or values of the nonprofit?

☐ Does the goal have predictable and acceptable effects on stakeholders?

☐ Does the goal consider the nonprofit's strengths and opportunities, weaknesses and threats?

☐ Does the description of the goal convey the level of application (organization, program, etc.)?

☐ Does the description of the goal convey the type of activities associated with the goal (activities versus outcomes)?

☐ Does the description of the goal convey timing information (start, stop and/or deadlines)?

☐ Does the description of the goal convey resource requirements?

☐ Is achievement of the goal realistic and achievable?

☐ Does working toward the achievement of the goal have more of an upside than downside?

What is the overall ranking of the goal ("1" is the highest) compared to other strategic goals (if known at this time)?

Worksheet #12: Strategies

Complete this worksheet for each strategy. (Small organizations might skip identifying strategies.)

Describe the strategy (see checklist below):

What strategic issue or strategic goal do these strategies primarily apply to?

What challenges might exist in implementing the strategy?

How might those challenges be overcome?

Validate the strategy using these criteria:

☐   Is the description of the strategy understandable and explainable?

☐   Is implementation of the strategy within the legal charter of the organization?

☐   Is the strategy in accordance to mission, vision and/or values of the nonprofit?

☐   Does the strategy have predictable and acceptable effects on stakeholders?

☐   Does the strategy consider the nonprofit's strengths and opportunities, weaknesses and threats?

☐   Does the description of the strategy convey the level of application (organization, program, etc.)?

☐   Does the description of the strategy convey the type of activities associated with the strategy (activities versus outcomes)?

☐   Does the description of the strategy convey timing information (start, stop and/or deadlines)?

☐   Does the description of the strategy convey resource requirements?

☐   Is implementation of the strategy realistic and achievable?

☐   Does implementation of the strategy have more of an upside than downside?

Worksheet #13: Action Planning

Action planning specifies who will do what and by when in order to achieve each goal and/or implement each strategy. (Small nonprofits might skip identifying strategies.) Complete this worksheet for each goal and/or strategy. The "Status and Date" column can be used to record when the plan was last monitored and the status of implementation. The format of the following worksheet might be helpful to you. Complete this worksheet for each strategy.

Actions for Goal or Strategy #	Date of Completion	Responsibility	Status and Date

Appendix H: Tools to Identify Strategies

1.   **Guidelines to Problem Solving and Decision Making**

2.   **Organic Philosophy of Problem Solving**

3.   **SWOT Grid Analysis**

4.   **Internal Problems and Strategies To Address Them**

5.   **Guidelines to Successful Organizational Change**

Tool #1: Guidelines to Problem Solving and Decision Making

This tool can come in handy, especially when analyzing strategic goals or issues and deciding what to do about them. The following highly rational approach is in sharp contrast to the organic approach described in "Tool #2: Organic Philosophy of Problem Solving" in this Appendix.

1. **Define the problem.**
    This is often where people struggle. They react to what they think the problem is. Instead, seek to understand more about why you think there is a problem.

    Defining the problem: (with input from yourself and others)

    Ask yourself and others the following questions:

    a) What can you *see* that causes you to think there is a problem?

    b) Where is it happening?

    c) How is it happening?

    d) When is it happening?

    e) With whom is it happening? (HINT: Do not jump to "Who is causing the problem?" When we are stressed, blaming is often one of our first reactions. To be an effective facilitator, planner or consultant, you need to address issues rather than people.)

    Write down a five-sentence description of the problem in terms of "The following should be happening, but isn't ..." or "The following is happening and should not be: ..." As much as possible, be specific in your description, including what is happening, where, how, with whom and why. (Your description of what should be happening often is a useful basis from which to generate descriptions of strategic goals, which are, after all, descriptions of what should be accomplished at some point in the future.)

    Defining complex problems:

    If the problem still seems overwhelming, break it down by repeating steps a)-e) until you have descriptions of several related problems.

    Verifying your understanding of the problems:

    It helps a great deal to verify your problem analysis by conferring with a peer or someone else.

    Prioritize the problems:

    If you discover that you are looking at several related problems, then prioritize which ones you should address first.

    Note the difference between "important" and "urgent" problems. Often, what we consider to be the important problems are really just the urgent problems. For example, if you are continually answering "urgent" phone calls, then you probably have a more "important" problem – that of needing to get a screening system for phone calls. The solving of important problems usually fixes the many urgent ones. Important problems deserve the most attention.

Understand your role in the problem:

Your role in the problem can greatly influence how you perceive the role of others. For example, if you are very stressed out, it will probably look like others are, too. Or, you may resort too quickly to blaming and reprimanding others. If you feel guilty about your role in the problem, you may ignore the accountabilities of others.

2. **Look at potential causes for the problem.**
It is amazing how much you do not know about what you do not know. Therefore, it is critical to get input from other people who might have noticed the problem and who are affected by it. It is often useful to seek advice from a peer in order to verify your impression of the problem.

   a) Collect input from other individuals one at a time (at least at first). Otherwise, people in groups tend to be inhibited about offering their impressions of the real causes of problems.

   b) Write down your opinions and what you have heard from others.

   c) Write down a description of the cause of the problem in terms of what is happening, where, when, how, with whom and why.

3. **Identify alternative approaches to resolve the problem.**
At this point, it is useful to keep others involved unless you are facing a personal and/or employee performance problem. Brainstorm for solutions to the problem. The brainstorming technique is described in PART III.

4. **Select an approach, or strategy, to resolve the problem.**
When selecting the best approach, consider:

   a) Which approach is the most likely to solve the problem for the long term?

   b) Which approach is the most realistic to accomplish for now? Do you have the resources? Are they affordable? Do you have enough time to implement the approach?

   c) What is the extent of risk associated with each alternative?

Reference the guidelines in the topic, "Criteria for Effective Goals and Strategies," in the subsection, "Ensure Strategic Thinking for Goals and Strategies," in the section, "Phase 3: Establish Strategic Direction," in PART II.

5. **Plan the implementation of the best alternative strategy.**
   a) Carefully consider "What will the situation look like when the problem is solved?"

   b) What steps should be taken to implement the best alternative to solving the problem? What systems or processes should be changed in your organization, for example, a new policy or procedure? Do not resort to solutions where someone is "just going to try harder."

c) How will you know if the steps are being followed or not? These are your indicators of the success of your plan.

d) What resources will you need in terms of people, money and facilities?

e) How much time will you need to implement the solution? Write a schedule that includes the start and stop times, and when you expect to see certain indicators of success.

f) Who will primarily be responsible for ensuring implementation of the plan?

Write down the answers to the above questions and consider this as your strategy or strategies.

Tool #2: Organic Philosophy of Problem Solving

"Solving Problems" or "Raising Consciousness"?

People in some cultures might believe that it can be quite illusory to believe that problems are identified and solved. These people might believe that the:

- Dynamics of organizations and people are not nearly so linear and mechanistic as to be improved by solving one problem after another.

- Quality of one's life comes from how one handles being "on the road," rather than from "arriving at the destination."

- Quality comes from the process of fixing problems, rather than from having fixed the problems.

- Organic approach to strategic planning is probably more effective than other major approaches, such as goals-based or issues-based.

If this perception is broadly held in the organization, then try to accommodate it through selection of an appropriate planning process (such as organic strategic planning) or other techniques, such as story telling. If the planning group includes some people with any of these views, then consider mixing the techniques in order to satisfy some of the people some of the time.

> *"All the greatest and most important problems in life are fundamentally insoluble ...*
> *They can never be solved, but only outgrown. This "outgrowing" proves*
> *on further investigation to require a new level of consciousness.*
> *Some higher or wider interest appeared on the horizon and*
> *through this broadening of outlook, the insoluble lost its urgency.*
> *It was not solved logically in its own terms,*
> *but faded when confronted with a new and stronger life urge."*

Carl Jung, Psychological Types, Pantheon Books: London, 1923.

Tool #3: SWOT Grid Analysis

A strategy is indeed strategic if it uses the organization's strengths to take advantage of opportunities, while shoring up weaknesses to ward off threats. The Grid can be very useful to planners when ensuring that their strategies are indeed strategic.

Kevin P. Kearns, in his article, "From Comparative Advantage to Damage Control: Clarifying Strategic Issues Using SWOT Analysis" (Nonprofit Management and Leadership, Volume 3 Number 1, Fall 1992, pp.3-22), provides a very useful approach to using SWOT information to organize and identify major types of strategies. Kearn's approach is to develop a SWOT analysis grid, which organizes the SWOT information into four quadrants. Kearn's approach includes labeling each quadrant according to a likely strategy to take regarding the nature of the information in that quadrant, as depicted below.

	Opportunities	**Threats**
Strengths	*Invest* Use the strengths to take advantage of the opportunities	*Defend* Use strengths to ward off threats
Weaknesses	*Decide* Decide whether to invest resources to shore up weaknesses to take advantage of opportunities, or divest areas of weakness	*Divest* Threats in this quadrant should be monitored and avoided as much as possible, without extensive investment of resources

The tool can be handy for planners when working from the various considerations described in the SWOT information and trying to decide what the nonprofit should do in the future in order to address those considerations.

Tool #4: Internal Nonprofit Organizational Problems and Strategies To Address Them

This tool helps planners to think about the specific kinds of issues in their organization and specifically what they might do about each. The following table depicts some of the most common:

1. problem areas reported by nonprofit personnel and/or revealed by assessments,
2. symptoms (presenting problems) reported by nonprofit personnel, and
3. action plans or solutions to address the problem areas.

Problem areas are associated with the organizational functions or areas of a nonprofit. The first column lists them in the ideal order in which they are planned in a typical nonprofit. For example, activities of the Board (the first row) ideally should precede coordinating activities in strategic planning (the second row), which, in turn, ideally precede coordinating program planning (the third row), etc.

Symptoms are associated with each problem area. One, some or all of the symptoms might be present. In addition, symptoms that appear in a particular problem area (e.g., program planning) are often caused by issues in an area listed higher up on the table (e.g., strategic planning). When you identify an area to work on, you may want to look up a row or two in the table to determine if you have symptoms in that area as well and therefore want to choose actions from the suggestions there.

A series of potential actions are associated with each problem area as well. You can select one, some or all of those actions. There are some basic requirements for effective action plans, which are requirements for effective change management, as well.

1. Follow principles of effective change management: include top leadership support, have champion and change agent, be developed and implemented as team effort, have vision and goals, be resourced, be widely communicated, etc.
2. Focus on changing the function/area of the organization in which the problem is most evident from the assessment, e.g., financial management, fundraising, etc.
3. Drive changes from at least one function/area level higher than the function/area in which problem is most evident.
4. Activities should realistically suit the expertise and resources of the client and consultant.
5. Integrate actions in an overall plan with suitable timing (start and finish dates) and sequence (order of activities).
6. Always address how staff will find resources to conduct new action plans, e.g., identify what they might stop doing now in their jobs in order to implement any new plans.
7. Include contingency plans so if action plans cannot be implemented, then other actions can be conducted in timely basis.
8. Include, even if only a rough, description of direction (goals) and methods (strategies) to achieve goals.

Tool #4: Internal Nonprofit Organizational Problems and Strategies To Address Them (Cont.)

NOTE: Some Board members choose not to use Board committees; thus, they should adapt the recommendations below to their particular Board structure.

Problem Areas	Typically Reported Symptoms	Action Plan(s) to Consider
Boards	• Low attendance • Burnout • Low participation • High turnover • No planning • Poor decision making • Conflict among Board members • Micromanagement	• Start Board Development Committee to oversee following actions. • Coach Chair on meeting management. • Give members something specific to do, including realistic goals (from strategic planning?), associate committees with goal(s), staff Board with skills to achieve goals, each committee develops specific work plan, each committee reports results at Board meetings. • Ensure Board staffing procedures are based on specific skills needed on the Board, and include training and provision of Board manuals. • Do two-hour Board training session each year to get all members on same "script"; include training about role of Chief Executive Officer. • Establish Personnel Committee to supervise Chief Executive Officer. • Ensure Board and Chief Executive Officer have annual goals. • Conduct Board and Chief Executive Officer Evaluation yearly. • Enact Board attendance policy. • Have clear Board member recognition procedures. • Rotate Board Chairs and Committee Chairs every two years.
Strategic Planning	• Lack clear focus for building programs and making major decisions • Frequent suggestions among Board and/or staff for new programs • Continual shortage of funds • Burnout among Board and/or staff • Poor program results	• Conduct strategic planning to determine organization's mission/purpose, optionally values, optionally vision, strategic goals, methods/strategies to work toward goals, and implementation plans that specify who will do what and by when and resources they need. • Ensure strategic planning is carried out completely, or on a renewal/update basis, at least once a year with Board and staff input. • Plan should be widely communicated and monitored.

Tool #4: Internal Nonprofit Organizational Problems and Strategies To Address Them (Cont.)

Problem Areas	Typically Reported Symptoms	Action Plan(s) to Consider
Program Planning (and inbound marketing)	- Shortage of resources for programs - Little or no results from programs - Frequent complaints from program staff - Numerous requests for funds to develop new programs - Conflict among program staff - Burnout among staff	- Conduct market research to clearly identify clients, which groups of clients to serve, their needs and wants, how to effectively meet their needs, what they are willing to "pay" for services, what resources are needed to provide the services, the cost of those resources and what the program must "charge" clients to benefit from the program. - Ensure staff is resourced (clear roles and time, energy and expertise) to carry out their roles in the program. Nonprofits rarely ask for help with "program planning," rather they ask for help with program advertising or evaluation, even though planning may be where they need help.
Management Development (includes management, leadership and supervisory development)	- Poor planning, organizing, leading and administration of resources - Lack of direction and guidance to staff - Conflict among staff - High employee turnover - Poor communications among staff and sometimes Board - Incomplete implementation and evaluation of programs	- Develop skills in leadership and management by providing training and opportunities to apply training (in order to develop skills) in: a) Basic skills in time and stress management. b) Planning process, including setting direction (vision and goals), methods (strategies) to achieve goals and resource planning to implement strategies c) Communications, including written and verbal, e.g., presentations, meeting management, etc. d) Basic skills in supervision, including setting goals, delegating, giving feedback, performance reviews and rewards e) Conflict management and facilitation.
Staff Burnout	- Frequent turnover - Frequent complaints and conflict - Compliance ("going through motions" on the job)	- Conduct strategic and program planning (see strategic planning actions listed above) for clear focus, roles and alignment of roles. - Assess staff needs for training, resources and supervision. - Ensure effective supervision, including mutually established goals, delegation, feedback, performance reviews and rewards. - (Be careful about initiating team building without first ensuring clear goals and roles via effective planning.)

Tool #4: Internal Nonprofit Organizational Problems and Strategies To Address Them (Cont.)

Problem Areas	Typically Reported Symptoms	Action Plan(s) to Consider
Fundraising (This is a frequently requested area of help, although the causes of problems often lie somewhere other than fundraising expertise.)	▪ Poor program evaluations ▪ Shortage of resources for programs ▪ Little or no results from programs ▪ Frequent complaints from program staff ▪ Numerous requests for funds to develop new programs	▪ Poor program planning, i.e., have not clearly identified client needs and/or ineffective methods to meet needs ▪ Little understanding of program clientele and results by fundraisers ▪ Poor communications planning regarding what messages should be conveyed to whom and how ▪ Lack of understanding of sufficient funding sources, how to approach them, accountabilities of who should approach them and/or administration/achievement of grant requirements ▪ Unrealistic expectation to integrate new programs
Advertising and Promotions (outbound marketing)	▪ Strong testimonials and results from participants of programs yet ▪ Little growth in programs ▪ Confusion among clients about program benefits and activities	▪ Develop and implement advertising and promotions plan including: what message to convey (e.g., communicating unique benefits of program, whom it serves, how to benefit from the program, examples of those who have benefited from the program, etc.), whom to convey the message to, how to convey it, who will convey it and by when and what resources they need to convey it ▪ Monitor status of implementation of the plan
Program Evaluation	▪ Confusion among staff about program ▪ Inability to successfully describe program to others ▪ Burnout among program staff ▪ Frequent complaints and conflict among staff ▪ Ineffective advertising and promotions ▪ Ineffective fundraising for program	▪ Conduct program implementation evaluation to determine if program was implemented as intended. ▪ Conduct program process evaluation to determine effectiveness and ineffectiveness of program process. ▪ Conduct program outcomes evaluation. ▪ Nonprofits often ask for program evaluation as means to verify to funders that programs are helping participants achieve intended outcomes (outcomes evaluation). Note that there are other advantages of program evaluation, e.g., to make sure the program is implemented as intended (implementation evaluation), improve how the program is operating (process evaluation), etc.

Tool #5: Guidelines to Successful Organizational Change

The implementation of any major strategy involves change to the organization. This tool helps planners to think carefully about the change and how it can best be carried out.

Change Efforts Fail Because of Forgotten Basics

The topic of organizational change has reached evangelical proportions. There is an explosion of literature about the subject and an accompanying explosion in the number of consultants who offer services in this general area. When organizations struggle to accomplish successful organizational change – whether in for-profit, nonprofit or government organizations – it is often because they have not consistently incorporated the most important basics of change into their change efforts. The following information includes the most important guidelines for successful organizational change.

What is "Organizational Change?"

Typically, the term organizational change is used in regard to organization-wide change, as opposed to smaller changes such as adding a new person or modifying a program. Examples of organization-wide change might include a major change in mission, restructuring operations, new technologies, mergers, major collaborations, "rightsizing," new programs such as Total Quality Management and Business Process Re-Engineering.

Some experts refer to the concept of "organizational transformation." While this concept certainly is a form of organizational change, organizational transformation refers to a fundamental and radical reorientation in the way the organization operates. An example would be completely changing an organization's structure from the traditional top-down, hierarchical structure to a large number of self-directing teams.

What Provokes "Organizational Change"?

Usually organizational change is provoked by some major outside driving force, for example, substantial cuts in funding, major new markets/clients or the need for dramatic increases in productivity/services. Typically, organizations must undertake organization-wide change to evolve to a different level in their life cycle, such as going from a highly reactive, entrepreneurial organization to more stable and planned development. Transition to a new Chief Executive can provoke organization-wide change when his or her new and unique personality starts to pervade the entire organization.

Why is Organization-Wide Change Difficult to Accomplish?

Typically, there is strong resistance to change. People are afraid of the unknown. Many people think things are already just fine and do not understand the need for change. Many are inherently cynical about change, particularly from reading about the notion of "change" as if it is a mantra. Many doubt there are effective means to accomplish major organizational change. Often there are conflicting goals in the organization, for example, to increase resources to accomplish change, yet concurrently cut costs to remain viable. Organization-wide change often goes against the very values held dear by members in the organization, that is, the change may go against how members believe things should be done. That is why much of organizational-change literature discusses needed changes in the culture of the organization, including changes in members' values and beliefs and in the ways they enact these values and beliefs.

Successful Organization-Wide Change – Some Specifics

1. Consider using a consultant. Ensure the consultant is highly experienced in organization-wide change. While many consultants refer to organizational change in their literature, many have not addressed organization-wide change. Ask to see references and check the references.

2. Have a change plan with goals. How do you plan to reach the goals, what will you need to reach the goals, how long might it take and how will you know when you have reached your goals or not? Focus on the coordination of the departments or programs in your organization, not on each part by itself. Have someone in charge of the plan.

3. Successful change must involve the very top management, including the Board of Directors (in the case of corporations) and the Chief Executive.

4. Usually there is a champion who instigates change by being visionary, persuasive and consistent. Often that champion is abysmal at driving execution of the change.

5. A change agent role is usually responsible to translate the vision to a realistic plan and carry out the plan. Ideally, the change agent has been a parent for a while.

6. Change is usually best carried out as a team-wide effort. "Lone Ranger" change efforts rarely succeed.

7. To sustain change, the structures of the organization itself should be modified, including strategic plans, policies and procedures. Preaching at people does not make for successful change.

8. When restructuring, end up having every employee ultimately reporting to one person, if possible, and each employee should know who that person is. Job descriptions are often complained about, but they are useful in specifying who reports to whom.

9. Delegate decisions to employees as much as possible. This includes granting them the authority and responsibility to get the job done. As much as possible, let them decide how to do an assignment.

10. Communications about the change should be frequent and with all organization members. Inexperienced managers often assume their people know as much as the managers do. Wrong! Therefore, over-communicate!

11. Ongoing forums should be held for organization members to express their reactions and ideas about the change plan. They should be able to express their concerns and frustrations as well.

Successful Organization-Wide Change – General Guidelines

1. Do not get wrapped up in doing change for the sake of change. Know why you are making the change. What goal(s) do you hope to accomplish?

2. The best approaches to address peoples' resistance to change are through increased and sustained communications and education.

3.   Widely communicate the potential need for change. Communicate what you are doing about it. Communicate what was done and how it worked out.

4.   Get as much feedback as practical from employees, including what they think are the problems and what should be done to resolve them. If possible, work with a team of employees to manage the change.

5.   The process will not be an "aha!" It will likely not be good as you had hoped, but not as bad as you had feared.

6.   Keep perspective. Keep focused on meeting the needs of your customer or clients.

7.   Take care of yourself first. Organization-wide change can be highly stressful.

8.   Do not seek to control change, but rather to expect it, understand it and manage it.

9.   Include closure in the change plan. Acknowledge and celebrate your accomplishments.

10.   Read some resources about organizational change, including new forms and structures.

Some Useful Resources about Organizational Change

 Free Management Library^{SM}, one of the world's largest collections of free, on-line, well-organized resources about personal, professional and organizational change at http://www.managementhelp.org/ on the Web.

 Changing the Essence by Richard Beckhard and Wendy Pritchard, Jossey-Bass, Inc., 1992. This book contains broad overview and useful guidelines about organization-wide change – a classic.

 Fifth Discipline by Peter Senge, Doubleday, 1990. A must-read for anyone wanting to understand how organizations really work and how to change them. This book explains that organizations are – and behave – very much like systems, like people, and must be treated accordingly.

 Making Sense of Life's Changes by William Bridges, Addison Wesley, 1980. This is one of the best books to explain how people react to, and can successfully respond to, change of any type.

BIBLIOGRAPHY

Boards of Directors

Field Guide to Developing and Operating Your Nonprofit Board of Directors, Carter McNamara, Authenticity Consulting, LLC, Minneapolis, MN, 2003.

The quality of the Board of Directors can make a big difference in the quality of the strategic planning process. This guidebook explains how to start a Board and nonprofit organization, or to fix a struggling Board. It also explains all of the activities required for effective Board governance and operations.

Consulting

Field Guide to Consulting and Organizational Development With Nonprofits, Carter McNamara, Authenticity Consulting, LLC, Minneapolis, MN, 2005.

This book provides complete, step-by-step guidelines to identify the most important issues in a nonprofit organization and how to successfully resolve each issue. Guidelines stress an approach that is highly collaborative in nature when working with the consultant. Focus is on a systems approach to ensure strong performance and learning during the consulting process.

Flawless Consulting: Guide to Getting Your Expertise Used, Second Edition, Peter Block, Jossey-Bass Publishers, San Francisco, CA, 2000.

Strategic planning is about change in organizations. This book is probably the best resource available on the realities of helping organizations to identify issues and guide them through change. The book is written in a very straightforward style, and contains checklists and procedures to guide you through the consulting process.

Data Collection and Evaluation

Qualitative Evaluation and Research Methods, Michael Quinn Patton, Sage Publications, Newbury Park, CA, 1990.

Provides comprehensive overview of qualitative research and data collection methods, many of which can be used in practical approaches to market research and program evaluation.

General Facilitation

Facilitation, Bentley, T., McGraw-Hill, Berkshire, England, 1994.

Provides a somewhat philosophical overview of facilitating, particularly about indirect facilitation. Readers would be best to review this book after having first reviewed more basic books on facilitation, including Clarke's book listed below.

The Skilled Facilitator: Practical Wisdom for Developing Effective Groups, Schwartz, R. M., Jossey-Bass Publishers, San Francisco, CA, 1994.

Provides a very comprehensive and useful overview of facilitation. It is somewhat academic, that is, research-oriented with theories, models and concepts. Readers might read this after reading a more basic, straightforward book, such as Clarke's listed below.

Technology of Participation: Group Facilitation Methods, Institute of Cultural Affairs, Phoenix, AZ, 1994.

Provided in the Institute for Cultural Affair's TOP facilitation workshop. Provides a straightforward overview of facilitating discussions, workshops and action planning techniques.

Who, Me Lead a Group? Clarke, J. I., Winston Press, Inc, Minneapolis, MN, 1984.

Beginning facilitators might read this straightforward book first to get an understanding of different types of meetings and then how to lead them.

Leadership and Supervision

Field Guide to Leadership and Supervision for Nonprofit Staff, Carter McNamara, Authenticity Consulting, LLC, Minneapolis, MN, 2002.

The most important determinant regarding whether a strategic plan gets implemented or not is the quality of the leadership and supervision in the organization. This guidebook provides complete, step-by-step guidelines to conduct the most essential activities in successful leadership and supervision in a nonprofit organization.

Nonprofit Strategic Planning

Five Most Important Questions You Will Ever Ask About Your Nonprofit Organization: Participant's Workbook, Peter F. Drucker Foundation, Jossey-Bass Publishers, San Francisco, 1993.

Top-level workbook guides organizations through answering five key strategic questions: What is our business (mission)? Who is our customer? What does the customer consider value? What have been our results? What is our Plan?

Strategic Planning for Public and Nonprofit Organizations, John Bryson, Jossey-Bass Publishers, San Francisco, CA, 1995.

Provides an extensive, well-organized and in-depth explanation of a 10-step strategic planning cycle that can be used in planning with organizations ranging from small to very large. This book is often referred to as the seminal source of expertise for nonprofit organizations.

Strategic Planning Workbook for Nonprofit Organizations, Revised and Updated, Bryan Barry, Wilder Foundation, St. Paul, MN, 1997 (651-642-4022).

Well-organized and very readable, top-level workbook provides guidelines and worksheets to conduct strategic planning for a variety of types, sizes and designs of nonprofit and public organizations.

Program Design, Marketing and Evaluation

Field Guide to Nonprofit Program Design, Marketing and Evaluation, Carter McNamara, Authenticity Consulting, LLC, Minneapolis, MN, 2003.

Programs are often the primary means by which nonprofits implement strategies from strategic planning. Therefore, programs must be carefully designed, marketed and evaluated. This guidebook includes complete step-by-step guidelines to successfully conduct those activities for the first time and on an ongoing basis.

Strategic Management

Strategic Management: Formulation, Implementation, and Control, Fourth Edition, John A. Pearce II and Richard B. Robinson, Jr., Irwin Publishing, Homewood, Illinois, 1991.

Explains the strategic planning process in the overall context of strategic management. Explains complete strategic management cycle, primarily for large for-profit corporations. Much of the information applies to nnprofits, including processes that nonprofits tend not to do, but should.

Index

Additional Titles Specific to Nonprofits

Field Guide to Developing and Operating Your Nonprofit Board of Directors

In our experience, nonprofit Boards rarely struggle because they do not understand advanced concepts. Rather, Boards struggle because they have not established all of the most critical, foundational processes to develop and operate a Board. This guide will help your Board establish those processes, whether you are just getting started or evolving to the next level of effectiveness. Comprehensive guidelines and materials are written in an easy-to-implement style, resulting in a highly practical resource that can be referenced at any time during the life of a Board and organization.

189 pp, comb-bound, 2003   Item #7110, ISBN 978-1-933719-01-6 / 1-933719-01-X $30

Field Guide to Leadership and Supervision for Nonprofit Staff

Top-level executives, middle managers and entry-level supervisors in nonprofit organizations need the "nuts and bolts" for carrying out effective leadership and supervision, particularly in organizations with limited resources. This guide includes topics often forgotten in nonprofit publications, including: time and stress management, staffing, organizing, team building, setting goals, giving feedback, avoiding Founder's Syndrome, and much more. It also includes guidelines to ensure a strong working relationship between the Chief Executive Officer and the Board.

204 pp, comb-bound, 2003   Item #7130, ISBN 978-1-933719-03-0 / 1-933719-03-6 $30

Field Guide to Nonprofit Program Design, Marketing and Evaluation

Nonprofits have long needed a clear, concise – and completely practical – guidebook about all aspects of designing, marketing and evaluating nonprofit programs. Now they have such a resource. This guide can be used to evolve strategic goals into well-designed programs that are guaranteed to meet the needs of clients, develop credible nonprofit business plans and fundraising proposals, ensure focused and effective marketing, evaluate the effectiveness and efficiencies of current programs in delivery of services to clients, evaluate program performance against goals and outcomes, and understand how a program really works in order to improve or duplicate the program.

252 pp, softcover, 2006   Item #7170, ISBN 978-1-933719-08-5 / 1-933719-08-7 $32

Field Guide to Consulting and Organizational Development With Nonprofits

This highly practical book combines the tools and techniques of the profession of Organization Development with the power of systems thinking and principles for successful change in nonprofits. The book also addresses many of the problems with traditional approaches to consulting and leading. The result is a proven, time-tested roadmap for consultants and leaders to accomplish significant change in nonprofits. You can use this book to accomplish change in small or large nonprofit organizations, for instance organizations that 1) have a variety of complex issues, 2) must ensure a strong foundation from which to develop further, 3) must evolve to the next life cycle, 4) need a complete "turnaround," 5) must address Founder's Syndrome or 6) want to achieve an exciting grand goal.

517 pp, softcover, 2005   Item #7180, ISBN 978-1-933719-00-9 / 1-933719-00-1 $58

Additional Titles of General Interest

Field Guide to Leadership and Supervision in Business

Top-level executives, middle managers and entry-level supervisors in organizations need the "nuts and bolts" for carrying out effective leadership and supervision, particularly in organizations with limited resources. This guide includes topics often forgotten in trendy publications, including: time and stress management, staffing, organizing, team building, setting goals, giving feedback, and much more.

204 pp, comb-bound, 2002   Item #7430, ISBN 978-1-933719-23-8 / 1-933719-23-0 $25

Field Guide to Consulting and Organizational Development

This highly practical book combines the tools and techniques of the profession of Organization Development with the power of systems thinking and principles for successful change in for-profits and government agencies. The book also addresses many of the problems with traditional approaches to consulting and leading. The result is a proven, time-tested roadmap for consultants and leaders to accomplish significant change. You can use this book to accomplish change in small or large organizations, whether the organization is dealing with a variety of complex issues or striving to achieve goals for the future.

499 pp, softcover, 2006   Item #7480, ISBN 978-1-933719-20-7 / 1-933719-20-6 $58

Authenticity Circles Program Developer's Guide

Step-by-step guidelines to design, build, manage and troubleshoot an Action Learning-based, peer coaching group program. The program can be used by consultants or an organization's leaders for training enrichment, problem solving, support and networking among peers.

127 pp, comb-bound, 2002   Item #7730, ISBN 978-1-933719-10-8 / 1-933719-10-9 $25

Authenticity Circles Facilitator's Guide

This guide describes how to organize, facilitate and evaluate peer coaching groups. Groups can be facilitated by an external facilitator or groups can self-facilitate themselves. It can also be used to recruit, develop and support facilitators of peer coaching groups. The guide includes appendices with worksheets for the facilitator's use and a handy Quick Reference tool.

114 pp, comb-bound, 2002   Item #7720, ISBN 978-1-933719-11-5 / 1-933719-11-7 $20

Authenticity Circles Member's Guide and Journal

This guide provides step-by-step guidelines for group members to get the most out of their Action Learning-based, peer coaching groups, including how to select goals to be coached on, how to get coached and how to coach others. The guide includes a journal of worksheets to capture the learning of the group members and a handy Quick Reference tool.

110 pp, comb-bound, 2004   Item #7710, ISBN 978-1-933719-12-2 / 1-933719-12-5 $15

Coming in 2008 – Watch our website for news!

Field Guide to Strategic Planning and Facilitation – *For business now too!*

Field Guide to Leadership and Supervision in Business – *Revised edition in softcover!*

Field Guide to Developing and Operating Your Nonprofit Board of Directors – *Revised edition in softcover!*

To order

To get your copies of these and other useful publications, contact us:

Online: http://www.authenticityconsulting.com/pubs.htm

Phone: 800.971.2250 toll-free in North America or 1.763.971.8890 direct

Mail: Authenticity Consulting, LLC
                 4008 Lake Drive Avenue North
                 Minneapolis, MN 55422-1508 USA